Jean Epstein

Manchester University Press

FRENCH FILM DIRECTORS

DIANA HOLMES and ROBERT INGRAM *series editors*
DUDLEY ANDREW *series consultant*

Chantal Akerman MARION SCHMID
Auterism from Assayas to Ozon: five directors KATE INCE
Jean-Jacques Beineix PHIL POWRIE
Luc Besson SUSAN HAYWARD
Bertrand Blier SUE HARRIS
Catherine Breillat DOUGLAS KEESEY
Robert Bresson KEITH READER
Leos Carax GARIN DOWD AND FERGUS DALEY
Marcel Carné JONATHAN DRISKELL
Claude Chabrol GUY AUSTIN
Henri-Georges Clouzot CHRISTOPHER LLOYD
Jean Cocteau JAMES WILLIAMS
Claire Denis MARTINE BEUGNET
Marguerite Duras RENATE GÜNTHER
Georges Franju KATE INCE
Jean-Luc Godard DOUGLAS MORREY
Mathieu Kassovitz WILL HIGBEE
Diane Kurys CARRIE TARR
Patrice Leconte LISA DOWNING
Louis Malle HUGO FREY
Georges Méliès ELIZABETH EZRA
François Ozon ANDREW ASIBONG
Marcel Pagnol BRETT BOWLES
Maurice Pialat MARJA WAREHIME
Jean Renoir MARTIN O'SHAUGHNESSY
Alain Resnais EMMA WILSON
Jacques Rivette DOUGLAS MORREY AND ALISON SMITH
Alain Robbe-Grillet JOHN PHILLIPS
Eric Rohmer DEREK SCHILLING
Bertrand Tavernier LYNN ANTHONY HIGGINS
André Téchiné BILL MARSHALL
François Truffaut DIANA HOLMES AND ROBERT INGRAM
Agnès Varda ALISON SMITH
Jean Vigo MICHAEL TEMPLE

FRENCH FILM DIRECTORS

Jean Epstein

CHRISTOPHE WALL-ROMANA

Manchester University Press

Copyright © Christophe Wall-Romana 2013

The right of Christophe Wall-Romana to be identified as the author of this work has been asserted by him in accordance with the Copyright, Designs and Patents Act 1988.

Published by Manchester University Press
Altrincham Street, Manchester M1 7JA, UK
www.manchesteruniversitypress.co.uk

British Library Cataloguing-in-Publication Data is available

Library of Congress Cataloging-in-Publication Data is available

ISBN 978 1 7849 9348 1 *paperback*

First published by Manchester University Press in hardback 2013

This edition first published 2016

The publisher has no responsibility for the persistence or accuracy of URLs for any external or third-party internet websites referred to in this book, and does not guarantee that any content on such websites is, or will remain, accurate or appropriate.

Printed by Lightning Source

Tous ces phares parlent une seule langue, celle des éclats de lumière que tous les navigateurs du monde comprennent.

[All these lighthouses speak but one language, that of light bursts, which all the navigators in the world understand.]

Jean Epstein, *Les Feux de la mer* (1948)

Contents

LIST OF PLATES	*page* ix
SERIES EDITORS' FOREWORD	xi
ACKNOWLEDGEMENTS	xiii
ABBREVIATIONS	xv
Introduction: Epstein at the crossroads	1
1 From literary modernism to *photogénie*	17
2 Avant-garde working-class melodramas	49
3 Technology, embodiment, and homosexuality	67
4 Brittany, the edge of the modern world	109
5 Documentaries and sound films	128
6 'A young Spinoza': Epstein's philosophy of the cinema	157
Conclusion: Epstein as pioneer of corporeal cinema	187
FILMOGRAPHY	201
SELECT BIBLIOGRAPHY	217
INDEX	220

List of plates

All plates appear between pages 97 and 108

1a Composite shot of Madeline, *La Chute de la maison Usher* (1928) courtesy of All Day Entertainment
1b A montage of stills of the Russian actress Alla Nazimowa in Epstein's *Bonjour cinéma* (1921)
2 Shivering curtain, *La Chute de la maison Usher* (1928) © La Cinémathèque française
3 Funeral procession with its hand-held 'heaving' shot, *La Chute de la maison Usher* (1928) © La Cinémathèque française
4 Jean (Léon Mathot) the melancholy dockworker, *Cœur fidèle* (1923) © Pathé Archives and © La Cinémathèque française
5 Marie (Gina Manès) and Petit-Paul (Edmond van Daële) on the first merry-go-round sequence, *Cœur fidèle* (1923) © Pathé Archives and © La Cinémathèque française
6 Third shot to last in the epilogue, *Cœur fidèle* (1923) © Pathé Archives and © La Cinémathèque française
7 Still from the vivisection scene of the inoculation of rabies in a rabbit, *Pasteur* (1922) courtesy of Institut National de l'Audiovisuel.
8a Peasant holding boy bit by a rabid dog, *Pasteur* (1922) courtesy of Institut National de l'Audiovisuel
8b Counter-shot of swooned boy's face, *Pasteur* (1922) courtesy of Institut National de l'Audiovisuel
8c Boy's crying face in Pasteur's imagination, *Pasteur* (1922) courtesy of Institut National de l'Audiovisuel
9 Two women dancing together, with a superimpression of Anna, *Le Lion des Mogols* (1924) © La Cinémathèque française
10 Protagonist getting in his car, shot through a vegetable cart, *La Glace à trois faces* (1927) © La Cinémathèque française

LIST OF PLATES

11 Protagonist in his automobile glass closet, *La Glace à trois faces* (1927) © La Cinémathèque française
12 Androgynous Jean (Nino Constantini), *Six et demi onze* (1927) © La Cinémathèque française
13 Jean shoots at the mirror, holding a camera, before killing himself, *Six et demi onze* (1927) © La Cinémathèque française
14 Photo strip from Jean's camera, dangling in front of Jérôme's eyes, *Six et demi onze* (1927) © La Cinémathèque française
15 Reflections on the Hispano-Suiza car, *L'Homme à l'Hispano* (1932) © DR / Collection Cinémathèque française
16 Pierre Batcheff in his mother's arms, *Le Double amour* (1925) © La Cinémathèque française
17a Composite shot of Pierre Batcheff, the singing 'Apache', the lute, and feather fan, *Le Double amour* (1925) © La Cinémathèque française
17b With three men circling each other, *Le Double amour* (1925) © La Cinémathèque française
18a Ambroise, *Finis Terræ* (1929) © Gaumont Pathé Archives and © La Cinémathèque française
18b Jean-Marie, *Finis Terræ* (1929) © Gaumont Pathé Archives and © La Cinémathèque française
19 Broken bottle with two small daisies, *Finis Terræ* (1929) © Gaumont Pathé Archives and © La Cinémathèque française
20 Ambroise's injured thumb, *Finis Terræ* (1929) © Gaumont Pathé Archives and © La Cinémathèque française
21 Example of intertitle verse, *Morv'ran* (1930) © La Cinémathèque française
22 A ghostly shirt, or the wind embodied, *Morv'ran* (1930) © La Cinémathèque française
23 Lighthouse keeper behind the lens, *Morv'ran* (1930) © La Cinémathèque française
24a Soizic showing her shy beauty to Rémy, *L'Or des mers* (1932) © La Cinémathèque française
24b Soizic trapped in quicksand, *L'Or des mers* (1932) © La Cinémathèque française
25 'Zip-line' shot of the quarry, found in both *La Bourgogne* (1936) and *Les Bâtisseurs* (1938) © Ciné-Archives – fonds audiovisuel du PCF
26 Two masons working on a cathedral, *Les Bâtisseurs* (1938) © Ciné-Archives – fonds audiovisuel du PCF
27 Animated cartoon depicting Le Corbusier's utopian social housing, *Les Bâtisseurs* (1938) © Ciné-Archives – fonds audiovisuel du PCF

Series editors' foreword

To an anglophone audience, the combination of the words 'French' and 'cinema' evokes a particular kind of film: elegant and wordy, sexy but serious – an image as dependent upon national stereotypes as is that of the crudely commercial Hollywood blockbuster, which is not to say that either image is without foundation. Over the past two decades, this generalised sense of a significant relationship between French identity and film has been explored in scholarly books and articles, and has entered the curriculum at university level and, in Britain, at A-level. The study of film as art-form and (to a lesser extent) as industry, has become a popular and widespread element of French Studies, and French cinema has acquired an important place within Film Studies. Meanwhile, the growth in multiscreen and 'art-house' cinemas, together with the development of the video industry, has led to the greater availability of foreign-language films to an English-speaking audience. Responding to these developments, this series is designed for students and teachers seeking information and accessible but rigorous critical study of French cinema, and for the enthusiastic filmgoer who wants to know more.

The adoption of a director-based approach raises questions about auteurism. A series that categorises films not according to period or to genre (for example), but to the person who directed them, runs the risk of espousing a romantic view of film as the product of solitary inspiration. On this model, the critic's role might seem to be that of discovering continuities, revealing a necessarily coherent set of themes and motifs which correspond to the particular genius of the individual. This is not our aim: the auteur perspective on film, itself most clearly articulated in France in the early 1950s, will be interrogated in certain volumes of the series, and, throughout, the director will be treated as one highly significant element in a complex process of film production and reception which includes socio-economic and political determinants, the work of a large and highly skilled team of artists and technicians, the mechanisms of production and distribution, and the complex and multiply determined responses of spectators.

The work of some of the directors in the series is already well known outside France, that of others is less so – the aim is both to provide informative and original English-language studies of established figures, and to extend the range of French directors known to anglophone students of cinema. We intend the series to contribute to the promotion of the formal and informal study of French films, and to the pleasure of those who watch them.

DIANA HOLMES
ROBERT INGRAM

Acknowledgements

I would like to thank Ulysse Dutoit for inviting his students to experience films and not just 'read' them, and Bertrand Augst for his kind and crucial encouragement with my budding work on Dulac and Epstein.

Research for this book has been supported at the University of Minnesota by a McKnight Land-Grant Professorship 2007–9, the Imagine Fund of the College of Liberal Arts 2010, and a sabbatical supplement award, 2011–12. I am very grateful to Matthew Frost at Manchester University Press for his kindness, patience, and flexibility. Portions of a chapter published as 'Epstein's Corporeal Vision', in Sarah Keller and Jason Paul (eds.), *Jean Epstein: Critical Essays and Translations* (Amsterdam: Amsterdam University Press, 2011) are reproduced here in chapter 1, courtesy of Amsterdam University Press.

This monograph would not have seen the light of day without access to Epstein's films and document archives. The staff and services of the Centre National du Cinéma at Bois d'Arcy have been helpful and attentive, in particular Fereidoun Mahboubi. The staff of La Cinémathèque française proved patient, generous, and understanding, especially Émilie Cauquy, Laure Marchaut, and Monique Faulhaber. The cheerful team at La Bibliothèque du film (BiFi) made archival work a new species of pleasure: thanks Régis Robert, Cécile Touret, and Waldo Knobler. My thanks also to Mélanie Herrick at the Musée Gaumont, and Agnès Berthola at Gaumont Pathé Archives, for guidance with rights and reproduction.

Sarah Keller (Colby College) and Jason Paul kindly invited me to the symposium on Jean Epstein they had organized at the University of Chicago in 2007, and it was a rare joy to meet other dedicated fans of Epstein. At this event I also met Tom Gunning whose unwavering support of my work since then has been an incredible gift. At the close of the symposium, I drew a mental outline of this book, so Sarah, Jason, and Tom were its gentle inspirers: thank you!

xiv ACKNOWLEDGEMENTS

I would like to thank my colleagues in film studies, at the University of Minnesota and beyond, from whom I keep learning so much, in particular Rembert Hueser, Jason McGraw, Shevvy Craig, Verena Mund, Charles Sugnet, John Mowitt, Richard Abel, Laurent Gaudio, Maria Tortajada, François Albéra, and Jennifer Wild. Finally, I would like to apologize to Chiara Tognolotti, who kindly sent me her book *Al cuore dell'immagine: L'idea di fotogenia nel cinema europeo degli anni Venti* (Bologna: La luna nel pozzo, 2005) as I was finishing the manuscript, so I was unable to incorporate more fully its remarkable analyses of *photogénie*.

For her gift of time and love, and for just about everything else too, I thank my wife and best friend, Margaret.

Abbreviations

To save space, I have used the following standard abbreviations for shot analysis.

- CU close-up (a face filling the screen or a small object/area)
- ECU extreme close-up (a small detail, part of something, an eye)
- ELS extreme long shot (persons too small to identify, aerial establishing shot)
- FS full shot (a person from the feet or knee up or equivalent)
- HA high angle (camera pointed downwards)
- LA low angle (camera pointed upwards)
- LS long shot (several persons in a large indoor or outdoor space or equivalent)
- MCU medium close-up (chest and face or a larger object/area)
- MS medium shot (a person from the waist up or equivalent)
- POV point of view
- VLS very long shot (a crowd or a very large space or expanse)

Introduction:
Epstein at the crossroads

Il n'y a pas d'histoires. Il n'y a jamais eu d'histoires. Il n'y a que des situations, sans queue ni tête; sans commencement, sans milieu, et sans fin; sans endroit et sans envers; on peut les regarder dans tous les sens; la droite devient la gauche; sans limites de passé ou d'avenir, elles sont le présent.

Jean Epstein (1974: 87 [1921a])[1]

Lumière vs. Méliès revisited

Jean Epstein opens his 1936 documentary *La Bourgogne* with a curious very long shot (VLS). A locomotive loudly speeds by a railroad crossing from left to right, while cars stack on both sides of the track. It's the kind of shot one expects from a realist drama, for instance in Renoir's 1938 adaptation of Zola's *La Bête humaine*, or the end of John Huston's *The Asphalt Jungle* (1950). A few minutes later, a continuous 360-degree pan – which is among the earliest use of this shot – shows us an unremarkable crossroad, La Rochefoucault near Montbard.[2] One branch runs to the north-east, linking Provence to Germany, the voice-over indicates, while the other goes to the north-west, linking

[1] 'There are no stories. There have never been stories. There are only situations, having neither head nor tail; without beginning, middle or end; no recto nor verso; they can be looked at from all angles; right becomes left; without limitations in the past or future, they are the present' (Jean Epstein, 1988: 242 [translation modified]).

[2] The first 360-degree pan is usually imputed to James Whale's *Frankenstein* (US, 1936), with a centripetal 360-degree pan around Paul Robeson in Whale's *Ol' Man River* (US, 1936). See Robertson (1991: 113).

Switzerland to Paris. It's a simple X in the middle of the non-descript countryside. The voice-over adds that it is a site of many car accidents, but oddly no cars can be seen. More shots of the deserted crossroad follow, with an ominous insistence.

We get the sense that Epstein is not so much documenting this place as reimagining it as an enigmatic symbol of his own life. After all, the north-east branch makes a straight line between Poland, where he was born, and Nice, where he discovered filmmaking, while the other road similarly links Switzerland, where he was raised, and Brittany, where he made some of his best films. Perhaps he has found something like the geographical fulcrum of his travels. In any case, this crossroad sequence illustrates a major question that runs through Epstein's filmmaking career: what separates the documentary, ostensibly beholden to reality – the cinema of the Lumière brothers – from a fiction film, a work of imagination – the cinema of illusion of Georges Méliès? It would be in keeping with Epstein's philosophy of cinema to present such a thorny problem in filigree, by filming a simple crossroad.

The epigraph above confirms that Epstein was explicitly rethinking fiction movie as a genre. According to him, dramatic movies ought not to be story driven, but built around a number of situations. What's the difference? In a typical Hollywood movie every action, line of dialogue, scene, or episode serves the narrative arc clearly and efficiently. So efficiently that we can talk of absolute narrative dominance reinforced by viewer expectation to form a closed commercial bond whereby buyers 'get' what they paid for. Though other avant-garde filmmakers were quick to peg him as a commercial director, Epstein refused this kind of closed aesthetics. His œuvre favours 'situations', that is, fragments or moments dislodged from the narrative, meant to be experienced and enjoyed for themselves, as direct presentations of the essence of cinema. We can think of situations as having a self-contained *poetic quality*, distinct from their *narrative value*. If fiction films correspond to novels in literature, Epstein's movies may be considered to embed wayward poems in their plot, in the very way Proust punctuates his narrative with sprawling descriptions and disquisitions that are almost stand-alone prose poems.

Epstein's quote certainly points us directly to Aristotle's theory of the three literary genres: the epic (or narrative), the lyric and the theatre. References to the 'head' and 'tail' and 'no beginning, middle, or end' cite almost verbatim the way Aristotle defines the epic – *haplèdiegetikê* – as a kind of animal body with a head and a tail. Epstein does not feel the need to make this explicit, however, thus illustrating a non-élitist intellectual ethics that attempts to couch complex ideas in approachable form. Greek thought and sexual tolerance matter to him deeply, as we will see, but not erudition. And while he delves into theoretical reflection he never seeks to gainsay a strategic advantage – as avant-gardes tend to do – only to clarify what we experience. To return to the citation as a whole, Epstein polemically rejects plot-driven cinema because it distracts viewers from the force and beauty of the filmic moments it is made of. What is beautiful, he suggests, is not the story – most plots follow stock fables anyway – but something about what is viewed and how it is viewed. In other words, a movie is not the *representation* of a pre-existing story, but the *presentation* of dramatic situations considered chiefly in how they appeal to our imagination and perception here and now. This, in turn, can help us to understand why poetry is so central to Epstein, together with *photogénie*, his term for the presentational force of certain shots or sequences.

By now, we have thrown out the window any notion that film theory in the silent era remained cursory until the likes of Sergei Eisenstein and Dziga Vertov produced sudden leaps. In *La Bourgogne*, Epstein overlays intimations of deadly crossings or accidents onto a bucolic evocation, grafting a potential drama on the sober documentary genre. In his 1927 fiction film *La Glace à trois faces*, a car accident puts an end to the story when a fateful bird hits the driver. The virtual accidents in the documentary and the actual accident in the fiction film illustrate the same idea: 'Without limits of past or future, [these situations] are the present.' Cinema, like history and life, takes place also in its accidents, that is, in the here and now, within the tensions that bind our present to past and future. It is significant, for instance, that *La Bourgogne* was shot in March 1936, at the very time the nearby Rhineland was being reoccupied by the Nazi regime with its expansionist agenda. The documentary, usually about present and past, can also refract the looming shadow of the future. Jean Epstein, famous yet misunderstood, original yet held to be idiosyncratic and poetic to a fault, consistently referred to by most critics as a key theoretician and yet substantially engaged with by very few of them, has been stuck at the crossroads of film history, in a past that has not yet been recovered.

This, at least, is the lasting ambiguity that accompanies Epstein's life, film work and writings. He is so central to French film history that the largest screening hall of the new Bercy Cinémathèque bears his name. And yet, only one of his more than forty films, *La Chute de la maison Usher* (1927), has been available to the public in VHS or DVD format until very recently, and only one book-length monograph on his work exists in French or English, published in 1964 and long out of print (Leprohon, 1964). For scholars and amateurs of silent cinema he has long been a star of steady first magnitude. Yet within cinema studies at large his aesthetics has waned before being fully investigated or understood. Diluted into a single word, *photogénie* (see chapter 1), his aesthetic project is equated with a naïve faith in the magic power of moving images, whereas Epstein insistently articulated *photogénie* in detailed corporeal, ethical and political terms as we will see. Meanwhile, thinkers of the cinema as diverse as Edgar Morin, Jean Mitry, and Siegfried Kracauer in the 1950s and 1960s, and Gilles Deleuze, Jean-Luc Godard, and Jacques Rancière in the 1980s and 1990s, have uniformly recognized in Jean Epstein both a remarkable filmmaker and among the first committed philosophical thinkers of cinema (see chapter 6). The time has come to take these influential figures at their word and give Epstein the critical appraisal that has been so long in coming. For his double attainment – as key director and pioneering theoretician – places him in the restricted company of Dziga Vertov, Sergei Eisenstein, Jean Cocteau, Pier Paolo Pasolini, and Jean-Luc Godard. Epstein is not only of the same stature as they are: he has informed their thinking much more directly, it would seem, than has yet been firmly established.

The aim of this book is to offer English readers the first comprehensive introduction to and preliminary study of Epstein's movies, film theory, and literary and philosophical criticism in the age of cinema. The book has in mind the many constituencies with which Epstein interacted over his lifetime: casual filmgoers, aficionados, researchers, teachers, students, historians, writers and artists, film archivists and museum curators, and movie industry professionals. In many ways, it is because his cinema and his thought have always aimed to address a plurality of recipients that Epstein has proved so resistant to being processed, distilled and pigeon-holed by film history.

INTRODUCTION 5

Biographical sketch: 1897–1953

Jean Epstein was born in Warsaw in 1897 of a Polish Jewish father and a non-Jewish French mother. In 1905, according to his younger sister Marie – who became an important filmmaker in her own right as well as a key member of the Cinémathèque – Jean discovered cinema in Abazzia, on the Adriatic coast (Leprohon, 1964: 12). After his father died in 1907, he and Marie were raised in Switzerland (he attended the Villa St Jean college in Fribourg), before coming to Lyon in late 1914, where he pursued medical studies. As the French joke goes, he never caught up with them, and was soon doing translation and editing work for Auguste Lumière, the co-developer with his brother Louis of the *Cinématographe*. Jean and his sister were already avid moviegoers by the time World War One broke out. But Jean became a true cinephile around 1915 while watching the Essanay comedies of Chaplin in London, before they were released in France the following year (Leprohon, 1964: 18–19, date corrected from 1914 to 1915).

In 1917 he made the key acquaintance of Abel Gance, at that time artistic director of the Film d'Art and an upcoming filmmaker, whom the powerful Charles Pathé groomed personally. Nine years older than Epstein and the illegitimate son of a Jewish father, Gance had been a would-be Symbolist poet and actor, turned scriptwriter in 1911, film essayist in 1912, then director of light melodramas and comedies the same year. In 1919, he wrote and shot *J'Accuse*, a bold and original *ménage à trois* plot unfolding into a biting indictment of war, which established his international reputation. In 1922 he released the big-budget *La Roue*, a railroad melodrama also featuring two men, father and son, vying for the love of a single woman whom the father adopted as a child. The innovation of this epic film recut several times at between four and six hours' duration and without a final edit, lay in its experiments with the rhythmic montage of composite shots of rails and electric wires that functioned clearly as a poetic nexus on the margins of the narrative. These sequences were ultimately gathered into a non-narrative short entitled *La Rose du rail*, shown and discussed widely in cine-clubs in the mid-1920s as encapsulating avant-garde aesthetics. Epstein and Gance must have felt an uncanny understanding of each other, as both fatherless one-time poets partly but not technically Jewish, and equally fascinated by the cinema's relationship with philosophy and by its capacity to envision social utopia.

6 JEAN EPSTEIN

By 1918, Epstein was writing poetry and poetic texts, some with obvious homoerotic tones (see chapter 3), and he was already jotting down theoretical reflections on the impact of mass culture, and in particular cinema, on modernist literature. Rather than a writer turned filmmaker (like Jean Cocteau), or a filmmaker turned writer (like Robert Bresson), Epstein remained all his life a cinephile writer and a writing filmmaker, often complementarily so, as when he penned two novels while shooting his Brittany films in the 1930s. In 1919, upon Gance's recommendation, Epstein contacted Blaise Cendrars to try to have his first critical writings published. Cendrars, who would assist Gance on the shooting of two films, was then literary editor at Éditions de la Sirène. He had been thinking about cinema's place in literature since 1912, and had just finished a series of texts on cinema (Cendrars, 2001). Cendrars obliged, and in 1921, Epstein's first book was published by La Sirène, *La Poésie d'aujourd'hui: un nouvel état d'intelligence* [*Today's Poetry: A New State of Mind*]. The book was accompanied by the publication of Epstein's complementary reflections, 'Le Phénomène littéraire' (1921c), in six back-to-back issues of *L'Esprit Nouveau*. This international journal, run by Ozenfant and Le Corbusier, was read by the artistic intelligentsia across the world, and soon the dadaist American journal *Broom* published an excerpt in English. This modicum of fame sadly triggered the jealousy of Cendrars who soon broke off relations with Epstein. Two other books nonetheless quickly followed at La Sirène: *Bonjour cinéma* (1921b) and *La Lyrosophie* (1922).

It was when visiting Cendrars in Nice in 1920 that Epstein discovered the strange world of the movie studio. There he caught a glimpse of the filmmaker and his future friend Germaine Dulac, 'a majestic, benevolent, and infinitely sympathetic woman', directing on a set (Epstein, 1974: 32). Cendrars and Epstein went to meet Gance in a rented villa, but the latter had already left. Epstein describes picking up a bit of film on the floor as 'a rush fragment, a relic', before pointing out how 'the pharmaceutical odour' from a box of reels mysteriously saturated the house (*ibid.*: 34). In other words, Epstein was hooked. We'll note that cinema figures as a vestige, that is, the material index and actual sensorial trace of something that has vanished, and at the same time promises a future revelation. This is the same forward–backward motion as in the epigraph or the shot of the crossroad. While in Nice, Cendrars assisted Gance on the shooting of *La Roue*, and Epstein occasionally helped out as well. But Epstein went back to Lyon, and in 1921 he launched a literary journal *Le Promenoir*. The success of *La Poésie d'aujourd'hui* brought him to Paris around the end of the year, at the invitation of Paul Laffitte, the owner of both La Sirène, and Le Film d'Art.

Through Laffitte, Epstein became assistant to Louis Delluc on the shooting of *Le Tonnerre* (1922) his first true cinema job, before Delluc recommended him to Marcel L'Herbier.[3] Thus before even starting his directing career, Epstein had rubbed shoulders with all the main representatives of the so-called French narrative avant-garde: Gance, Dulac, Delluc, and L'Herbier. In passing, there are several terms to refer to this group of filmmakers. 'The first French avant-garde', distinguishes them from the dadaist/Surrealist filmmakers Fernand Léger, Man Ray, Luis Buñuel and René Clair forming the second French avant-garde. 'Impressionist cinema' refers to the manipulations of film images (composites, slow motion, deformation) often, but not always, present in the films of the first French avant-garde. I follow here Richard Abel who opts for 'the French narrative avant-garde', to underline the fact that these filmmakers aimed to alter narrative from the inside, and also to suggest that there were other contemporary movements, e.g., the Danish narrative avant-garde (Abel, 1984: 279–94).

Interning at La Sirène, Epstein also met Jean Benoit-Lévy in a neighbouring office (Vignaux, 2007: 82). Formerly from Pathé, he had just launched his own production company (in educational films), and would become the most prolific French documentary filmmaker into the 1950s. Benoit-Lévy and Marie Epstein would go on to make films together, for instance co-directing *La Maternelle* (1933), a proto-Front Populaire docufiction. Benoit-Lévy put Epstein in charge of his first directing job: a docufiction on France's iconic hero Louis Pasteur that came out in 1922, launching his directing career for good.

Between 1923 and 1929, Epstein directed and often produced nearly twenty fiction films. They were adaptations from literature

3 Marie Epstein adds in a radio programme that 'Jean faisait tous [l]es découpages [de *Tonnerre*], indiquant le nombre de tours de manivelle pour chaque surimpression, l'objectif, le diaphragme, mais improvisait au tournage' ['Jean did all of *Le Tonnerre*'s découpages, specifying the number of crankturns per superimpression, and the kind of lens and diaphragm, but he improvised during the shooting'] (Douek and Krauss, 1998).

such as *L'Auberge rouge* (1923) after Honoré de Balzac, *Mauprat* (1926) after George Sand, *La Glace à trois faces* (1927) after Paul Morand and *La Chute de la maison Usher* (1928) after Edgar Allan Poe. He also wrote original scripts for *Cœur fidèle* (1923), or co-wrote them with Marie for *L'Affiche* (1924), *Le Double amour* (1925), and *Six et demi onze* (1927), or with other writers such as Ivan Mosjoukine for *Le Lion des Mogols* (1924). Around 1927–28, financial and personal reasons that included wanting to work away from Paris, led him to undertake a then rare experiment: the shooting of a film entirely on location with a small technical team and non-professional actors. This decision was also the result of his abiding interest in the coastal communities of Brittany whose harsh sea-centred lifestyle, scarcely affected by the tumultuous mutations of modernity, was closely intertwined with the dynamic, indeed kinetic, environment of water and wind. After *Finis Terræ* (1929) – among his undisputed masterpieces – Epstein shot four other fiction films in Brittany, two of them with sound, including his final masterpiece, *Le Tempestaire* (1947), and a docufiction on light-houses for the UN that was to be his last film in 1948.

During the 1930s, Epstein turned largely to documentary work. He had shot his first fully documentary film in 1923 on the eruption of Mount Etna – a film that is sadly lost. He directed over twenty documentaries between 1929 and 1948, ostensibly for material reasons, which did not, however, preclude a clear social and political intent. Indeed, the bulk of his documentary production coincided with the rise of social and labour movements that led to the Front Populaire in mid-1930s France, and Epstein fully committed himself to supporting it. The suspicion among Surrealists and more recent film critics that his embrace of commercial movie-making implies conservative leanings is put to rest by the careful study of this documentary work. The Surrealist poet Robert Desnos, for one, must have known this well when he collaborated with Epstein on the 1938 documentary, *Les Bâtisseurs*. Archival documents reveal that Epstein also believed in equal pay, since on his *Artères de France* (1939), the director (Epstein), assistant director (René Lucot), scriptwriter/voice talent (Champly), and editor (in this case, Epstein too) were paid the same.[4]

With the onset of World War Two in 1939, then the Occupation of the North of France in 1940, and all of France after 1942, Epstein was all but forced to place his directing career on hold, since he would

---

4 Fonds Epstein, Collection Cinémathèque Française, BiFi, 77B20.

have been classified as Jewish by the Vichy regime. We know he was in the crosshairs of virulent anti-Semites such as Lucien Rebatet who, in his 1941 anti-Semitic pamphlet *Les Tribus du cinéma et du théâtre*, attempted to discredit Abel Gance based on the fact that he was a friend of Jean Epstein, and thus probably also a Jew:

> Jusqu'ici, parmi les metteurs en scène, le contingent des Juifs reste modeste. Le plus notoire est Jean Epstein. Il est juif avant tout par son esthétisme ambitieux et composite. Ses écrits – car il a noirci aussi du papier, la *Lyroscopie* [sic] entre autres – sont d'un amphigouri fort révélateur également de l'esprit juif. J'allais placer à côté d'Epstein Abel Gance. On assure qu'il aurait fait la preuve d'un aryanisme suffisant ... Rien, cependant, n'exhale un fumet juif plus prononcé que le messianisme primaire et vaniteux de *Prisme*, le journal intime où il assure s'être mis tout entier. (Rebatet, 1941: 8; Marie Epstein is 'denounced' on 28)[5]

Little is known of his whereabouts during the war, although letters place him in Paris, then later in Vichy where Marie Epstein worked in a service assisting the wounded and displaced after 1943.[6] Marie states that both Jean and she were arrested by the Gestapo in February 1944 and released only through the intervention of friends, while Jean himself mentions an arrest by the Gestapo in May 1944 (Leprohon,1964: 58). In a letter to the Red Cross, Epstein writes that he was 'démissionné d'office [de la Coopérative de Production des Artisans d'Art du Cinéma] par la Préfecture de Police de Paris, sur ordre des Allemands en Novembre 1940, dépouillé de son mobilier personnel, emporté par les Allemands, le 7 février 1941, objet d'un mandat d'amener de la Gestapo depuis le 8 février 1944, arrêté par les Allemands le 9 mai 1944, relâché par la suite'.[7] What is certain is that

---

5 'Until now, among directors, the Jewish contingent remains modest. The most notorious is Jean Epstein. He is a Jew above all through his ambitious and composite aestheticism. His writings – for he also inked pages, la *Lyroscopie* [sic] among others – are a mishmash also very much typical of the Jewish mind. I was going to set next to Epstein Abel Gance. We are assured he has demonstrated a sufficient Aryanism ... Nothing, however, exhales a more pronounced Jewish reek than the primitive and conceited messianism of *Prisme*, the personal journal in which he boasts of having depicted himself entirely.'

6 Among the supporters Epstein may have relied on in Vichy was Jacques Chevalier, the author of a book Epstein adapted in documentary form as *L'Arbre ou le pas de la mule* (1930), who was Secrétaire d'état in Vichy from late 1940 to mid-1941.

7 'forcibly demoted [from la Coopérative de Production des Artisans d'Art du Cinéma] by the Préfecture de Police de Paris on German orders in November

the landlord of the apartment of Marie and Jean (they lived together for most of their lives) stole all their property under cover of Vichy's anti-Semitic laws. Countless letters of Jean to post-Liberation authorities attest to this, and also that the two never recovered anything.[8]

After the Liberation, Epstein played a substantial part in the institutional reconstruction of French cinema, since some of his friends occupied high positions in new state-supported film organizations. For instance, the Institut des Hautes Études de Cinéma was co-directed by Marcel L'Herbier and composer Yves Baudrier (who wrote the score for *Le Tempestaire*). He gave lectures and led courses on cinema at the newly created Institut de Filmologie as well as at the Institut des Hautes Études de Cinéma, and continued publishing articles in important journals, such as Jean-Paul Sartre and Maurice Merleau-Ponty's *Les Temps Modernes* (Le Forestier, 2009). But with the exception of his last two Brittany films, he no longer directed. Epstein is said to have been dogged by alcoholism in his final years: his last book posthumously published was to be entitled *Alcool et cinéma*. It is unclear whether it was the cause or result of his impossibility to work in films, or for that matter whether it was connected to lifelong personal tensions such as being neither Polish nor French, neither fully a Jew nor a Gentile, or being obliged to anchor his movies around heterosexual melodramas while being himself a homosexual unable to come out of the closet. When he died in 1953, Marie organized a collective homage at the *Cinémathèque* where she had been working closely with its founder, Henry Langlois. A handful of speakers who included Jean Cocteau gave him a simple and sober eulogy.

Epstein in semi-oblivion

That Epstein has become such an oxymoronic *fameux inconnu* (famous unknown) may be ascribed to various contingencies and choices that shaped his career, as well as to the evolution of film studies after his death. He started work in cinema in the early 1920s, in a precarious

---

1940, deprived of his own furniture taken away by the Germans on 7 February 1941, subject to an arrest order by the Gestapo since 8 February 1944, arrested by the Germans on 9 May 1944, subsequently released' (Fonds Epstein, Collection Cinémathèque Française, BiFi, 189B42).
8 *Ibid.*

time for the French movie industry that had lost its early global dominance in the course of World War One. When it began reconstructing, French cinema registered the new hegemony of Hollywood's high-quality studio system productions, with which it tried to compete for the domestic market. Epstein joined the loose group of filmmakers known retrospectively as the first narrative avant-garde. They borrowed some of Hollywood cinema's newest features, in the wake of Griffith, Ince, and DeMille; e.g., quicker pacing and editing, careful lighting and cinematography, more attention to realism, superimposed intertitles, etc. They also tried to develop an 'avant-garde' cinema reflecting social concerns closely linked to the Paris cine-club network that encouraged and discussed such movies. For instance, Jacques Feyder's *Crainquebille* (1922) and Germaine Dulac's *La Souriante Madame Beudet* (1923), make use of ample composite shots to bring focus in their realist fictions respectively to an orphan and a destitute working-class old man, and to a psychologically abused woman. This dedication to a hybrid of popular and experimental cinema, however, quickly proved commercially unviable. By 1929, the compounding impacts of poor box-office receipts, the global economic crisis, and the arrival of the talkies decimated this avant-garde wing of silent French cinema. Seemingly less radical than subsequent avant-gardes from dadaist film onwards, the group disappeared from both public and critical awareness roughly from the mid-1930s to the late 1970s. Abel writes that, 'by the end of the silent film period, Jean Epstein was the most prominent, and controversial, filmmaker in the French narrative avant-garde' (1984: 284). Oblivion of the movement has accordingly meant that Epstein was relegated to limbo.

To economic, technical, historical, and archival contingencies (film preservation had barely begun, and movies released in too few prints often quickly vanished), there were added a number of personal decisions. Like his friends Germaine Dulac and Abel Gance, Epstein was unwilling to compromise his ideals of cinema beyond a certain point. This complicated relationships with producers and financial backers who naturally pushed for established formulae. Such an uncompromising attitude, combined with Epstein's idiosyncratic approach to hybridizing fiction and documentary genres would have become even less feasible after the talkies brought drama and theatrical dialogue to the forefront. In a letter of 8 June 1930, he writes: 'I am going through a year in which almost every day carries for me an acute money problem.'[9] Moreover, the political climate of the early 1930s likely accentuated his break with fiction cinema, since most of his documentary work was shot in the period leading to or during the Front Populaire, and it displays explicit anti-fascist ideas holding the collective to be a source of empowerment and freedom more powerful than the state. This documentary work subsequently all but disappeared from public view into a few archives, further obscuring a key period in Epstein's late career.

After his death, the fate of Epstein became even more bifurcated. At the Cinémathèque, Marie Epstein kept the memory of her brother's œuvre alive, and thanks to her efforts the growing circle of international film archives and festivals, film historians and specialized journals – including *Les Cahiers du cinéma* – never lost sight of Epstein's contribution. But this was not the case with the burgeoning milieu of academic film studies. In the 1960s, in spite of isolated attempts by scholars from the US, Epstein dropped out of the new canon of film theory. Regarding Epstein's contribution to *filmologie*, for instance, Antoine Le Forestier wonders expressly, 'why has *filmologie* totally erased any reference to [Epstein], whereas some of the works it produced clearly betray his influence?' (2009: 135). André Bazin, certainly among the key references in the 1960s and 1970s, had little use for Epstein's brand of realism, in spite of his admiration for Flaherty's Epsteinian docufiction, *Louisiana Story* (1948). In the Anglo-American academy, the single most decisive factor in Epstein's oblivion lay with the strategic condemnation of the narrative avant-garde group by André Breton and Luis Buñuel, at a time when Surrealism set out to take over the mantle of radical avant-garde in cinema after 1929. Subsequently, in both France and the Anglo-Saxon world, Breton and Buñuel's skewed assessment became something of a diktat, or at least a cliché, so that film theory's subsequent turns towards Marxism, the critique of the cinema apparatus and feminism throughout the 1970s and 1980s largely ignored the narrative avant-garde.

In the late 1970s, amnesia began subsiding when scholars at the Congress of Brighton programmatically decided to focus on the silent period within the already fast-diversifying field of academic film studies grounded in sound cinema. Simultaneously, Epstein's theoretical work was published almost in its entirety by Pierre

9 *Ibid.* 16B12.

Leprohon, at the publishing house of poet and communist sympathizer Pierre Seghers. The 1978 Brighton Congress and this publication no doubt explain the relative return of Epstein to the horizon of major film thinkers of the 1980s such as Gilles Deleuze and Jacques Rancière. Finally, in 1998, Jacques Aumont organized a large international conference on Jean Epstein at the Cinémathèque française, and the published proceedings represent the first important critical work on Epstein, with several studies following suit, especially in Italy, by Laura Vichi and Chiara Tognolotti. The new Cinémathèque's main screening hall at Bercy was named after Jean Epstein in 2005, obliquely in homage to Marie Epstein who had died in 1995. Finally, in 2007, the first conference in the English-speaking world devoted to Epstein was held at the University of Chicago, under the auspices of Tom Gunning, and a second collection of critical articles resulting from it, edited by Sarah Keller and Jason Paul, and published in 2012. The present book partakes of the renewed interest in Epstein studies that this conference instigated.

Why Epstein matters today

We might ask plainly what makes Epstein's films and writings relevant to cinema studies today, beyond the concern of a few impassioned historians of the silent era? The present book is written in the hope of providing specific and detailed answers. But a quick response would be this: in displacing in his films and writings all the canonical boundaries that have since then come to be accepted between the viewer and the film, fiction and documentary, cinema and literature, art and commerce, entertainment and politics, modernity and tradition, straight and queer, scopophilia and bodies on display – among many other binaries – Epstein transmits to us a challenging invitation to question all such dichotomies within our new regime of post-digital and distributed moving images. Strangely, the inherent experimentalism of French cinema in the 1920s seems much closer to our new yet unsettled digital regime, than it does to the 'mainstream' studio-centred cinema that took place in between. It is because of his very marginality that Epstein can now help us to rethink both cinema and moving images more broadly, outside of entrenched ways of thinking. In the conclusion, I will argue more specifically that Epstein's novelty

– and main legacy – consists of having shifted the centre of gravity of film thinking towards the mediating role of the body, including the queer body, as well as filmic and pro-filmic materiality. Until now, cinema theory has largely resisted the call of the sensorial by defining itself mainly through questions of illusion, suspicion, projection, control, and representation that remain woefully disembodied, indeed at times anachronistically Cartesian. Epstein opened and reopens today the corporeal horizon within which cinema has developed and changed, every step of the way.

Here is a quick synopsis of the book. Chapter 1 will look at the foundational pair of books Epstein published in 1921–22, amounting to a general critique of modernism in the new technological age, comparable to that of Walter Benjamin. As his interests in poetry dovetailed with his passion for cinema, we will analyse his movie remix of Edgar Allan Poe tales, *La Chute de la maison Usher* (1928) as a work reflecting on and transmuting the aesthetic legacy of Symbolism. Chapter 2 approaches Epstein's melodramatic films of the 1920s from the purview of social contestation, focusing on three: the dark and beautiful Marseille port masterpiece *Cœur fidèle* (1923); the rejection of high birth for the barge life in *La Belle Nivernaise* (1924); and a working-class mother in mourning struggling against corporate advertising in *L'Affiche* (1924). Chapter 3 turns to Epstein's technological, corporeal, and psychosexual view of cinema. This will point us in two seemingly opposite directions: the non-human nature of the gaze and intelligence of the apparatus, and the corporeal affects they magnify. We will show that the apparent opposition between human and non-human does not hold, and that Epstein's view of embodiment, including queer sensibility, brings them together. The films discussed include *Le Double amour* (1925), a melodrama about gambling with a clearly homoerotic episode; *Six et demi onze* [6 ½ x 11] (1927), a story in which a photograph acts as a protagonist; *La Glace à trois faces* (1927), an adaptation of a short story by Paul Morand about the glass closet and an automobile; and *L'Homme à l'Hispano* (1932), a sound melodrama in which an automobile and foreclosed heterosexuality go together. Chapter 4 analyses the Brittany period of Epstein and his resolute embrace of a (pre-) neorealist documentarian ethos. The chapter focuses on *Finis Terræ* (1929), among Epstein's most important films, and the new practice of filmmaking within a local community. Chapter 5 explores his documentary production as a whole in its social and political advocacy of labour and workers' participation. This chapter also analyses his philosophy of sound and its application to sound films, in particular *Le Tempestaire* (1947), his last masterpiece. Chapter 6 focuses on film philosophy rather than film theory per se to show how Epstein constructed through cinema a new way of understanding reason, reality, sensation, and perception in the wake of Spinoza. The chapter then turns to more recent cinema thinkers (Deleuze and Rancière) to explore the extent to which Epstein's cinema contributed to their own thought. The conclusion relates Epstein's legacy to subsequent developments in world cinema, particularly with regard to cinematography, the focus on the body, and the temporal intensification of the present that links them. We will follow briefly how these practical ideals made their way into films by Robert Bresson, Steven Soderbergh, and Ang Lee.

References

Abel, Richard (1984), *French Cinema: The First Wave, 1915–1929*, Princeton: Princeton University Press.

— (ed.) (1988), *French Film Theory and Criticism*, vol. 1, 1909–29, Princeton: Princeton University Press.

Aumont, Jacques (ed.) (1998), *Jean Epstein: cinéaste, poète, philosophe*, Paris: La Cinémathèque française.

Cendrars, Blaise (2001), 'L'ABC du cinéma' (1917 [1919]), *Tout autour d'aujourd'hui, œuvres complètes*, vol. 3, Paris: Denoël.

Douek, Simone and Mireille Krauss (1998), 'Jean Epstein, Les mardis du cinéma', radio programme aired on 19 April, Institut National de l'Audiovisuel.

Epstein, Jean (1921a), *La Poésie d'aujourd'hui, un nouvel état d'intelligence*, Paris: Éditions de la Sirène.

— (1921b), *Bonjour cinéma*, Paris: Éditions de la Sirène.

— (1921c), 'Le Phénomène littéraire', in Aumont (ed.), *Jean Epstein*, 39–85.

— (1922), *La Lyrosophie*, Paris: Éditions de la Sirène.

— (1974), *Écrits sur le cinéma*, vol. 1, Paris, Éditions Seghers.

— (1976), *Écrits sur le cinéma*, vol. 2, Paris: Éditions Seghers.

— (1988), 'The Senses 1(b)', in Abel (ed.), *French Film Theory and Criticism*, vol. 1, 241–6.

Le Forestier, Laurent (2009), 'Entre cinéisme et filmologie: Jean Epstein, la plaque tournante', in François Albera and Martin Lefebvre (eds), *La Filmologie, de nouveau, Cinémas* 19: 2–3 (spring), 113–40.

Leprohon, Pierre (1964), *Jean Epstein*, Paris: Éditions Seghers.

Rebatet, Lucien (1941), *Les Tribus du cinéma et du théâtre*, Paris: Nouvelles éditions françaises.

Robertson, Patrick (1991), *The Guinness Book of Movie Facts and Feats*, New York: Abbeville Press.

Tognolotti, Chiara (2005), *Al cuore dell'immagine: l'idea di fotogenia nel cinema europeo degli anni Venti*, Bologna: La luna nel pozzo.

Vichi, Laura (2003), *Jean Epstein*, Milan: Editrice Il Castoro.

Vignaux, Valérie (2007), *Jean Benoit-Lévy ou le corps comme utopie: une histoire du cinéma éducateur dans l'entre-deux-guerres en France*, Paris: AFRHC.

1

From literary modernism to *photogénie*

Mass culture and cinepoetry

Born in 1897, Jean Epstein belongs to the generation that came of age during the protracted carnage of World War One, as did André Breton (b. 1896), Tristan Tzara (b. 1896), René Clair (b. 1898), or László Moholy-Nagy (b. 1895). Recall that this was not one conflict among many, but the deadliest war in history, with more than 30 million dead, and an average of over 3,000 soldiers killed *daily*. Such mad figures resulted from unprecedented technological 'progress' deployed on all sides: huge-calibre canons, machine guns, carpet-bombing, grenades, minefields, asphyxiating gas, tanks, and air bombardment. Europe's supposedly enlightened civilization of democracy and positivism had turned cannibalistic and sadistic. The two determining figures in Epstein's early career, Blaise Cendrars and Abel Gance, were both survivors of the carnage. The bodily marks they bore and the lessons they drew would not be lost on Epstein as he launched on his radical path.

As soon as the war appeared close to an end, after it became clear the US would enter the conflict in 1917, artistic reactions accelerated in European capitals. In France, intellectual circles reconnected with the pre-war avant-garde ferments, transfiguring war trauma into absurdist and dada comedies, such as the ballet *Parade* by Cocteau, Diaghilev, Satie, and Picasso, and *Les Mamelles de Tirésias* by Apollinaire. Both performances, interestingly, include references to film, particularly American movies, which had flooded the home market during the war, once and for all dethroning France as the global leader in the film industry. Nevertheless, regardless of differences between specific movements and inspirations, 1917 signals the year when avant-garde works as a whole integrate references to cinema.[1]

The 1913 avant-garde of the 'banquet years' (pace Roger Shattuck) had been ecstatic and optimistic. Things were different this side of the war. The 1917 avant-gardes wondered how to save a shred of forward-thinking from the overwhelming sense of bankruptcy of the pre-war ideals. On the bright side, the Tramp films of Chaplin arrived in France in 1916, offering wonderfully inventive variations on the figure of the *clown triste* who overcomes the ruins. For artists and intellectuals, Chaplin had as much global importance as the infamous mutinies of French soldiers at the front in 1916 and the October Revolution in Russia in 1917 – and for the same reason: it showed that for too long the lower classes had disproportionately shouldered the human cost of so-called progress. In Gance's 1919 film *J'Accuse*, the war dead come back from the tomb, horribly disfigured, mutely accusing the living of having died for nothing. Gance featured actual disfigured veterans known as *gueules cassées* ('broken mugs'), among whom Blaise Cendrars made a cameo, since he'd lost his right arm at the front. Of course, in the film the living had no retort. European modernity had argued that utopia and humanism ultimately outweighed the negative aspects of innovation, exploitation, alienation, and colonization. Post-war modernism faced a radical quandary: what should now be the project of modernity? How could science, nationalism, commerce – even intellectuals themselves, who had been largely pro-war as a class whether in France or Germany – be trusted? What kind of art might guide the social ethos of Europe back from the brink?

While Epstein scarcely refers to World War One in his writings or film work, it is clearly from this set of urgent questions that he began reflecting on art and literature. Like his contemporaries Tzara and Breton, Epstein started from the diagnostic that instrumental reason alone was no longer a valid basis for the future of Western civilization and culture. Tzara famously rejected reason altogether to pursue the radical negation and absurd protests of dada, while Breton opted for unreason, automatism, the marvel of mythical events and the unconscious of Freud. Epstein, by contrast, took a third way, at once more

---

[1] Guillaume Apollinaire, Max Jacob and Maurice Reynal founded the *Société des amis de Fantômas* in 1913, but Futurism was the first organized movement to claim cinema's centrality as early as 1916, Lista (2008).

concrete, less centred on the artist as unique guide and, on the face of it, much more far-sighted. What science and art had overlooked and misunderstood, he began to suspect, was the perennial bad child of Western Judeo-Christian thought: the body. And not just the body in the abstract, nor merely bourgeois domesticated sexuality, but the larger body social – the bodily needs and experiences of the working masses.

Epstein began articulating this alternative argument in the years 1919–20, and it informs his first book, *La Poésie d'aujourd'hui: un nouvel état d'intelligence* (1921) as well as related essays concurrently published in six issues of the journal *L'Esprit nouveau* under the title 'Le Phénomène littéraire'. The argument also runs through his second and third books written in 1921–22: *Bonjour cinéma* and *La Lyrosophie*. Let us delve into this original theory of social embodiment and aesthetic transformation, since it aims to explain how cinema is especially suited to modernity's needs and how it is poised to become the ascendant medium.

La Poésie d'aujourd'hui: un nouvel état d'intelligence (1921)

> The poet must become more and more comprehensive, more allusive, more indirect, in order to force, to dislocate if necessary, language into his meaning. (A brilliant and extreme statement of this view, with which it is not requisite to associate oneself, is that of M. Jean Epstein, *La Poésie d'aujourd'hui*.)
>
> (T.S. Eliot, 1975: 65 [1921])

Epstein's central assumption in *La Poésie d'aujourd'hui* is that urban masses live in a state of semi-exhaustion and affective and sexual frustration resulting in a nervous condition that has initially little to do with what goes on in the mind. This is what he calls '*la fatigue*'. Moreover, for him exhaustion and pent-up feelings are directly linked. Because we are exposed to constant sensorial jolts in our means of transportation and repetitive tasks in our workplaces, our bodily capacities naturally become blunted, like the diminishing response to an ongoing stimulus. And because we belong to a systems-central industrial world that streamlines our experiences, our affective capacities are rarely solicited in their fuller spectrum and thus appear dormant, diffuse, or dammed up. Epstein does not see fatigue as a loss or shortage of energy, but rather as a state of sensorial and affective anaesthesia. The solution to both forms of anaesthesia consists in finding new routes to and from the subconscious (*le subconscient*). That is what modernist literature and especially poetry proposes to do, according to him, quite programmatically. The riddle of modernism, after the devastations of World War One, can only be solved by coming up with a new art that can heal the anaesthesia and trauma of the masses. And the paradigm for such a new art is very simply cinema. The intermittency, shock and speed that cause fatigue and sensorial erosion in the first place are, as it were, native to the film apparatus, and thus the latter is ideally suited to healing our sensing bodies in a homeopathic way.

To begin unpacking this conceptual programme, it is crucial to point out the difference between the *subconscious* and the *unconscious*. Epstein considered Freud's theory of the unconscious as some secret chamber or locked room within the bourgeois soul, as amounting to little more than a cheap device found in cheap novels (and films) such as those of detective Nick Carter. In 'Freud ou le nick-cartérianisme en psychologie' (1922c), Epstein affirms that our thought processes are too complex to encrypt only one (latent) message in any (manifest) expression. After a convincing critique of the arbitrary determinism Freud displays in the analysis of dream, Epstein concludes – rather hastily – that psychoanalysis therefore is mere delirium. However partial this view is, Epstein does hone in on the problematic (and necessary) lack of evidence for Freud's unconscious, and its resemblance to a novelistic ploy whereby only the psychoanalyst is capable of reading a missing or purloined document. Although he is not entirely fair to Freud – whom, however, he was among the first to read in France – Epstein rejects the Freudian unconscious principally because it is made of specific *thoughts* and *words*, rather than something much more bodily.

If we indeed repress anything – Epstein is not opposed to the process of repression – it is sensorial impressions, affective comportments, unsettled sexual desires, curtailed emotions, interpersonal mistakes, etc. For Epstein it makes no sense to believe that these would be first translated into words and thoughts then stored in some recess of the mind. Instead of words or signs, what we repress is sentient, motile, alive: 'Cette vie a été appelée vie végétative, vie sympathique. C'est une vie sourde, profonde, active, silencieuse, animale' (Epstein, 1921a:

153).² Repression and fatigue – including of a sexual nature (*ibid.*: 32) – impress themselves onto our bodies. According to Epstein, the fascination for this bodily subconscious is precisely what characterizes modernism: 'Non seulement l'esprit moderne se laisse envahir par la vie végétative, mieux il va au devant d'elle, se penche sur sa rumeur, l'ausculte, la scrute, l'interroge et en attend beaucoup de merveilles' (*ibid.*: 156).³ This attention to one's own bodily states, with a view to intellectualizing it down the road, Epstein calls 'coenaesthesis', which he defines as 'le visage physiologique du subconscient', 'the physiological face of the subconscious' (*ibid.*: 83). Coenaesthesis is the root of the aesthetic impulse, rather than intellection, and Epstein radically takes for granted 'la nonparticipation [sic] de la volonté, du jugement, du libre choix, etc. à l'émotion esthétique' ['the non-participation of will, judgement, free choice, etc., in aesthetic emotion'] (*ibid.*: 32).

The originality of this thesis consists in positing an embodied layer of repressed or delayed experiences that informs new artistic stances and innovations almost *materially*, although through the crucial mediation and interpretation of the artist. The reason cinema becomes central within such a model is that the film apparatus is much closer to the chain: fatigue → subconscious → coenaesthesis → aesthetic production than is the word-based intellectual process. So cinema becomes the medium where coenaesthesis discloses itself, and a homeopathic remedy is proposed to heal fatigued perception.

Epstein does not stop there. He goes on to isolate a number of formal features in the modernist writings of poets such as Max Jacob, Jean Cocteau, Guillaume Apollinaire, Louis Aragon, etc., and compares each of them on the one hand to specific perceptual and cognitive properties, and on the other hand to technical possibilities of the cinema. Hence the 'esthétique de succession' ['aesthetics of succession'], that he describes via the quick visual touches present in poems by André Salmon or Blaise Cendrars (*ibid.*: 74–6), keeps cerebral excitation up by stimulating surprise and variation. In turn, this drive for succession, as 'l'utopie physiologique de voir ensemble' ['the physiological utopia of seeing everything at once'], is directly

---

2 'This living layer has been called vegetating or sympathetic life. It is a veiled, deep, active, silent, and animal life.'

3 'Not only does the modern spirit accept the invasion of this vegetating life, but it goes ahead to meet it, it bends over its rumours, sounds it out, scrutinizes it, questions it and expects from it great marvels.'

satisfied by film technology's quick and angular succession of shots approximating 'le cercle parfait du simultanéisme impossible' ['the impossible simultaneism of the perfect circle'] (*ibid.*: 173). Proximity, mental quickness, suggestion, sensuality, metaphor, and ephemera constitute other elements of modernity that cut across poetry, psychology, and film in such a way that Epstein is led to posit a new realm that fuses all three – what he calls 'the unique intellectual plane'. We'll return to this complex idea later on, but for now let us note that modernist poetry becomes in large part the transcription of events taking place in the bodily subconscious, the importance of which was disclosed through movie-viewing.

La Poésie d'aujourd'hui mentions no specific movies, and it furthermore singles out pulp literature – which he calls 'sub-literature' – as a direct inspiration to modernist poetry before cinema, especially in its reliance on melodrama. Now, for avant-garde thinkers like Breton, Tzara, and Adorno, the melodrama's celebration of the status quo and its manipulative play of identification, render it unsuited to artistic revolution and instead a substantial tool for conservative forces. Here again, Epstein sees things otherwise. For him, the melodrama provides satisfaction to any number of authentic drives – justice, an ethical worldview, happy endings – and any number of causes for despair – loneliness, exploitation, disappointment, everydayness. Sure, melodramas *are* cultural opiates; yet taking the psycho-physiological needs of the working masses seriously, rather than holding such needs to be delusions and capitulation, represents a rare recognition by an intellectual of the actual embodied condition of mass workers. Epstein's aesthetic choices always privilege the embodied other (actual working-class persons) over avant-garde ideological stances, especially when they aim to overcome mass culture as if in all its aspects it was a political bad object.

This theory about modernist poetry should appear to us striking in a variety of ways. To begin with, it precedes by fifteen years similar concerns from the mid-1930s about mass phenomena and the culture industry analysed within both the Frankfurt School in Germany and the Collège de sociologie in France. More specifically, Epstein's medical training allows him to anticipate Benjamin's Freudian invocation of shock and innervation to try to explain the psychic and corporeal effects of film (see the section on *photogénie* and aura, below). Although several ideas akin to those of Epstein's book were floating in the late war journals such as *SIC*, *Nord-Sud*, *Littérature*, *Le Film*, or *L'Esprit nouveau*, no one had yet sought to fully integrate modernity, poetry, cinema, melodrama, the body's inner sense, and psycho-physiological research within a single framework. It shouldn't surprise us then that, in spite of several positive reviews, the book's holistic thesis remained too far ahead of its time. Within film studies, we have to wait for André Gaudreault and Tom Gunning's 'cinema of attractions', in the early 1980s, to find a comparable focus on the *positive* perceptual and embodied impact of the apparatus on spectators. In biographical terms, it should be noted that medical student and would-be poet Epstein finds a way to link his two avocations: medicine and poetry. He does so, it seems, on behalf of a third passion that will soon subsume them both: cinema. His book is then not theory for the sake of theory, but a pragmatic groundwork for his own metamorphosis into a filmmaker.

His second book, *Bonjour cinéma* (1921b), confirms the reorientation of his thought towards film culture, while paradoxically remaining within writing and poetry. This hybrid book, which expands and illustrates the theses of *La Poésie d'aujourd'hui*, mixes theory and verse, photos and drawings, cinephilia and star mania, and presents its own table of contents as a movie programme, each chapter corresponding to a different film (Keller, 2012). The book cover shapes the letters of the word *'cinéma'* into a movie projector, thus representing visually what *La Poésie d'aujourd'hui* had called for: 'Pour ainsi, se mutuellement soutenir, la jeune littérature et le cinéma doivent superposer leurs esthétiques' ['in order to shoulder each other, this new literature and the cinema must superimpose their mutual aesthetics'] (Epstein, 1921a: 170). *Bonjour cinéma*, I have claimed elsewhere, exemplifies a new kind of poetry that has shadowed cinema from its very beginnings up to the contemporary period and may be called cinepoetry (Wall-Romana, 2012a). While the book contains some of the germinal essays for Epstein's thought, and thus for film theory of the 1920s, notably 'Grossissement', 'Le Sens 1bis', and 'Ciné Mystique', it has only been republished once in 2000 in a very limited run (Epstein, 1993).[4] Moreover, these essays are currently available in English or in the French collected works only as stand-alone fragments broken from the book's formal, textual, poetic, and visual whole. Indeed, the norms

---

4 'Magnification' and 'The Sense 1b' can be found in Abel (1988: 235–46).

of humanities scholarship (including film studies) have too often excluded as non-essential visual material understood to be merely illustrative. A keen and beautiful work such as *Bonjour cinéma* reopens for us the productivity of multimedia and multisensorial responses to cinephilia, while questioning the filters that have unfairly excluded them from the accepted purview of scholarly and film studies.

Epstein's first two books traverse and subvert a number of aesthetic separations that have become standard within modernist criticism. While it is clear now that mass culture and new technologies of reproduction fascinated artists and writers from the 1840s onward, the process whereby, say, cinema enters literature, has been thought of as a one-way aestheticization of the apparatus, that is, literature lending its prestige to its young sister cinema. Poet Vachel Lindsay's 1915 book, *The Art of the Moving Picture*, makes the point through its title alone. It is a process of purification and sublimation. Eisenstein's comparison of silent cinema with Japanese haiku accomplishes a similar ennobling gesture on literature's side. Epstein goes about it in exactly the opposite way: 'Si vraiment "la machine à écrire", le "cinéma", le "chewing-gum", le "Gutenberg 24-19" ne peuvent entrer dans l'alexandrin sans le faire sauter, quoi d'étonnant qu'il ait sauté' ['If it is true that the "typewriter", "cinema", "chewing-gum", "Gutenberg 24-19 [phone number]", cannot figure in the alexandrine without blowing it apart, we should not be surprised if it blew apart'] (*ibid.*: 121). The medium migration is *from* technics *to* literature. Such transmigration of course comes with an ideological inversion: the technical products that were mainstream, commercial, and conservative are transfigured into a new species of aesthetic, and often, critical poetic objects. Directors of the French narrative avant-garde straddled sometimes uncomfortably this bridging of narrative mainstream and poetic experimentalism: for Epstein the filmmaker, this two-way street would prove equally a financial necessity and a critical virtue. Nonetheless, Epstein distinguished himself from other artists and filmmakers by developing a theory of the specificity of the film medium that, in profound ways, locates him right across the great divide between so-called high and low culture. This is what he called *photogénie*.

Photogénie

The word '*photogénie*', literally meaning 'created by light', was first used by astronomer François Arago in 1839, to refer to his friend Louis Daguerre's new photographic process. British photographer William Fox Talbot also used 'photogeny' to denote photography the same year. Gradually, however, the French noun shifted from the technology itself to its object, connoting the special aptitude of a model, a thing or a scene of lending itself well to photographic capture. Let us note in passing that such a shift signals an adaptation in sensory cognition. For to say that something is 'photogenic' before it is photographed means that the observer can look at a real scene with her naked eye and foresee or imagine its photographic representation. Better yet, when she beholds a scene or thing the observer develops a sense of what the photograph will feel like, and in so doing, we might say that she changes places with the camera. In this sense, even before Epstein, *photogénie* signalled a brand new cognitive–sensorial technology at play *within* human vision.

With regard to cinema, the term '*photogénie*' was scarcely used before Louis Delluc harnessed it in 1919 as a broad didactic slogan calling attention to the special nature of filmic images.[5] In the mid-1920s, after Delluc's early death, Epstein became its foremost proponent, notwithstanding the fact that his mentor, the poet Blaise Cendrars (as we saw, a collaborator of Abel Gance, the 'master' of early *photogénie*), objected that the word was, '*cucul-praline-rhododendron*' (Epstein, 1974: 32). This slang expression that telescopes words for the ass, a sweet, and a plant means at once 'cheesy' or 'schmaltzy', in a melodramatic sense, and 'airy-fairy' in a sense that is not devoid of effeminate or homosexual connotations (see chapter 3). Over a span of thirty-odd years, and crossing into the revolution of synchronous sound in cinema, Epstein enriched his understanding of *photogénie* but never wavered from his commitment to it as the essence of cinema: he reasserts it in his last (posthumously) published text, *Alcool et cinéma* written in the 1950s, commenting on how 'la photogénie s'introduisit subrepticement dans les œuvres filmées' ['*photogénie* surreptitiously inserted itself in the movies'] (Epstein, 1976: 177).

---

5 Colette and Henri Diamant-Berger's reference to 'photogenic arc' lamps in 1917 are possible sources for Delluc's updating the term (Delluc, 2002: 227, fn. 230). The most thorough discussion of *photogénie* is in Abel (1988: 95–124).

Together with '*cinégraphie*', which has to do with the overall rhythm of a movie and is obtained through editing, *photogénie* became one of the motivational refrains of 1920s filmmakers: historians Nourredine Ghali and Richard Abel have painstakingly shown the sophistication and diversity of its use in the silent period (Ghali, 1995: 123–36; Abel, 1988: 95–124). For all that, it remains a fuzzy concept, and film scholars often equate *photogénie* with an unqualified fetishism for the apparatus and a naive aestheticism of the filmic image for its own sake.[6] We will recall that a similar reproach was aimed at the Symbolists: that of foregoing subject matter and content altogether for the sake of a hyper-aestheticized vision of art and medium, further radicalizing the art-for-art's-sake of the Parnassians. We will delve into Epstein's characterization of *photogénie*, then turn to his best-known film, *La Chute de la maison Usher*, which deals with the legacy of Symbolism.

Epstein sees *photogénie* not as a partial feature (the camera for Arago, or the photogenic object or face), but as a total relation between *pro-filmic reality*, what stands in front of the camera, *filmic images*, and the *embodied viewer*. A canonical definition is given in 'De quelques conditions de la photogénie' (1923), collected in *Le Cinématographe vu de l'Etna* (1926): 'J'appellerai photogénique tout aspect des choses, des êtres et des âmes qui accroît sa qualité morale par la reproduction cinématographique' (Epstein, 1974: 137).[7] *Photogénie* is thus foremost the melding of the filmic with the pro-filmic: instead of offering a devalued copy or simulacrum of the model, less essential than or separated from it, film enhances the model's 'moral quality.' The latter is a fuzzy expression in French, since 'moral' ranges from the spiritual to the ethical and social, and 'quality' has the Bergsonian ring of duration (vs. 'quantity' which, for Bergson, is a purely spatial notion). Fortunately, Epstein twice alters his definition, to add that only 'mobile aspects' are photogenic, and further on that 'seuls les aspects mobiles et personnels des choses, des êtres et des âmes peuvent être photogéniques' ['only mobile and personal aspects of things, beings and souls can be photogenic'] (Epstein, 1974: 138, 140). Here the 'moral' would

---

6 Turvey (2008) views *photogénie* as a 'category mistake'. See Wall-Romana (2012b), for a rebuttal.

7 'I will term photogenic any aspect of things, beings and souls that enhances its moral quality through cinematographic reproduction' (Abel, 1988: 314 [translation amended]).

seem to have merged with the 'personal' in a way that suggests that *photogénie* is partly an experience of the viewer rather than an objective quality. At the very least, putting on the same plane 'things, beings, and souls', *photogénie* is the experience whereby animism, anthropomorphism, reified glamour, and idealism slip in and out of each other.

Though Epstein warns that 'you fall flat on your face trying to define it' (*ibid.*: 91), from the examples he provides we can infer the following. First, *photogénie* is a hyper-aesthetic phenomenon, that is, a *heightened mode of viewing* through which things and beings animated by film appear more intense to perceivers. Second, *photogénie* involves some kind of *emotional response by the perceiver* to this heightened mode of appearance, relatively independently from the contents of film images themselves. Third, Epstein writes that, 'la photogénie se conjugue aux [sic] futur et à l'impératif. Elle n'admet pas l'état' ['*photogénie* is to be conjugated in the future and imperative. It is never a state'] (*ibid.*: 94). This indicates that temporality and the virtuality of something to come, as well as some kind of interpersonality – since the imperative is a command of someone to someone else – organize the force-field of the movie-viewing experience. This echoes Bergson's focus on duration as becoming, while adding to it an intersubjective dimension, that of a call, an interpellation from someone or something. The mobile–temporal aspect of *photogénie* may reflect its closeness to arts of time such as music and poetry as well as to the phenomenology of temporal retention and protention.[8] But this personal and transpersonal aspect also evokes the allure of film stars (indeed, the trivial sense of 'photogenic' in movie culture) adding a sensual sense of promise, obsession, and pleasure for the viewer.

At his most aphoristic, Epstein formulates *photogénie* as 'logarithmes sensoriels' ['sensorial logarithms'] (*ibid.*), an apt expression conveying the way filmic images *compress* the sheer density of sensorial impressions within a photogenic moment. This also confirms that the medium of film is tightly intertwined for Epstein with bodily affects and non-visual sensations. Certainly, one of the most original aspects of his theory of *photogénie* is that it involves sensations *besides* vision, and in some way evinces the very root of sensation, that which the body has of itself:

---

8 These are Edmund Husserl's terms for our sense of time in how it gathers what has just happened (retention) and projects towards what is going to happen (protention), see Wahlberg (2008: 24).

> L'inconstance, le vague du temps vécu proviennent de ce que la durée du moi est perçue par un sens intérieur complexe, obtus, imprécis: la cénesthésie. Celle-ci constitue le sentiment général de vivre, dans lequel se somme et confond une foule de sensations indistinctes, recueillies par la sensibilité très imparfaitement consciente, de nos viscères. Sensibilité primitive, fœtale, très animale ... (*ibid.*)⁹

Coenaesthesis is generalized self-sensation, the sensing of one's self-sensing, the getting in touch with one's corporeal subconscious, as we have seen from *La Poésie d'aujourd'hui*.¹⁰ The screen is photogenic in that it discloses the coenaesthesis of the actors, the way their bodies express – or better, incarnate – their corporeal subconscious, as a means to invite the viewer's body to get in touch with his or hers. The screen, we might say, is the porous membrane through which two kinds of self-sensation interface, for and within the viewer. Epsteinian *photogénie* is then a total and triadic relation between the viewer as embodied and self-sensing, the pro-filmic as material and embodied as well, and the filmic as an interface where they encounter each other in a virtual or imaginary realm that provides a kind of virtual embodiment for the viewer.

Epstein's conception of movie-viewing might appear complicated and far-fetched. Our popular model of vision has images come through our eyes into our brain, which then deciphers their meaning. The body seems to play no part. Without entering into a long discussion for which there is no space here, let us say only that contemporary perception science rather sides with Epstein than our popular model. For one thing, it has long been known that there can be no vision without corroborative experience from other senses. Both Bergson and Maurice Merleau-Ponty insist that vision is a mode of testing the world relying on virtual body experiments via the other senses.¹¹ Moreover, vision does not merely *receive passively* what we see: it *actively produces* it. Indeed, it does so by sampling a few cues from the field of vision, extrapolating them with the help of past visual

---

9 'The inconstancy and fuzziness of lived time are due to the fact that the ego's duration is perceived by a complex, obtuse, imprecise inner sense: coenaesthesis. It constitutes the general feeling of living, in which a host of indistinct sensations coalesce and fuse, collected by the very imperfectly conscious sensibility of our viscera. A primitive, foetal, and very much animal sensibility...'
10 For the intellectual history of the sense of sensing and coenaesthesis, see Heller-Roazen (2007).
11 Bergson (1990).

experiences mixed with other sensations to give form to what it sees. In other words, we see by fitting what we have seen and felt before onto our field of vision, in what one researcher calls 'enactive vision'.[12] This is not very far from Epstein's idea that things and bodies move on-screen in such a way that they resonate with our affects so that we can experience and know them. Certainly, Epstein's *photogénie* is the most complete theory of filmic vision until what is known as 'apparatus theory' in the 1970s by the likes of Christian Metz, Jean-Louis Comolli, Jean-Louis Baudry, and Laura Mulvey, all of which largely discounted the productive aspect of the viewer's sight.[13]

Photogénie vs. aura

Epstein's *photogénie* also shares central features with one of the most celebrated critical concepts of the 1930s: Walter Benjamin's aura. *Both photogénie and aura stage a scene of beholding between a subject and an object-field in which a crucial qualitative change results from cinematic mediation and nothing else.* The canonical formula of the aura, from Benjamin's 'The Work of Art' essay is, 'A strange weave of space and time: the unique appearance of a distance, however near it may be' (2002: 104–5). Both *photogénie* and the aura are hyperactive middle terms that alter time and space. Epstein writes in the 1920s: 'l'aspect photogénique d'un objet est une résultante de ses variations dans l'espace-temps' ['the photogenic aspect of an object results from its variations in space-time'] (1974: 139; Abel 1988: 316) and in the 1950s, 'la photogénie est liée au mouvement soit de l'objet cinématographié, soit de l'appareil, soit de la lumière' ['*photogénie* is linked to the movement either of the filmed object, of the camera, or of the light'] (Epstein, 1974: 177). This deserves emphasis in terms of aesthetic philosophy. No longer is immediacy between subject and object privileged or even posited, as was the common premise of both Romanticism and Realism. On the contrary, a new form of semi-agency or imaginary agency arises between and mediates them – and has to do with cinema. Benjamin's auratic 'distance' proceeds also from cinema, as is plain from another quote of the essay: '[F]or the first time – *and this is the effect of film* – the human being is placed in a position where

12 For this discussion, see Merleau-Ponty (2002); Noé (2006).
13 See Rosen (1986).

he must operate with his whole living person, while forgoing its aura' (2002: 112). In other words, cinema's pressure destroys auratic distance, but also generates a new mode of bodily experiencing. Thus, while Benjamin's aura as a qualitative loss is the exact opposite of *photogénie* as a qualitative enhancement, both describe the very same phenomenon at the level of the body: a qualitative shift in the mode of embodiment due to cinema and cinema alone.

We can push the similarity further. The close-up, quite hyperbolically, is 'cinema's soul', Epstein writes, adding immediately: '[le gros plan] peut être bref, car la photogénie est une valeur de l'ordre de la seconde' ['it may be brief, for *photogénie* is a value of the order of the second'] (Epstein, 1974: 94; Abel, 1988: 236). This suggests Abel Gance's rapid edits of medium close-ups and iris shots during Eli's flashback as he is about to fall from the mountain in *La Roue* (1922), or Epstein's own *Cœur fidèle* (1923) with the famous merry-go-round sequence (see chapter 2). But rather than isolated or still close-ups, Epstein favours a sequence of shots of alternating scales. Hence he states that 'la danse du paysage est photogénique' ['the dance of the landscape is photogenic'] (Epstein, 1974: 94; Abel, 1988: 237), not any one shot of the landscape in particular. Epstein propounds shot variation around close-ups, for example describing an actual dance filmed with a mobile camera taking very close shots of dancers, then pulling back to their periphery (Epstein, 1974: 95; Abel, 1988: 237). I belabour the importance of scale shift here because of Benjamin's enigmatic and quasi-filmic staging of the aura: 'To follow with the eye ... a mountain range on the horizon, or a branch that casts its shadow on the beholder is to breathe the aura of those mountains, of that branch' (2002: 105). In her essay on Benjamin's aura and the aura hysterica (the alteration of perception prior to an epileptic seizure), Ulla Link-Heer points out an instance of a hill returning Marcel's gaze in Proust's *La Recherche* as a possible source for Benjamin's image (2003: 122–3). Yet a more complete similarity is found in the first section of *Le Cinématographe vu de l'Etna*, where Epstein writes:

> L'une des plus grandes puissances du cinéma est son animisme. A l'écran, il n'y a pas de nature morte. Les objets ont des attitudes. Les arbres gesticulent. Les montagnes, ainsi que cet Etna, signifient. Chaque accessoire devient un personnage. (1974: 134)[14]

---

14 'One of cinema's greatest powers is its animism. On the screen there is no still

Of course, this is just the kind of magical animism Benjamin warns against: cinema's fake 'mass existence' replacing the 'unique existence' of things to satisfy 'the desire of the present-day masses to "get closer" to things' (2002: 104). Yet Epstein's animism is not 'a passionate concern for overcoming each thing's uniqueness' as Benjamin puts it, but exactly the contrary: a desire to preserve the singular character and movement (gesture) of a thing. This is what Epstein calls 'le personnage du regard' ['the persona of the gaze'] (1974: 140; Abel, 1988: 317) that is, the gaze-like presence that emanates from an object when it is filmed. That is why the third definition of *photogénie* is crucial – 'mobile and personal aspects of things' – because, like philosopher Emmanuel Levinas who holds the face/gaze as the irreducibly human, this 'persona of the gaze' of the filmic image is foremost ethical. This explains Epstein's paradigmatically photogenic objects – a telephone, a gun, a door handle – in that they convey interhuman involvement: these objects crystallize intersubjectivity into a mobile material form that the film discloses as a kind of gesture. Hence, while Benjamin's scepticism about cinema (at least at one pole of his thought)[15] follows the traditional charge that it offers a mere kinetic copy of reality, Epstein's model theorizes *photogénie* from an ethical standpoint as that attribute of the filmic that discloses the human gaze and interhuman relations implicated in all things. While such 'return of the gaze' is fundamental to the aura, for Benjamin the ethics of the returned gaze implies the *exclusion* of technological mediation, whereas for Epstein it denotes its inclusion.[16] Nonetheless, as quasi-photo negatives of each other, *photogénie* and the aura are plainly two differing views on the same phenomenon.

Was Benjamin in the 1930s aware of and perhaps influenced by Epstein's theoretical work from the 1920s? The question is worth asking, and I believe Benjamin at the very least knew *of* Epstein's *photogénie*. The direct link between them is Léon Pierre-Quint, the

---

life. Objects have attitudes. Trees gesture. Mountains, like this Etna, signify. Each element of staging becomes a character.'

15 For Benjamin's fundamental ambivalence see Hansen (2002).
16 It is in the context of Baudelaire's condemnation of the daguerreotype that Benjamin formulates the auratic gaze: 'Experience of the aura thus arises from the fact that a response characteristic of human relationships is transposed to the relationship between humans and inanimate or natural objects ... To experience the aura of an object we look at means to invest it with the ability to look back at us' (2003: 338).

French critic who wrote the first book on Proust in 1925, and was, as Benjamin's 'Paris Diary' of 1930 attests, Benjamin's closest friend in Paris, both men sharing a daily breakfast (1999: 340, 350). As Michael Jennings (2004) has indicated, when Benjamin turned his attention towards popular culture and cinema, around 1924, after his failed *Habilitation*, he became close to the *Gestaltung* group of Berlin for whom photo-montage and film constituted an intermedia franca where all arts could meet. Hans Richter was its main figure and a journal was launched in 1922 around Moholy-Nagy, El Lissitsky, and Mies van der Rohe. Yet the prototype of such post-war inter-art journals was *L'Esprit Nouveau*, edited by Ozenfant and Jeanneret (later to be known as Le Corbusier) starting in 1920. It is in that journal, as we saw, that Epstein published 'The Literary Phenomenon', which ran through six issues. Perusing the list of *L'Esprit Nouveau* subscribers for the years 1920–21, we in fact find the names of Moholy-Nagy, Lissitsky, and Tzara – among hundreds of well-known artists (Brancusi, Duchamp, Pound, Stevens, Gide, Fauré, etc.).[17] If Benjamin did not directly discover Epstein in *L'Esprit nouveau*, certainly the latter's theories were widely disseminated within the *Gestaltung* group.

The footnotes to the 'Work of Art' essay mention several books in French, including *L'Art cinématographique* (Benjamin, 2002: fn. 3, 14, 15, 20). The latter is a 1927 collection of essays on cinema by Germaine Dulac, Abel Gance, Lionel Landry, and Léon Pierre-Quint, the second of an eight-volume series. Taken together, these four essays may be seen to push the narrative avant-garde theory in a direction very close to what Benjamin would theorize after Freud as innervation (*Bahnung*) – the counter-impulse capable of undoing the anaesthetic effects of shock or trauma by reviving the path of the original impulse. In her essay, Dulac writes for instance: 'It was cinema which revealed progressively to us the presence within our unconscious [*inconscient*] of a new emotional sense allowing for our sensorial comprehension of visual rhythms' (1927: 32). Minus the idea of rhythm, this progressive new sense of 'sensorial comprehension' is closely related to Benjamin's innervation via the optical unconscious (Hansen, 2002: 52–5). Now, it is the essay by Léon Pierre-Quint – from which Benjamin cites a passage citing Pirandello – that establishes a link between Benjamin and Epstein. In it, Pierre-Quint tells of his

17 www.fondationlecorbusier.asso.fr/fondationlc.htm, cf. 'Fonds,' 'Éditions,' 'Revues,' '*L'Esprit nouveau*', accessed 21 February 2009.

FROM LITERARY MODERNISM TO *PHOTOGÉNIE* 33

recent conversion to cinema in the following terms: 'The ray of light from the "surreal eye" as Mr. Jean Epstein puts it, has lit my darkness' (1927: 2). He adds, 'A wholly new image ... prolonging the reach of our senses, creates in ourselves a stimulation until now unknown in our consciousness' (*ibid.*: 20). This 'prolonging' into a 'new stimulation' has aspects of both the innervation via the optical unconscious and *photogénie* as adumbrated by Epstein himself. A third passage by Lionel Landry, who refers to several films of Epstein, including *Le Lion des Mogols* (1924), reads: 'Should we hope that, through a fusion, a progressive simplification, through some unconscious "facilitation" of associations [*'frayage' inconscient d'associations*], a pure cinematic sensibility might be created?' (1927: 80–1). The word 'frayage' is the sanctioned translation of Freud's 'Bahnung' into French from *Beyond the Pleasure Principle*, and it is here directly linked to the questions of a 'new emotional sense', or 'cinematic sensibility', or prolonged sensory experience, all three authors examine in a clearly Epsteinian way.

From this quite sophisticated volume, Benjamin excises for the 'Work of Art' essay three flat-footed passages from the most exulted of the four essays, that by Abel Gance. Benjamin wilfully leaves the link between *photogénie* theory and the optical unconscious by the wayside.[18] His citational strategy aims only at illustrating, 'the obtuse and hyperbolic character of early film theory', in how 'these theoreticians ... attribute elements of cult to film – with a striking lack of discretion' (Benjamin, 2002: 110). As for Epstein's comment about the 'surreal eye', it concludes the 1923 essay, 'Of Certain Conditions of Photogeny', collected in *Le Cinématographe vu de l'Etna* (1926), a book Pierre-Quint obviously read carefully. In view of his conversion, it is quite probable that he gave it to Benjamin to read, or at minimum talked to him about Epstein's *photogénie*.

As Miriam Hansen's recent recovery of Benjamin's aura prior to 'The Work of Art' essay attests, the tactical dissolution of the aura occluded 'broader anthropological, perceptual-mnemonic, and visionary dimensions' (2008: 338) in Benjamin's earlier work,

---

18 We may wonder how Benjamin chanced upon volume 2 only. In volume 1, René Allendy's 'The Psychological Value of the Image', defines an optical unconscious, concluding that, 'a deep knowledge of the affective value of images and unconscious processes would be the indispensable know-how of the filmmaker' (1926: 103).

not inimical in my view to Epstein's *photogénie*. Both share several profound inspirations: the sensory nature of remembrance and childhood mediated by Proust, a paradoxical temporality of past and becoming informed by, but distinct from Bergson, and the Kabbalah as a messianic mode of *making present* rather than representation (Epstein, 1922a and in Aumont, 1998: 119–24). Among more minute similarities, we could mention 'le Phénomène littéraire' (Epstein, 1921c) which opens with a long section on modernity's technological erasure of distance, '*le loin*', in terms that were reprised by Valéry's 1933 'The Conquest of Ubiquity', an excerpt of which opens the last version of 'The Work of Art' essay.

It isn't very difficult to see why Benjamin would repudiate *photogénie*. Epstein embraces neither the Hegelian dialectic (rejected in *La Lyrosophie*) nor Marx's dialectical materialism, nor even Freud's rationalization of the unconscious. Epstein's financial backers were the white Russian émigrés of the production company Albatros – the landless white bird of long migrations. Moreover, Benjamin attempted to get close to André Breton from the late 1920s onwards, and, as we will see later, Epstein was among a small group of writers who had the misfortune of using the word 'surréalisme' (invented by Apollinaire) prior to Breton – who then insisted on making the word his and his alone. Finally, Epstein managed to antagonize both Buñuel and Artaud while shooting *La Chute de la maison Usher*, so that Benjamin's future, which lay with the Surrealists, dictated negative references to the *photogénie* school and silence about Epstein – regardless of deeper affinities. That Benjamin's position was strategic rather than substantial might be confirmed by the stance of his friend and editor Sigfried Kracauer in his *Theory of Film*, written during the war. In it, Kracauer freely refers to Epstein: in fact, he does so more than to Béla Balázs, Fritz Lang, and Hans Richter combined. Certainly, Kracauer would have discussed such an important theoretician and filmmaker directly with Benjamin. We can only hope that a reference to Epstein in Benjamin's manuscripts or correspondence might shed more light on the very likely influence of *photogénie* on the latter.

Photogénie vs. Soviet montage

Louis Delluc's book *Photogénie*, and selected writings of Epstein around the reworked concept of *photogénie*, made their way into the circles of filmmakers reinventing Soviet cinema in the 1920s. By and large, their appraisal was violently negative, due to several factors. First, they conflated Delluc's and Epstein's notions of *photogénie*, without looking to differences beneath the surface lyricism and the phenomenological fetishism of the filmic evidenced in both theoreticians but in different ways. It is paradoxical that thinkers such as Vsevolod Pudovkin, Viktor Pertsov, and Sergei Eisenstein should end up condemning *photogénie* for its *superficial* euphory – its reverence for filmic surfaces and its political naïveté – when the core of Epstein's thought lay with the psycho-physiological conditions of the working body. A second factor was that the movies released in 1925 in the Soviet Union were Epstein's weakest, *La Belle Nivernaise* and *La Goutte de sang*, the latter being a film whose direction Epstein had in fact abandoned. These choices must have resulted either from the indifference of French distributors or the calculation of Soviet censors – or both. We can hardly blame the condemnation of these two films by Pudovkin and Eisenstein in 1925, even though they direly misrepresent the œuvre of Epstein.[19] In 1929, Eisenstein voiced interest for *La Chute de la maison Usher*, a film on which he comments on the basis of press reports only since he had not seen it (1969: 43–4). Finally, apart from the difficulty of viewing Epstein's best movies, it appears that some of Epstein's writings published in Eastern Europe were among his most homoerotic, in particular 'Le Bel Agonisant', published in the international journal *Zenit* in Zagreb in 1922 (Epstein 1922b). Given the homophobia of the Soviet regime, Russian filmmakers counting on official support would certainly have disowned Epstein, at least publicly. Had the Russian montage school seen *Cœur fidèle*, with its incisive didactic–rhythmical editing and its stark social realism, Epstein would have likely become a more active and positive influence on Soviet cinema. Of course, his association with the Russian émigrés of the production company Albatros around Alexandre Kamenka and Mosjoukine had all but foreclosed that eventuality.

19 For the reception of *photogénie* in the URSS, see Widdis (2003: 64–7).

La Chute de la maison Usher (1928)

Let us now turn from Epstein's theory of *photogénie* and its reception to one of his masterpieces: *La Chute de la maison Usher*. For a long time it was the only one of Epstein's films available on VHS or DVD, so it makes sense to begin with it since it is his best known. As a mash-up of Edgar Allan Poe's poetic tales, it is also Epstein's most literary film, or at least the film in which questions of adaptation and cross-medium transfers – which he had been thinking about since he first gauged the importance of the movies for poetry around 1918–19 – are the most prominent. The choice of Poe is very deliberate, since he was the tutelary figure for the two poets who bookend French Symbolism: Baudelaire as initiator and Mallarmé as epitome. Since both of them translated Poe into French, it is possible that Epstein saw his work as a continuation of theirs, but in a new kind of transmediation. In a short article of 1928 about the film, Epstein accuses 'satanizing' Baudelaire of mischaracterizing Poe by deforming his 'mélancolie et recherche magique de l'innocence perdue' ['melancholy and magical quest for lost innocence'] (1974: 187). Baudelaire, Epstein goes on to write, is all angles, plosive sounds and broken glass, whereas Poe is rounded and resonant like soft-sounding 'Ulalume'. No surprise then, concludes Epstein, that Baudelaire's French so often mistranslates Poe's English (*ibid.*: 188).

But why would Epstein, after having so carefully redefined the modernist literature and poetry from the 1910s to 1920s, now turn back to the movement against which, in large part, modernism had been reacting: Symbolism? While modernists embraced the vibrant, machine-aided, mass environment of new cities, the Symbolists, so the cliché goes, had dreamed of quiet and utopian retreats to behold love and art's beauty, and, in a more decadent version, exercise freely their morbid instincts. But is this what is really going on in *La Chute de la maison Usher*? Why, then, was Epstein attempting in 1928 to explore the source œuvre for French Symbolism?

Before letting the film answer this question, we can point to a useful counterpart: a movie of the same title made the same year by James Sibley Watson in Rochester. With German Expressionism-like angular decors, a plethora of optical distortions, and maniacal acting, the quick-pacing and dream-like aesthetics of Watson's movie make it a modernist pastiche, an experimental attempt to restage the atmosphere of Poe as a neo-Gothic cinematic extravaganza. By comparison, Epstein's decors have little to do with Murnau's, the film's pacing is excruciatingly slow, and the shooting took place in and around a real castle of the swampy region of Sologne. Although Epstein's film features composite and slow-motion shots, they do not aim for Watson's stylized perceptual distortion. In other words, Epstein is not at all attempting to modernize Poe or adapt the sensibility of his texts into tenets of modernism, unlike Watson, who was the director of the central organ of American literary modernism: the journal *The Dial*.

Epstein's streamlined narrative centres on Roderick Usher, the scion of a lineage of men who are cursed with the mania of painting their wives' portrait, with fatal results. Indeed Roderick's wife Madeline, while modelling for him, falls down, seemingly dies and is buried. Soon, however, Roderick begins to suspect that she was not dead, and at the eleventh hour, she comes out of her crypt. Ultimately, Roderick, Madeline, and the visiting friend through whose POV we enter the film, escape the manor that quickly crumbles, consumed by flames. The film combines the main storylines of Edgar Allan Poe's 'The Fall of the House of Usher' and 'The Oval Portrait', with passing references to 'Ligeia' (her name appears on the frame of a painting) and 'The Pit and the Pendulum', as we see shots of the clock's weight in MCU swinging like a sharp blade towards viewers. The conceit common to the two main stories is retained: that of encountering a strange situation through the eyes of a perplexed visitor.

With the visitor opening up the movie, Epstein shows that he is very much interested in questions of POV and contrasts of subjective vs. objective vision. These questions are fundamental for fiction cinema, and even more so in the case of fantastic fiction which relies on the protagonist's and the viewer's uncertainty as to whether something happened or not, and whether it was supernatural or not. Readers and viewers alike generally know a little more than protagonists do, but they experience a little less. We might say that the fantastic genre is animated by a desire for exchange: viewers would gladly give up some knowledge to see more, while protagonists would gladly give up some of their experience to finally know what's what. At one point, Roderick gently pushes his visiting friend out of the manor to work alone on his Madeline painting, and we exit with him. Until then, we had seen everything through the visitor's POV. But after the outdoors shift, when the film returns indoors, it is no longer led by the visitor's eyes. Hence when we encounter Roderick again, the narrative POV is uncertain: are we in a more omniscient mode allowing us to peer on Roderick? Or are we now seeing things through the POV of his nearmadness? Once Madeline seemingly dies, the visitor returns, but we are no longer aligned with his POV. The conceit of the fantastic has thus been translated by Epstein into an innovative decentring of POV allowed by the film medium.

As for the narrative itself, it can be broken down into five parts. First comes the laborious arrival of the visitor to the House of Usher and his discovery of Roderick's condition and obsession. Second, around 9:40, a breeze starts blowing inside the manor – a supernatural wind of madness signalling other oddities and introducing the first slow-motion and quick edit sequences. We see, for instance, the still image of Madeline's portrait beginning to animate itself, representing the transfer of life from her to it. Third, at about 17:30, Roderick begins the fatal session of painting that culminates with Madeline's syncope and fall, while his friend is out of doors. Fourth, we have probably the most important part, from a fade to black at 29:20, when the friend comes back in to find Madeline on the ground, to about 44:20 when her coffin is nailed shut in a funeral crypt across a lake. It is crucial because narratively very little happens, and the nervous tension that inhabits Roderick is progressively transferred to us, through a curiously visceral mixture of impatience, sympathy, and boredom. Finally, from around 45, after Madeline is entombed, to the end (65), we wait, with Roderick and his friend, again quite excruciatingly, until she comes back from the dead. The manor collapses as soon as Madeline reappears, but without killing Madeline and Roderick, as it does in Poe's tale.

Richard Abel and John Hagan have given excellent accounts of some of the technical felicities of the movie, such as an early transition between a shot of Roderick painting Madeline's cheek and a shot of Madeline feeling herself as though pricked on the cheek – a match based on mysterious remote touching or hyperesthesia (Abel, 1984: 465–6; Hagan, 1977). Hyperesthesia is said of people such as Roderick according to Poe, who have such a highly developed sensibility that everything is unbearably amplified or magnified for them. By contrast, his visiting friend seems to suffer from hypoesthesia: poor eyesight and poor hearing (he uses glasses and a horn). This is another conspicuous trope of desired but impossible exchange:

less acuity for the one, more for the other. Later, Roderick sings a song on his guitar, and Epstein inserts 16 shots in quick, rhythmic succession, by batches of 4, over 30 seconds, to weave a visual equivalency to the rhymed stanzas of the song. The cross-cut shots show trees, lakes, and the skies of Sologne, the marshy region of France where the shooting took place (later the main location of Renoir's 1938 *La Règle du jeu*), and they form a tantalizing correspondence with the poem 'The Haunted Palace', which figures in Poe's 'The Fall of the House of Usher' and is quoted in the movie. Let us note that in this sequence filmic gestures (strumming the guitar) suggest music, while sung poetry is rendered through extra-diegetic images of nature; the sequence coming to a close when Roderick puts down the guitar with one hand to take hold of his palette with the other, in order to resume his vampiric painting. At the close of the following sequence, Madeline falls in slow motion, in a very choreographic way underscored by a composite MS of multiple exposures of her face superimposed through stop action (see Plate 1a). Thus, in this narrative studded with technical bravura, but whose gist is ultimately difficult to discern, we are invited to think about the senses – over-acute or dulled – and the arts – painting, music, poetry, and to a lesser extent, dance and architecture. Madeline's chrono-photographic seizure is significantly similar to an illustration of three superimposed takes of Alla Nazimowa's face in *Bonjour cinéma* (see Plate 1b). We can interpret both images as pointing towards the continuum from immobility to motion formed by still photography, chrono-photography, slow-motion film, and normal speed cinema. Yet instead of seeing this continuum as a historical or temporal progression, the movie flattens evolution and makes use of all these techniques side by side. Finally, the movie is remarkable for the sheer abundance of references to the elements: land (the manor, the ground, trees), water (lakes, rain pools, rivers), air (sky, the mysterious and omnipresent rustle), and especially fire (candles, fireplace, and the final deflagration). These are of course the four elements of the system of Aristotle, to which he added a fifth – the so-called *quintessence*, the mysterious element called 'ether'. It is described as neither wet nor dry, neither hot nor cold, incapable of transformation, while moving in circles. Like cinema, then? Roderick flips through pages of a treatise on magnetism, illustrated with a large horseshoe magnet with lines of forces streaming between its two poles (29:30). It is clear that Epstein is pointing to cinema itself as a new kind of materiality that transcends the four elements and thus approximates ether. Appropriately, by the 1920s, film projectors were all powered by electricity, the fifth element that powered modernity.

For Abel, Epstein's film is centrally about Roderick's fetishism, his misogynistic death drive directed at reducing Madeline into a mere likeness. His drive is ultimately countered by her rebirth in the crypt saturated with nature, symbolized especially by shots of two copulating toads. Reference to magnetism and magical arts in both the film and Poe's work might confirm Abel's reading, since the toad can symbolize the transformations leading to the birth of the philosopher's stone in alchemy.[20] That is certainly a valid interpretative approach to the film. Another would be the mute jealousy of the house physician whose nose-pincers, upon the arrival of the older male visitor and competitor (since the visitor immediately monopolizes Roderick's warm attentions), reflect light directly and menacingly back at the viewer, as if threatening to make the screen blank. The intimation of a triangular contest between men, even without overt signs of a sexual nature, is clearly supported by the treatment of Madeline as a fourth wheel, with little actual screen time. But does it make sense to consider this movie primarily as a critique of hetero-patriarchal or homosocial practices when the bulk of the film is non-narrative and points clearly elsewhere?

A more comprehensive way to understand this film might be to see it as a cryptic manifesto amalgamating the sensorial aims of Symbolism and modernist currents. This requires a short detour through French Symbolism, a loose literary movement taking place between 1860 and 1900, which included well-known poets such as Charles Baudelaire, Arthur Rimbaud, Paul Verlaine, and Stéphane Mallarmé; lesser-known authors such as Marceline Desbordes-Valmore, Saint-Pol-Roux, Sâr Peladan, Remy de Gourmont, and Albert Kahn; and young writers who would distance themselves from it and forge their own paths such as Paul Claudel, André Gide, and Paul Valéry. The stale version of Symbolism reduces it to a radicalization of the Parnassian doctrine of art for art's sake, leading to the artist's retrenchment from ordinary life in the name of aestheticism (Bürger, 1984). However, this can only be a mere caricature. Mass culture and popular culture, in particular the cabaret, the theatre, and

20 See Prinke (1991).

technologies linked to performances, play too much of a central role in Symbolism to warrant the indictment of isolationism. Théophile Gautier, the novelist and poet who coined the expression 'l'art pour l'art' in a complex and ironic text, was an avid traveller, chronicler and photographer, and even wrote an essay on 3D photography in the 1860s.

The *poète maudit* figure proposed by Verlaine in his eponymous book of 1884 is much more representative of Symbolist ideals: that of marginal and under-appreciated artists, intent on experimenting with sex, drugs, alcohol, altered perception, and self-destruction, dedicated to their task and knowledgeable about their art, and writing puzzling or obscure texts disavowed by bourgeois mores and institutions. Rimbaud (b. 1854), the brilliant bisexual seer and reformer of French poetry, was of course foremost on Verlaine's mind. For Baudelaire and Mallarmé, however, the crucial figure was Edgar Allan Poe (d. 1849), for two main reasons. First, Poe was a keen chronicler of the broad spectrum of impressions, emotions, instincts, drives, affects, and sensations – close to what Epstein means by coenaesthesis – which intrigued thinkers and researchers of the 1860-90 era and led to the heydays of psychological research, psycho-physics, psychiatry, hypnosis, and psychoanalysis (Crary, 2001). The fantastic set-up of his tales generally conceals precise psychological observations, e.g., schizoid dissociation ('The Imp of the Perverse') or voyeuristic identification ('The Man of the Crowd'). Second, Poe was also something of a contrarian theoretician. He represented for instance in 'The Philosophy of Composition' that he had set out to write his heavily rhyming poem 'The Raven' by using a purely logical process for picking subject matter, words, rhymes, and rhythm based on the effects they would have on the reader. We know that he wrote that piece after the poem, so it is an *ex post facto* explanation stemming both from a heightened theoretical animus and a taste for mystification. These three aspects – exploring arcane psychosomatic forces, seeking for theoretical relevance, and performing on the brink of mystification – were followed by subsequent Symbolists. Baudelaire's 'spleen' and interest in synaesthesia and Swedenborgian correspondences, and his texts on drugs and wine that are part autofiction and part theory, bear this point. So do Rimbaud's hallucinated poems in *A Season in Hell* and *Illuminations*, and his theory of self-mortifying 'seeing' in his famous 'Lettre du voyant.'

We can then readily see how these tenets of Symbolism dovetail with the concerns of Epstein as theoretician of *photogénie*, and author of a treatise on homosexuality (see chapter 3) and a manuscript entitled *Alcool et cinéma*. Both Rimbaud, about whom he wrote two long pieces, and Remy de Gourmont, the leader of late Symbolism (see chapter 6), were major influences on Epstein, together of course with Poe. The most productive way to understand his film, *La Chute de la maison Usher*, might be as a radical and rearguard attempt to deploy the cinema as a modernist medium furthering the meditations of Symbolism on matter, sensation, and embodied thought. While a good deal of the avant-garde movements in the 1900–30 period, from Jules Romains' Unanimism to L'Esprit nouveau, Apollinaire, Cubist and dada poetry, and Surrealism, sought to elude the gravitational pull of Symbolism, Epstein understood the greater continuity at play between Symbolist aesthetics and film. In this, he proved as remarkably prescient as did after him André Bazin and Stanley Cavell who both saw in Baudelaire a precursor of the moving image (Bazin, 1981: 61; Cavell, 1979: 41–6).

The interconnections between early cinema and Symbolism are indeed multiple and varied. Here are a few salient examples. Émile Cohl, the pioneer of animation, belonged to the circles that Verlaine frequented (the Cros brothers' *Hydrophobes*); Villiers de l'Isle-Adam foresaw the invention of cinema by Edison in *L'Ève future* (1886); Mallarmé was the first poet to write about the cinema in 1897, likely because of Villiers' novel; Remy de Gourmont wrote two pieces on the cinema in 1897 and 1907; and journalist Jules Huret, the author of a defining 1891 study on Symbolism was an ardent supporter of the Lumière's *Cinématographe* in his regular reports in *Le Figaro* throughout 1896 (Wall-Romana, 2012a).

The works of Jonathan Crary on nineteenth-century optics and psychology, the study of the predecessor technologies to cinema from dioramas and panoramas to the daguerreotype (about which Poe wrote a remarkable piece in 1840), and more generally the turn of the humanities towards visual studies, make such connections much more productive than they were a generation ago. The theme of the flat image coming to life, which is after all at the core of Epstein's *La Chute de la maison Usher*, clearly links Fantastic and Symbolist literature to cinema. Hence the short trick films of Georges Méliès showing a painting or the queen on a playing card stepping out of the frame or card, pick up exactly where Jules Gautier's 1834 short story, 'Omphale', in which a tapestry with a female likeness ravishes a young man in his dream (Gautier, 1902), or Oscar Wilde's 1890 *The Picture of Dorian Gray*, written when Wilde was living in Paris close to Symbolists, had left off. *La Chute de la maison Usher* proceeds from a similar amalgamation of Symbolism with cinema, largely inspired by Epstein's pioneering study of how cinema was inflecting modernism. The cultivation of borderline sensations and affects, inter-art experimentation, a reflection on the experiential warp of time and matter – all these Symbolist creeds could be rendered and reinvigorated by the cinema apparatus.

Such a 'rearguard' effort, as would be expected, failed to convince audiences who saw in the film an influence of German Expressionism, albeit wrong-headedly as Leprohon notes (1964: 46). Perhaps 'German', as in the time of Dreyfus, was already a code word for 'cosmopolite', i.e. Jewish. But this was also the heyday of Surrealism and it didn't help any that Epstein had fired his assistant, Luis Buñuel, midway through the shooting (for disrespecting Abel Gance), nor that he had turned down Antonin Artaud, desperately wanting to play Roderick, when both were ascending stars in the movement. That Epstein did not pursue this Symbolist–modernist fusion after *La Chute de la maison Usher* likely says more about the state of artistic debates and production financing in this period than about his own commitments. A 1928 telegram to Abel Gance tells us that after shooting his next film, *Finis Terræ* (see chapter 4), Epstein was thinking of tackling a *Damnation of Faust* – another favourite Symbolist theme.[21] As we will see in chapter 6, Epstein's overall philosophy – as distinct from his limited theory of *photogénie* – never became inimical to the philosophy of Symbolism.

But let us return in closing to the convergence of Symbolism, the fantastic, and cinema. A novella from 1895 entitled *La Deux Fois Morte*, by Jules Lermina, may help us to understand the *mise en abyme* of cinema in the 'living portrait' of Madeline as other than a kitsch remembrance of Méliès films. The novella also takes place in a manor of Sologne and follows a similar storyline as Epstein's film. A man comes to visit his friend after his wife has died. How she died has to do with her uncanny love for her husband, which is described as a kind

---

21 Fonds Epstein, Collection Cinémathèque Française, BiFi, 16B12.

of hypnotic attachment so intense that her life-force was ultimately sucked away from her and into him. That is exactly the intimation of Epstein's film: Madeline's life-force is sucked away and transferred to the painting. The life-force, again pictured as a quintessential energy, is what triggers the fantastic novella's plot through the fact that the widower is dangerously wasting away. As the friend ends up discovering one night, the reason for this wasting is that the widower has found a way to invert the life-current: he can now extract it from his heart in order to recreate his wife, or at least, a 3D projection of her that floats in the room as a faint blue light. The novella was written in 1895, the very year cinema was implemented, and this mode of animated projection clearly bears the marks of the new medium. In the end, the role of the visitor is to save his friend by making him stop this self-destructive fantasy in order to embrace normal mourning. In other words, he must let go of his wife and let her die a second time – hence the title.

The Aristotelian ether that Lermina laboriously describes with a lexicon of energy, 'current' or 'blue light' has to be imagined by the reader. By contrast, Epstein spends as little time as possible showing us the portrait of Madeline becoming animated or explaining why it does so. The quintessence of cinema, its animation, shows itself in the frame, redoubled as it were, since it is the very same animation we witness in the 'rest' of the film outside the frame of the painting – from Roderick's slightly out-of-focus face in CU staring at the camera (like a portrait in the frame of the screen), to the liquid wax of the candelabra dripping as a material correlative to Madeline's body wreaked with gravity as she falls in slow motion, to the curtains heaving unnaturally as though to express ambient affects, to the prick Madeline feels on her cheek as Roderick paints the same part on the canvas (see Plate 2). There is no need for supernatural representations, for gaudy rays or luminescent eyes. No need for special effects to suggest those indescribable phenomena which writers of the fantastic almost invariably call a 'phantasmagoria', that is, a phenomenon whose origin or nature cannot be gauged. Of course, *Phantasmagorie* was a Gothic spectacle invented in the late 1790s by Belgian showman and hot-air balloon flyer Robertson, using magic lanterns on wheels and projecting images of ghosts in the dark – a clear antecedent of both cinema and the fantastic. So we might say that Epstein restitutes to the apparatus of the visual and spectacular the phantasmagoria that fantastic literature had translated into a trope of narrative uncertainty.

In *La Chute de la maison Usher*, Epstein finds remarkable ways to construct uncertainty using purely visual and sensorial means. When they think Madeline dead, Roderick, the bespectacled physician, the visitor and the butler carry her coffin through a clearing towards the crypt. We see superimposed shots of thin candles, falling leaves, and branches on the slow-motion MS of the walking men, and this is akin to a literary phantasmagoria combining a funeral with nature's autumnal death. But then Epstein keenly places the hand-held camera close to the ground, with the cameraman walking backwards in front of the men (see Plate 3). The camera moves up and down in an undulating and slightly nauseous manner. This can only be to bestow to the viewers a *bodily* sense of how it feels to be Madeline locked inside the coffin, thus surreptitiously injecting her POV in the shot, in a way that could not be rendered in a textual equivalent. With this camera movement that has no name (a motion sickness shot?), Epstein creates a medium-specific phantasmagoria nonetheless rigorously in line with Symbolism's fascination with precise accounts of bodily experience. Madeline's cryptic POV is also an indication of the central place of the reader/spectator in Symbolist art, which Epstein comments on in his writings: 'l'écran cinématographique est ce lieu où la pensée actrice et la pensée spectatrice se rencontrent et prennent l'aspect matériel d'être un acte' ['the screen of cinema is that place where acting thought and viewing thought meet and take on the material aspect of being an action'] (1974: 187). Earlier in the movie, Roderick approaches the painting that has just animated itself, and Epstein shows us his torn face in a CU counter-shot that indicates he is at once its agent and its fascinated spectator. The *mise en abyme* of cinema via the painting thus also serves to suggest the reversibility of makers and viewers, reinforcing the intersubjectivity at the heart of *photogénie*.

La Chute de la maison Usher becomes a much less difficult movie to watch when it is properly related to Epstein's deep understanding of the stakes of Symbolism in exploring jointly intermedia arts and medium specificity, sensory, and affective experiences (from anaesthesia, to kinaesthesia, synaesthesis, hyperesthesia, and coenaesthesis), and the variety of material effects that shape our sensory and cognitive life. Seen in this light, *La Chute de la maison Usher* represents a rearguard manifesto calling for the reintegration of Symbolism's corporeal savvy within new currents of modernism. The film's ending might then show the couple and the doctor as figures of survival of the collapse of the Symbolist edifice. Certainly, the move from the unbearable inside to the open air outside signals a similar turn in Epstein's career towards filmmaking in exteriors. As Malcolm Lowry understood when he saw the movie, it is a clear affirmation of a new beginning: 'But in the film ... she came back in time, as it were with the doctor's help, to save him: they went out into the thunderstorm, but into new life' (Ackerley et al., 1984: 37). It is noteworthy that two other important filmmakers were struck by this re-entry of fantastic protagonists into the natural world: Charles Laughton, whose *The Night of the Hunter* (1955) shows an LS of the two children in a rowboat with a toad in the foreground citing Epstein's similar shot of toads in front of Madeline's crypt, and George Franju in *Les Yeux sans visage* (1959), whose faceless female protagonist exits her prison at night in the last sequence, letting her white garments flow in the wind – in just the same manner as the white veils of Madeline freed from the crypt.

References

Abel, Richard (1984), *French Cinema: The First Wave, 1915–1929*, Princeton: Princeton University Press.
— (ed.) (1988), *French Film Theory and Criticism*, vol. 1, 1909–29, Princeton: Princeton University Press.
Ackerley, Chris, Lawrence Jon Clipper, Malcolm Lowry (1984), *A Companion to Under the Volcano*, Vancouver: University of British Columbia Press.
Allendy, René (1926), 'La Valeur psychologique de l'image', *L'Art cinématographique*, vol. 1, Paris: Alcan.
Aumont, Jacques (ed.) (1998), *Jean Epstein: cinéaste, poète, philosophe*, Paris: La Cinémathèque française.
Bazin, André (1981), 'Théâtre et cinéma', *Qu'est-ce que le cinéma?* Paris: Le Cerf.
Benjamin, Walter (1999), *Selected Writings*, vol. 2, 1938–1940, Howard Eiland, Michael W. Jennings, and Gary Smith (eds), Cambridge: Harvard University Press.
— (2002), 'The Work of Art in the Age of Its Technological Reproducibility', in Howard Eiland and Michael W. Jennings (eds), *Selected Writings*, vol. 3, 1935–1938, Cambridge: Harvard University Press, 101–33.
— (2003), *Selected Writings*, vol. 4, 1938–1940, Howard Eiland and Michael W. Jennings (eds), Cambridge: Harvard University Press.
Bergson, Henri (1996 [1896]), *Matter and Memory*, N.M. Paul and W.S. Palmer (trans.), New York: Zone Books.

Bürger, Peter (1984), *Theory of the Avant-Garde*, Michael Shaw (trans.), Minneapolis: University of Minnesota Press.
Cavell, Stanley (1979), 'Baudelaire and the Myth of Film', *The World Viewed*, Cambridge: Harvard University Press, 41–6.
Cendrars, Blaise (2001), 'L'ABC du cinéma' (1917 [1919]), *Tout autour d'aujour d'hui, œuvres completes*, vol. 3, Paris: Denoël.
Crary, Jonathan (2001), *Suspensions of Perception: Attention, Spectacle and Modern Culture*, Cambridge: MIT Press.
Delluc, Gilles (2002), *Louis Delluc 1890–1924, l'éveilleur du cinéma français au temps des années folles*, Périgueux: Pilote 24 éditions.
Delluc, Louis (1920), *La Photogénie*, Paris: Maurice de Brunoff.
Dulac, Germaine (1927), 'Les esthétiques, les entraves, la cinégraphie intégrale', *L'Art cinématographique*, vol. 2, Paris: Alcan.
Eisenstein, Sergei (1977), *Film Form: Essays in Film Theory*, New York: Harcourt.
Eliot, T.S. (1975), 'The Metaphysical Poets [1921]', in Thomas Stearns Eliot and Frank Kermode (eds), *Selected Prose of T.S. Eliot*, New York: Harcourt, 59–67.
Epstein, Jean (1921a), *La Poésie d'aujourd'hui, un nouvel état d'intelligence*, Paris: Éditions de la Sirène.
— (1921b), *Bonjour cinéma*, Paris: Éditions de la Sirène.
— (1921c), 'Le Phénomène littéraire', in Aumont (ed.), *Jean Epstein*, 39–85.
— (1922a), *La Lyrosophie*, Paris: Éditions de la Sirène.
— (1922b), 'Le Bel Agonisant', *Zenith* 14 May.
— (1922c), 'Freud ou le nick-cartérianisme en psychologie', in Aumont (ed.), *Jean Epstein*, 139–46.
— (1926) *Le Cinématographe vu de l'Etna*, Paris: Les Écrivains réunis.
— (1974), *Écrits sur le cinéma*, vol. 1, Paris: Éditions Seghers.
— (1976), *Écrits sur le cinéma*, vol. 2, Paris: Éditions Seghers.
— (1988), 'The Senses 1(b)', in Abel (ed.), *French Film Theory and Criticism*, vol. 1, 241–6.
— (1993), *Bonjour cinéma*, Paris: Galerie Maeght.
Eisenstein, Sergei (1969), *Film Form: Essays in Film Theory*, Jay Leyda (trans.), New York: Houghton Mifflin Harcourt.
Gautier, Théophile (1902 [1834]), 'Omphale', *The Works of Théophile Gautier*, vol. 11, New York: International Publishing, 269–85.
Ghali, Nourredine (1995), *L'Avant-garde cinématographique en France dans les années vingt, idées, conceptions, théories*, Paris: Paris expérimental.
Hagan, John (1977), 'Cinema and the Romantic Tradition', *Millennium Film Journal* 1(1), Dec., 38–51.
Hansen, Miriam (2002), 'Benjamin and Cinema: Not a One-Way Street', in Gerhard Richter (ed.), *Benjamin's Ghosts: Interventions in Contemporary Literary and Cultural Theory*, Stanford: Stanford University Press, 41–73.
— (2008), 'Benjamin's Aura', *Critical Inquiry*, 34(2) (winter).
Heller-Roazen, Daniel (2007), *The Inner Touch: Archaeology of a Sensation*, New York: Zone Books.
Jennings, Michael (2004), 'Walter Benjamin and the European Avant-Garde', in David S. Ferris (ed.), *The Cambridge Companion to Walter Benjamin*, Cambridge: Cambridge University Press, 18–34.

Keller, Sarah (2012), 'Poetry and Cinema in *Bonjour cinéma*', in Sarah Keller and Jason Paul (eds), *Jean Epstein: Critical Essays and New Translations*, Amsterdam: Amsterdam University Press, 265–71.
Kracauer, Siegfried (1960), *Theory of Film: The Redemption of Physical Reality*, New York: Oxford University Press.
Landry, Lionel (1927), 'Formation de la sensibilité', *L'Art cinématographique*, vol. 2, Paris: Alcan, 51–81.
Le Forestier, Laurent (2009), 'Entre cinéisme et filmologie: Jean Epstein, la plaque tournante', in François Albera and Martin Lefebvre (eds), *La Filmologie, de nouveau, Cinémas* 19(2–3) (spring), 113–40.
Leprohon, Pierre (1964), *Jean Epstein*, Paris: Éditions Seghers.
Lermina, Jules (2010 [1895]), *La Deux fois morte*, Paris: Livres généraux.
Lindsay, Vachel (2000 [1915]), *The Art of the Moving Picture*, New York: Modern Library.
Link-Heer, Ulla (2003), 'Aura Hysterica or the Lifted Gaze of the Object', in Michael Merrinan and Hans Ulrich Gumbrecht (eds), *Mapping Benjamin: The Work of Art in the Digital Age*, Stanford: Stanford University Press, 122–3.
Lista, Giovanni (2008), *Le Cinéma futuriste*, Paris: Paris expérimental.
Merleau-Ponty, Maurice (2002 [1945]), *The Phenomenology of Perception*, Paul Kegan (trans.), London: Routledge.
Noé, Alva (2006), *Vision in Perception*, Cambridge: MIT Press.
Pierre-Quint, Léon (1927), 'Signification du cinéma', *L'Art cinématographique*, vol. 2, Paris: Alcan, 2–20.
Prinke, Rafal (1991), 'Hunting the Blacke Toade: Some Aspects of Alchemical Symbolism', *Hermetic Journal* 14: 78–90.
Rosen, Philip (ed.) (1986), *Narrative, Apparatus, Ideology*, New York: Columbia University Press.
Turvey, Malcolm (2008), *Doubting Vision: Film and the Revelationist Tradition*, Oxford: Oxford University Press.
Wahlberg, Malin (2008), *Documentary Time: Film and Phenomenology*, Minneapolis: University of Minnesota Press.
Wall-Romana, Christophe (2012a), *Cinepoetry: Imaginary Cinemas in French Poetry*, Fordham: Fordham University Press.
— (2012b), 'Jean Epstein's Corporeal Vision', in Sarah Keller and Jason Paul (eds), *Jean Epstein: Critical Essays and New Translations*, Amsterdam: Amsterdam University Press, 51–73.
Widdis, Emma (2003), *Visions of a New Land: Soviet Film from the Revolution to the Second World War*, New Haven: Yale University Press.

2

Avant-garde working-class melodramas

In the previous chapter, we discovered the broad conceptual range of Epstein's master word, *photogénie*. What it seeks to link are: the embodiment of the viewer and the actors; the cinema apparatus as positive and ethical mediation (compared to Walter Benjamin's aura-damaging mediation); and a paradoxical aesthetics at once avant-garde and utterly modernist, and rearguard in insisting that sensorial experiencing in the cinema remains haunted by the ghost of Symbolism. This complexity explains how easy it has been for audiences and even critics to misread *La Chute de la maison Usher* as a mere kitsch reaffirmation of art-for-art's sake, if not a simple ghost story.[1] Such simplifications are due in large part to the unavailability of Epstein's first two books in which he approaches cinema as psycho-physiologically homeopathic, that is, capable of healing the depleted sensibility characteristic of the life of the masses within urban modernity. Indeed, what makes *photogénie* ultimately ethical and political is its function – at least, ideally – as pragmatic remedy for the psychosomatic damage to the working classes. In this chapter we will further unpack this social aspect of Epstein's *photogénie*, to understand how it represents an implicit programme and informs the narrative and stylistic choices of his early fiction films in the 1920s.

Avant-garde melodrama

Epstein's film production in the early 1920s centres on melodramas and literary adaptations. *Cœur fidèle* (1923), *La Belle Nivernaise* (1923),

[1] Kyrou (1963: 79) sees the film as a mere ghost story.

Le Lion des Mogols (1924), *L'Affiche* (1924), and *Le Double amour* (1925) are melodramas. *L'Auberge rouge* (1923), *Les Aventures de Robert Macaire* (1925), and *Mauprat* (1926) adapt literary works of Honoré de Balzac for the first, Benjamin Antier, Armand Lacoste, and Alexandre Chapponier (under the title *L'Auberge des Adrets, aventures véridique de Robert Macaire et son ami Bertrand*, which Epstein likely discovered in the edition by Jules Lermina illustrated by Émile Cohl) for the second, and George Sand for the last. The literary adaptations are very much uneven. *L'Auberge rouge* skilfully melds through a single crime two distinct periods: the rise of the bourgeois class in the 1820s, subsequent to the suppression of the aristocracy in the aftermath of the Revolution in the 1790s. Technically, the film deploys inventive angles and composite shots to suggest the same kind of POV uncertainty that Epstein would more fully explore in *La Chute de la maison Usher*. Richard Abel has provided a detailed description of this film, suggesting that it was the first in which Epstein began applying the theoretical research of *La Poésie d'aujourd'hui* and *Bonjour cinéma*, notably by experimenting with the use of free visual motifs in lieu of explicit narrative discourse, whether through filmed scenes or intertitles (Abel, 1984: 351–9). Eptein's other 1920s adaptations have less to offer. *Les Aventures de Robert Macaire* is a five-part comic serial whose protagonist is a traditional French outlaw figure escaping authorities through trickery and disguise. Although slim in terms of cinematographic innovations, it does typify Epstein's interest for social marginals and pariahs, clearly echoing the Punch-and-Judy mockery of the police that Chaplin revived, very much aware of its oppositional register. As for *Mauprat*, it is a morally edgy narrative about an outlaw character who, cornered by police in a country castle, wields the threat of rape to coerce a noblewoman into helping him, even though he is in love with her. But this work too is filmically uncompelling, in spite of its critique of heterosexual desire's violence. Hence with the exception of *L'Auberge rouge*, these literary adaptations do not appear to break new ground, nor do they illustrate the promise of an alliance with literature – in particular poetry – to further the medium of cinema, that Epstein's two early books had announced.

Surprisingly, it is with melodramas that Epstein succeeds in furthering the avant-garde aesthetics he has examined in his book. To us, who come after the radical experiments by the so-called structuralist filmmakers in the US beginning in the 1940s, or the New

Wave movement in France in the late 1950s, putting melodrama and avant-garde together feels oxymoronic if not sacrilegious. We take it for granted that such films as Maya Deren's *Meshes in the Afternoon* (1943) and Godard's *Breathless* (1959) share an avant-garde ethos that developed in directions precisely antagonistic to the culture industry's hegemony of melodrama. While this is certainly the case after World War Two, the situation is quite different in the inter-war period when the question was already debated. Notably in 1926–27 a virulent discussion took place in the French press between defenders of dramatic and narrative movies and proponents of 'pure cinema' (Ghali, 1995: 205–27). The latter reproached the former for adhering to the dramatic coherence of a story, scenario, or literary adaptation that does not allow the medium of film to express optimally its own specificity or essence.

The 'pure cinema' filmmakers wanted to do away with plot, anecdote, intertitles, description, and traditional dramatic protagonists, in favour of a variety of new aspects such as abstraction, geometry, studies of light and forms, non human-centred documentaries, non-traditional narratives based on poetic forms rather than linear prose, or a mixture of all these. Epstein, together with Dulac, Jacques Feyder, and Gance, had in many ways precipitated this debate since their early 1920s films cultivated a difficult compromise: combining formal and stylistic innovation alongside an incontrovertibly melodramatic core, occasionally even in a comic vein, as in René Clair's *Paris qui dort* (1924) or Marcel L'Herbier's *Feu Mathias Pascal* (1925). In any case, the 'pure cinema' debates accelerated the perceived divergence between the categories 'avant-garde' and 'dramatic' in the late 1920s. This is most notable in the famous anti-dramatic trio of films funded by the Count and Countess de Noailles: Dalí and Buñuel's *Un Chien andalou* (1929), Cocteau's *Le Sang d'un poète* (1930), and Man Ray's *Les Mystères du Château de dé* (1930). Of course, the arrival of sound in French cinema in 1929–30 completely reshuffled the cards. But as Richard Abel has pointed out, Epstein and the narrative avant-garde put pressure on two genres in particular which they sought to reinvent: the bourgeois melodrama and the realist film (Abel, 1984: 286). In a way, we can think of Epstein's particular position in the early 1920s as one attempting to combine avant-garde aesthetics with working-class melodrama to craft a new form of social realism.

The very history of melodrama as a genre lends itself to such reinventions. A melodrama may be minimally defined as a narrative punctuated with sensational and sensationalized events causing the emotional state of the protagonists to become amplified to the point of exaggeration. For Epstein, some of the key features characteristic of the new poetics of mass modernity consisted in the recourse to artifice, simplification, and schematization (Epstein, 1921a: 13, 48). Melodrama seems well suited to these aims. Research on modern melodrama has squarely located its origins in the aftermath of the French Revolution when the monarchic monopoly placed on theatre and theatrical dialogue was relaxed or lifted. As a result, while popular cabaret-like shows had previously included only non-verbal elements (music, dance, costume, pantomime, painted canvas, etc.), around the 1790s dialogue was grafted onto them under the oxymoronic tag *pantomime dialoguée*. Wildly popular, this new genre diversified and was soon adapted to print, from librettos to pulp novels, assisted by the boom of the newspaper in 1830s France through which the *feuilleton* became its primary vehicle. By the 1840s in both French and English, 'melodrama' came to denote the new and immensely popular and serial fiction of Charles Dickens or Alexandre Dumas. It is noteworthy that Epstein's three literary adaptations should focus on the very 1820–40 period that saw melodramatic novels reaching pre-eminence – particularly those of Balzac and Sand – as if he were consciously revisiting the genealogy of the melodrama.[2]

In his writings, Epstein refers interchangeably to serialized novels, pulp fiction, popular literature (which he calls sub-literature), and melodrama. He also understands the dynamics of the melodrama well enough to point out that within a few years of the invention of cinema, melodrama had begun migrating from the stage and the book to the screen – and history has proved him right (Epstein, 1976: 57). Across media, Epstein sees melodrama as regulated by a single goal: to trigger such emotional and physical responses among viewers as to refresh their affective life and put them in better touch with their subconscious rendered opaque by the pressures of modern life. In his recent study of melodrama and early American cinema, critic Ben Singer concurs: what tearjerkers and cliffhangers have in common is that they were 'designed to create a nervous charge in the spectator, a kind of sensory excess' meant to replenish their sensibility (2001: 40).

---

2 This could be said too of Prévert and Carné's *Les Enfants du paradis* (1945), taking place precisely during the Restoration and July Monarchy around the shift from pantomime to melodrama.

What happens to that psychosomatic excess is the big question for criticism. In the cathartic and conservative view of Aristotle, this charge is evacuated or purged, returning to a kind of zero degree affective state so the citizen can go back to serving the collective interests of the community. Melodrama, in such a model, acts as the regulative opium of the people (to cite Marx on religion), doled out by the dominant political and economic class as an effective soporific in order to defang the masses and increase control over them. This, in any case, has been the exclusive consideration of melodrama for oppositional thinkers on the left, from Berthold Brecht to Guy Debord. It is precisely what led Theodor Adorno and Max Horkheimer to tag this leveraging of sentimental entertainment with the pejorative moniker 'the culture industry'.

However, we should question such an easy assimilation of melodrama with political conservatism, since it arose as an oppositional genre to the monopoly on and censorship of theatre. Moreover, it is clear that melodramatic movies have often served as pretext to give voice to under-represented classes within a modern public sphere dominated by the educated ambitions and social mores of the middle class. Workers, women, foreign and ethnic minorities, and children, have gained social recognition and civil rights often on the heels of well-publicized melodramatic movies. One can think of Chaplin's Essanay productions around the Tramp character, such as *The Kid* (1921), echoed in France by Feyder's *Crainquebille* (1922), both movies about a poor orphan boy. Oscar Micheaux's *The Symbol of the Unconquered* (1920) uses melodrama to deepen black communities' understanding of the dilemmas of racial identity and especially the ambiguities of 'passing'. The multiplication of melodramatic serials in which women were not only the lead but performed physical feats until then reserved to males, heightened the reconsideration of women's rights. This was the case in Pathé's path-breaking *The Perils of Pauline* (1914), in which it was well advertised that the actress Pearl White did all her own stunts. In other words, melodrama can become an effective counter-discourse when it focuses on that part of the population of a democracy that philosopher Jacques Rancière calls the *demos* – those who have neither political voice nor representation. Although short of constituting what Rancière (2010) calls a *dissensus*, that is, a direct political action of the demos against the consensus, melodrama cannot simply be neutralized as mere culture industry opiate.

Epstein was very well aware of the broad spectrum of the melodrama ranging from psychophysiological catharsis to ideological formation, and from the appeal of identification to the enlargement of social rights. But his interest as a filmmaker and a theoretician lay neither in melodrama per se, nor in the purging process. In explaining his 1923 film *Cœur fidèle* (see below), he indicates that he used a melodramatic framework for two reasons: first, to reach a large public and show that its taste for melodrama was malleable; and second to deconstruct the genre itself by coming up with a melodrama 'tellement dépouillé de tous les artifices ordinairement attachés à ce genre ... qu'il parviendrait à se rapprocher du genre noble, par excellence, la tragédie' ['so devoid of all the artifices usually attached to this genre ... that it would get closer to the noble genre par excellence, tragedy'] (Epstein, 1974: 124). His social programme is therefore twofold: to provide a finer yet approachable narrative vehicle to the general public, and to pursue the tacit politics of melodrama in substituting lower-class protagonists to tragedy's noble heroes without lessening their virtue.

More pragmatically, Epstein displaces and transforms the strictures of the melodrama because his movies and his theories do not revolve around climax and resolution. Instead, they attempt to suggest that the energy of viewing may be better spent by creatively attending to the very dynamics of the shot or sequence. In *Bonjour cinéma* he writes for instance:

> Généralement, le cinéma rend mal l'anecdote. Et 'action dramatique' y est erreur. Le drame qui agit est déjà à moitié résolu et coule sur la pente curative de la crise. La véritable tragédie est en suspens. (Epstein, 1921b: 30)[3]

Suspension, as Epstein means it, is akin to dramatic suspense, but for a crucial difference. Both suspense and suspension evince in the viewer a pleasurable tension of uncertainty and delay. But, in suspense, that tension points narratively forward, by playing with answers to the question: 'what will happen next?' How will Cary Grant escape the police waiting for him at the train station in Hitchcock's *North by Northwest*? By contrast, in Epsteinian suspension, the build-up comes entirely from the virtuality generated by the filmic images in

---

3 'Generally speaking, cinema does not render narrative well. And "dramatic action" is a mistake here. A drama that acts is already half-resolved and glides on the curative slope of the crisis. True tragedy is in the suspension' (Abel, 1988: 42 [translation modified]).

the present. The questions are thus: 'what is happening now?' 'what am I experiencing as the viewer?' 'what am I discovering within while seeing this?' It is this free, imaginative, and highly intensified state of possibilities produced by a certain slackness or delay within the action that generates the dramatic charge of *photogénie*.

The opening shot of Hitchcock's *Marnie* (US, 1964) is a dolly ECU on a yellow mass. As the dolly slows down a little, forming a CU, we identify this object as a handbag held under a woman's arm. When the dolly stops altogether, the woman keeps walking away from the camera, and an MS lets us see her hair and high heels. Finally, she stops on the empty and silent train station platform in an LS. If we watch this single shot as *suspense*, then we're in the narrative economy that awaits the next shot for an explanation. Hitchcock obliges, of course, with a sudden cut and a man in MCU uttering the simple word 'robbed!' But if we experience the *suspension* of *photogénie*, we would note how strange it is that this shot places us in the position of shadowing a single woman in a deserted public place, looking at the bag's folds with their hard-to-miss resemblance to vaginal labia before realizing she wears a jet-black wig. In a subtle and forcible way, we are made to wonder about her, desire or identify with her, before ultimately separating ourselves from her as the camera subliminally commands us to do – all in the space of ten seconds. As soon as the second shot appears, Epstein's suspension has made way to Hitchcock's suspense, and *photogénie* has been subsumed by narrative. This example is useful to gauge Epstein's attempt to alter the formula of the melodrama by optimizing and multiplying situations of suspension, while defusing the kinds of logical expectations that fuel narrative suspense.

Singer's book cites the work of another scholar, Lea Jacobs, whose research focuses on isolating melodrama's key constituent as the 'situation' (Singer, 2001: 41–4), which accords well with Epstein's use of the same word. For Jacobs, a situation implies a deadlock, a twist, a stall, an impasse, either in the plot or in the organization of a scene or shot, or in the psychological or moral make-up of a protagonist. Rather than leading to the next narrative unit with continuity and efficiency, the situation draws attention to its awkward present tense, to its unclear roots in past situations, to its current inextricability – that is to say, to where it will *not* lead. (Hitchcock's protagonist Marnie incarnates this situational suspension in a very literal way since her psychological blockage structures the movie as a series of thwarted escapes.) Singer refines Jacobs' situation-centred model of melodrama by isolating five main constitutive elements that he finds omnipresent in American melodramatic movies of the 1900–20 period: (1) pathos, both in the form of viewer's pity for the protagonist and viewer's self-pity implying identification; (2) emotional outbursts of the protagonists; (3) moral polarization of the plot into absolute good vs. evil; (4) non-classical narrative form indulging in coincidences, subplots, piecemeal episodes, and sudden resolutions; and (5) spectacular sensationalism, often combining violence and realism (ibid.: 44–58). Epstein's theory of sentimental 'sub-literature' in *La Poésie d'aujourd'hui* broadly conforms to these parameters, and that book lists comparable features: (1) a logical plot (2) that exudes sadness (3) with good-or-bad protagonists (4) struggling over strong moral values, (5) the plot aiming for a 'fair and hygienic outcome' (Epstein, 1921a: 5–6). We are now equipped to examine in what ways Epstein adapts these melodramatic and pulp features to the screen, and how he transforms some of these elements into a more explicit social critique.

Cœur fidèle (1923)

Shot from a scenario Epstein wrote himself over the course of one night – and indeed the plot is utterly simple – *Cœur fidèle* is a triangular melodrama. It focuses on Marie (Gina Manès), a young woman and orphan exploited by a bistro-owning couple in Marseille's industrial port. To make matters worse, these bad parents 'gave' her to the local bully, Petit-Paul (Edmond van Daële), seemingly in exchange for his protection of the bistro. Her true love is a dockworker and dreamer, Jean (Léon Mathot) (see Plate 4). The first part of the film revolves around the bistro, the simmering conflict between Jean and Petit-Paul, and the respective longings of Jean and Marie for each other. It climaxes with a fist fight between Jean and Petit-Paul, following which the latter takes Marie to a merry-go-round (see Plate 5). During the fight, as Jean wrests Petit-Paul's knife from him, he accidentally wounds a policeman who had intervened. Jean is jailed for a year. When he comes out, he goes in search of Marie who has had a child to Petit-Paul in the meantime. The latter is now a drunkard who beats her, spending all the money she earns so she cannot even buy medicine for their sick child. Jean locates Marie and elicits the help of her neighbour, a young woman with a crippled leg (played by Marie Epstein) who sympathizes with Marie. Egged on by false rumours that Jean and Marie are having an affair, Petit-Paul arrives home drunk, finding Jean who has come to help with the child's medicine. To prevent Petit-Paul's eruption of violence, the neighbour sneaks through the front door, shoots him, and he dies next to the baby in the crib. Jean and Marie are reunited in a second merry-go-round sequence but neither of them shows any mirth. A short puzzling epilogue closes the film. The (critical) viewer is thus left with several questions: does the melodrama respect the absolute separation of good vs. evil? Is the sensationalist ending 'hygienic'? Are the outbursts of passion more important than the almost constant curtailing of emotion? And, taking our distance from the narrative, in what ways do the shot structure and the editing inflect this film which, according to its most loving interpreter, 'contient dès le départ tout l'art d'Epstein' ['contains from the onset all of Epstein's art']? (Hillairet, 2008: 32).

Pierre Leprohon complicates the answer by indicating that the film was altered both by the censors and the producers. Epstein was forced to cut down the fist fight and remove shots of a child imitating the limping neighbour, as well as of a second gunshot.[4] The Pathé producers also asked him to shorten the merry-go-round sequence and cut several composite shots of faces and water (Leprohon, 1964: 34–5). The film's violent realism seems to have bothered the censors, while its rhythm was thought by the producers to impede the melodramatic plot. A long sequence of over two minutes remains, with Jean daydreaming about Marie, whose face in CU and upper body in MS come and go out of the sea, transforming her into a hybrid of deadly siren and drowned Ophelia. These are clear instances of imaginary suspension diametrically opposed to narrative suspense. As for the merry-go-round ride sequence that takes place just before the fight, so original were its quick edit and subjective POVs that it brought immediate recognition to the movie and Epstein's cinematographic

---

4 According to Jean Tédesco, who presented in 1924 Epstein's 'director's cut' to Sorbonne students, four scenes were eliminated: the child imitating Marie's limping, the fight between the two men when an officer is knifed (that scene is in the existing version), Petit-Paul throwing a big rock at the heart drawn in chalk, the long sequence of the death of Petit-Paul who was shot twice (it is very short, with only one shot in the existing version), Gauthier (1999: 155).

vision among the Paris intelligentsia. Leprohon is right in affirming that, 'this melodrama was the pretext for an experimental movie' (*ibid.*: 34).

Richard Abel provides a masterful commentary of the movie that examines in details several key sequences, especially the beautiful opening sequence of Marie's automata-like actions, shot in typical Epsteinian close-ups (1984: 359–66). He explains in particular how, in editing his film, Epstein carefully set the length ratio of shots that follow each other or alternate between two protagonists, in order to emphasize a dramatic crescendo or an unequal power relation. According to Abel, Epstein also multiplied the use of dissolves and superimpressions in order to articulate Marie's subjective POV in a complex manner. Thus her face is overlaid or alternates with shots that inform us of her depressed and fugal state. An empty truck goes left to right then right to left, detritus flotsam undulates sickeningly against a quay. These shots, for Abel, signify her feeling trapped.

But we might also say that these are less *symbolic* images of her entrapment than *direct communications of sensations and affects to viewers*. The to-and-fro routine of the truck is in fact broken up by a shot loading it with coal, weighing it down, while at that moment Marie is so burdened herself, so paralysed, that she cannot even move to get the wine that she's asked to fetch. As for the flotsam, it objectifies physically for us, in us, the sickening and ebbing affects of fear lodged inside her – all at once fear of her bosses and Petit-Paul, and fear for herself and Jean. The movie's images are keyed on *sensation*, they are not representations or symbols. These sensations of heavy to-and-fro and deep disgust resurface in the merry-go-round sequence much celebrated as the bravura piece of Epstein's early filmic œuvre. That sequence begins when Marie is made to go on the fair ride by Petit-Paul who tells her that 'we will get married on the wooden horses', a first intimation that he plans to force himself on her. The quick edit of LSs and CUs of the fair rides filmed under various angles again gives a dizzying physical correlate to the distress and disgust Marie feels towards Petit-Paul, who kisses her on the ride, and soon pushes her towards the hotel. Epstein summarizes the role of the merry-go-round by writing that with it, 'le tragique ainsi centrifugé décuplerait la photogénie et ajouterait celle du vertige et de la rotation' ['tragedy centrifuged thus would multiply *photogénie* tenfold and add [the *photogénie*] of vertigo and rotation'] (Epstein, 1974: 59). Affect at its most sensorial clearly takes centre stage over plot, pity, and even the imperative of expressing the protagonists' excessive emotions as such. Abel's indication that audiences were very unhappy with this merry-go-round sequence goes a long towards attesting that it broke the melodramatic norms they expected (1984: 363).

Classic melodrama demands that injustice be reversed even, Epstein points out in *La Poésie d'aujourd'hui*, if it leads to 'une justice très artificielle' ['a very artificial justice'] (1921a: 21). The working masses, physically and psychologically exhausted, require the conceptual salve of the 'tropismes élémentaires' ['elemental tropisms'] (ibid.: 15) of good and evil, as well as the clear victory of the former over the latter 'grâce à la force physique que [la sous-littérature] représente, et qui est à la fois sa tare et sa qualité' ['through 'the physical force that [subliterature] stages, and which is at once its weakness and its better quality'] (ibid.: 17). Traditional melodrama, in other words, dreams up forcefully non-realist and clean resolutions.

Sensational as it may be, the resolution of *Cœur fidèle* does not fit this mould. It comes right out of the *faits divers* pages of the newspaper and seems far from hygienic – as the censors sensed. Placing side by side in MS then MCU Petit-Paul's bloodied face and the baby's head, the movie proposes a visual correspondence between them, as if both were equivalent, the baby being Petit-Paul in flashback, or becoming Petit-Paul in flash forward. Any one of these possibilities violates the strict moral polarity of good vs. evil. In the end, *Cœur fidèle* disrupts the economy of melodrama in two main ways: it refuses to let the catharsis of denouement erase the social squalor from which all the protagonists suffer, and it frustrates the happy ending because both members of the couple have experienced irreversible shocks or traumas. The sensorial maiming that unfair jailing and sexual servitude have brought about in Jean and Marie cannot be readily undone any more than the lack of social and economic justice can be easily corrected. This is what the neighbour with the crippled leg *incarnates*: the sheer impossibility of wholeness. More problematic yet for the melodrama, in the second half of the film, Petit-Paul is shown to be just as much a prisoner of his own violence as Marie is. Epstein's portrayal, while not sympathetic, keenly exposes his pain and his humanity. In a 1924 conference, Epstein indicates that he sees Petit-Paul as a Dionysian type compared to Jean's more Olympian (Nietzsche would say, 'Apollonian') character (Epstein, 1974: 124).

60 JEAN EPSTEIN

Again, such a dialectical or gnostic view definitely exceeds the moralistic yield of melodrama.

Commentators of the movie have also paid insufficient attention to the way Epstein closes his film. Right after Petit-Paul's slow death, Epstein inserts a title card: 'Cœur fidèle: Épilogue'. We then see a shot of fireworks, several shots of Jean and Marie on the merry-go-round looking pensive, shots of the neighbour with the baby, images from a kaleidoscope, and a single title card: 'Love allows one to forget everything else'. Here is a découpage of this fairly long epilogue that lasts approximately 2 min. 22 sec.:

1. Card: 'Cœur fidèle / Épilogue' (4 sec.).
2. VLS: completely dark exterior night (false fade-in from black) with twirling then cascading fireworks on a high mast with a crowd of very small heads at the bottom; false fade-out (29 sec.).
3. MS: double iris fade-in; Jean and Marie on the merry-go-round (21 sec.) double iris dissolve.
4. MCU: jump-cut to Jean and Marie on the merry-go-round; fade to black (9 sec.).
5. HA/LS: fade from black on the neighbour sitting on the stairs holding the baby; fade to black (15 sec.).
6. Same as 4, with iris out (5 sec.).
7. CU: Marie on the ride looking sideways towards Jean; cut (10 sec.).
8. CU: Jean on the ride looking straight at the camera; cut (4 sec.).
9. VLS: cascading fireworks on the ground with a crowd in front (9 sec.).
10. Card: 'L'amour permet de tout oublier' (4 sec.).
11. Composite: 11a=CU pan of flowers + 11b=ECU on flowers (3 sec.), dissolve.
12. Composite: same as 11 + 12a = CU iris of Jean and Marie cheek-to-cheek (2 sec.) dissolve.
13. Composite: 12a + 13a = ECU of kaleidoscopic image rotating (20 sec.) dissolve.
14. Composite: 12a + 14a = ECU on words written in charcoal on wall 'For / Ever' (2 sec.) dissolve.
15. Iris out on 12a to leave only 14a (2 sec.).
16. White lead (less than 1 sec.).
17. Card: 'Fin' (2 sec.).

We should note first the plethora of words that signal an ending: 'Épilogue', 'oublier', 'for/ever', 'fin'. Not only do they not mean the same thing, in the case of the last two, their meaning is antithetical. It is as if Epstein were trying all at once to evoke in us both the end of the movie and its persistence in our memory. He might also be attempting to give a different ending to the melodramatic plot than to the visual–filmic work. This would explain why he sets the melodramatic shots (3–8, 12a) within a sequence of poetic and extra-diegetic shots (1–2, 9–11, 14a–17) that both frame and overlay them. The two shots of fireworks (2 and 9) are especially intriguing. Of course, aerial fireworks are often used to foreshadow sex, for instance in Hitchcock's notorious sequence in *To Catch a Thief* (US, 1955). This may in part be the case here, since Petit-Paul after all had taken Marie to the fair with the idea of having sex with her in a nearby hotel. In the shot 'Love allows one to forget everything' following immediately on the second fireworks shot, 'love' might mean (also) sex. The huge and bright fireworks with the very small crowd visible at the bottom of the shot seem, however, to have a different meaning. They mirror the movie theatre itself, with our rows of heads outlined against the bright lights of the screen. The kaleidoscope has also been compared to the projection of a movie, for instance in a book by Irène Hillel-Erlanger, the film production partner and lover of Germaine Dulac. Her 1919 *Voyages en kaléidoscope* stages a modern fable about a mystical film apparatus that may be used either for the benefit of all or the power of a few. In Hillel-Erlanger's tale, as in Epstein's epilogue, the kaleidoscope has the ambivalent function of either gathering fragments into an image, that is, bringing isolated viewers into a new mobile social whole, or else hypnotizing each viewer individually so that no collective effort can emerge.

With these closing *mise en abyme* references to the film apparatus, Epstein's *Cœur fidèle* may be questioning the nature of our own *fidelity* to cinema, perhaps by asking whether we love the medium enough to loosen up the strictures of melodrama and reinvent the genre so as to serve better and otherwise the somatic needs and aspirations of the masses. This transpires in the very divided form of the Epilogue, as well as in the insistent gap or slash in the words 'for ever' and 'for/ever' written on two walls (see Plate 6).[5] Are we willing to complicate the

---

5 On both walls 'forever' accompanies the word Shandon and on one wall the year 1903 or 1908. Shandon is a central neighbourhood of Cork (Ireland), which was a world centre for shipping meat and butter until the 1920s.

'ever after' of melodrama by remembering the nervous condition or trauma that set the stage, and from which the working-class protagonists cannot be so easily purged? It is far from accidental that a French viewer would pronounce 'forever' the same way as '[il] faut rêver', that is, 'one must dream'. With this bilingual palimpsest, Epstein concludes with a note of utopia – yes, love is possible and must be sought – immediately complicated by the shadow of dystopia – and no, social ills and wounds don't just disappear with a happy ending.

La Belle Nivernaise (1923) and *Sa tête* (1929)

We reserve for the next chapter a set of Epstein's melodramas that involve in various degrees technology and a queer critique of heterosexuality, which we will address together. Here we will examine briefly two melodramas that seem more related to *Cœur fidèle*: *La Belle Nivernaise* (1923) and *Sa tête* (1929).

The first, adapted from a novella by Alphonse Daudet, tells of Victor, an abandoned boy adopted by Louveau, the father of a family living and working on a commercial barge. As he grows up, Victor falls in love with the daughter, Clara. Epstein shows them going out together around town, and watching a flickering seventeenth-century costume drama at the movie theatre – a rare instance of a film within the film in Epstein's œuvre. But Victor's real family is the wealthy Mangendre, who tracks him down and asks Louveau to give him back. While the latter leaves to discuss the situation with Mangendre, the drunk sailor of the barge chooses this moment to attempt rape on Clara, wounding Victor when he defends her. The barge then floats away rudderless, towards a dangerous water-lock, but the sailor falls off and drowns, and Victor and Clara save the day. Victor is subsequently sent to school in the care of the Mangendres but misses the barge and takes ill. At one point Epstein shows Victor hallucinating Clara in superimposition over a reproduction of the smiling *Virgin Mary* of Leonardo (45) – a shot foreshadowing Madeline's live semblance caught in a painting. Clara ultimately comes to him and Mangendre agrees to let him go back to the barge life. Clara and Victor are reunited in a happy ending.

This commercial fare with stock characters shows the social incisiveness of *Cœur fidèle* by sheer contrast. The camera work and editing are fairly standard, with one notable exception. Having fended off the drunk sailor who then drowned, Victor and Clara attempt to steer the barge away from a hazard. Rather oddly, Epstein decided to affix the camera on the top of the rudder, outside the deck, so that when Victor and Clara push against the rudder's handle, they are controlling the camera that pans accordingly (36). This original shot – perhaps too original here – might serve to suggest that the two lovers are now steering their own destiny. Jean Renoir likely took notice, for he uses a similarly mechanical pan in *La Règle du jeu*. At the climactic moment when Schumacher aims at Jurieux, a subjective shot lets us see the gun barrels jutting out in the foreground, rotating right as they track Jurieux in the middle ground, before shooting at him. Renoir must have strapped together the gun and the camera on a turret and it creates a kind of fateful pan similar to Epstein's shot.

Much more experimental is the 1929 melodrama *Sa tête*, whose curious title is never clearly explained. It likely refers to the accidental death of a banker when *his head* hits a safe. The originality of the film lays in its non-linearity. We begin with an intertitle card bearing an apology of realism: 'Ce film est un simple fait divers dépourvu de tout accessoire dramatique et intrigues policières traditionnelles. Note de l'éditeur' ['This film is a simple news item devoid of any traditional dramatic accessories or crime plot. Editor's note']. The opening sequence shows a young couple, Blanche and Jean, consulting a tarot reader. The CUs on Blanche's face are out of focus (but not those on Jean's face), and in one shot Jean looks at something without a counter-shot showing us what it is. Epstein is clearly going against the grain of seamless continuity. A cross-cut scene then shows two older men: one uses a toy guillotine to cut a cigar, the other shakes so badly he can barely hold his glass. An intertitle card then introduces a new location, 'Livilliers, Seine-et-Oise'. We are on a farm and in the fields a young man (Jean) embraces an older woman, likely his mother. Two men in hats walk around the farm, talk to the woman, and ultimately put manacles on Jean. The diegesis continues in this puzzling fragmentary fashion, alternating flashbacks with the present time of Jean's pre-trial hearings. Slowly, the viewer pieces together the following plot. Blanche slept with her boss, the banker, in order to secure a job for her no-good brother Paul. Then Blanche met Jean, an apprentice automobile designer with little money. Confronted by the banker for his sub-par work, Paul shoves him, the banker hits his head and dies, and Paul steals money from the open safe. Jean is wrongly arrested for the murder, and yet, as we witness through the POV of the overwhelmed mother who sits outside the judge's chambers, he is ultimately found innocent. Although Blanche's promiscuity comes out in the open, Jean stays with her. However, Jean's mother returns to the farm, all alone, while children and old crones make fun of her. The end.

In spite of the viewer straining to figure out who is who in the oddly framed, gauzy lens, or ECU shots of sequences that are difficult to locate within a sequence of events, *Sa tête* is a brash attempt to renew narrative form. The film holds surprising shots and odd scenes, such as a completely abstract shot of a play of light resembling an imaginary flower (40:8), and a 'free attraction' at the fairground that consists of women in skirts willingly walking on a small bridge so men stationed underneath can look up their skirts. Socially, it raises the bar for male viewers, since they are invited to identify with a protagonist in love with a woman who has 'slept with the boss'. Like Renoir in *Le Crime de monsieur Lange* (Fr., 1934), Epstein then critiques the way a power differential in the workplace can be leveraged for sexual abuse. The editing uses ellipses, unexplained cross-cuts, dislocated flashbacks, while the camerawork frames off parts of the actors' bodies and plays with focus and POV. The melodramatic anchor of the film is the uneducated mother and widow lost in a justice system that does not bother to explain anything to her, and confused by amorous relations too different from her own. In spite of her reciprocated love with her son, in the end she is left alone, aloof, more shaken than relieved by the touch of fate. We are reminded of the second title card of the film that reads 'Coïncidences ... / Chance ...' ['Coincidences ... Luck ...']. The impression left on the viewer is indeed one of the sheer contingence of events which is reflected by the disorder of the montage and the partial resolution of the plot: the insistence, as in *Cœur fidèle*, is on the marks and after-effects that events produce rather than on the complete purging of a happy end.

Another film of Epstein would deserve to be discussed with these two melodramas: *L'Affiche* from 1924. Unfortunately, for legal reasons tied with inheritance conflicts, as of 2010 the film can no longer be shown even at *La Cinémathèque française*, which owns a copy. Signed by Marie Epstein, the plot is the most classically melodramatic of all of Epstein's films. It recounts in flashbacks how a young woman named

Marie met a handsome rich man at a *guinguette* (an outdoor bar in the countryside).

After they flirt and dance together, a final CU on a broken champagne glass suggests consummation. Three years later, she is left with a baby and only a card with the name of the man, Richard. Penniless, she enters the baby in a competition for the best-looking baby in France and wins. The insurance company which organized the contest plasters the photo of the baby – 'named Richard like you', as someone portentously tells the handsome son of the boss – all over Paris. Soon after, baby Richard dies. The grieving mother is haunted by the ubiquitous posters, hallucinating at one point that they too show her baby dead. When she confronts the head of the company, he hides behind the law giving him the rights to the photo. So she goes around Paris at night and tears down the posters. She is caught and Richard, the son of the head of the company, meets her at the police station, where they recognize each other. In a subplot, Richard's sister was deathly ill and had begged her father, the head of the company, to take down the posters out of pity for Marie. He agreed and she is soon cured, so nothing impedes the union of Richard and Marie. Sandy Flitterman-Lewis takes this film to address the relationship between parents and children, and reveals that Marie Epstein found the idea in a *fait divers* regarding the death of the baby featured in the famous soap advertisement 'Bébé Cadum'.[6] We note also the importance of photography as the site of a class conflict between female working-class advancement and male corporate greed. Since the slogan on the insurance ad is about protecting one's children's future, the photo as medium also renders porous the line between life and death, chance and money, and present and future. Published accounts of the film point to a largely unremarkable cinematography, apart from a few sequences of hopeful dreaming (the baby shown sitting in front of piles of gold) or nightmarish hallucinations (the dead baby on the posters).

Although these three films may not be his strongest melodramas, taken together they nonetheless sketch a panorama of frictions and misrecognition across classes within the socio-economic landscape of contemporary France. While falling short of *Cœur fidèle*'s precise study of the waterfront underworld of Marseille, *L'Affiche*, *Sa tête*,

---

6 Fitterman-Lewis (1996: 145–7). For another description of the film, see Vichi (2003, 81–5).

and *La Belle Nivernaise* emphasize the wayward role of desire at the borders between classes, in a vein that recalls eighteenth- and nineteenth-century sentimental novels. What is new, however, is the explicit plight of working women facing sexual exploitation akin to rape, and the fate of children out of wedlock who get lost, become sick or die. Such storylines may not be rare in 1920s or 1930s French cinema, yet taken together they yield a tangible social and gender critique beneath the melodramatic surface.

References

Abel, Richard (1984), *French Cinema: The First Wave, 1915–1929*, Princeton: Princeton University Press.

— (ed.) (1988), *French Film Theory and Criticism*, vol. 1, 1909–29, Princeton: Princeton University Press.

Adorno, T. and Horkheimer, M. (2002), *The Dialectics of the Enlightenment*, Stanford: Stanford University Press.

Epstein, Jean (1921a), *La Poésie d'aujourd'hui, un nouvel état d'intelligence*, Paris: Éditions de la Sirène.

— (1921b), *Bonjour cinéma*, Paris: Éditions de la Sirène.

— (1974), *Écrits sur le cinéma*, vol. 1, Paris: Éditions Seghers.

— (1976), *Écrits sur le cinéma*, vol. 2, Paris: Éditions Seghers.

Fitterman-Lewis, Sandy (1996), *To Desire Differently: Feminism and the French Cinema*, New York: Columbia University Press.

Gauthier, Christophe (1999), *La Passion du cinéma: cinéphiles, ciné-clubs et salles spécialisées à Paris de 1920 à 1929*, Paris: AFRHC.

Ghali, Nourredine (1995), *L'Avant-garde cinématographique en France dans les années vingt, idées, conceptions, théories*, Paris: Paris expérimental.

Hillairet, Prosper (2008), *Cœur fidèle de Jean Epstein, le ciel et l'eau brûlent*, Crisnée: Yellow Now.

Hillel-Erlanger, Irène (1996 [1919]), *Voyages en kaléidoscope*, Paris: Allia.

Kyrou, Ado (1963), *Le Surréalisme au cinéma*, Paris: Le Terrain vague.

Leprohon, Pierre (1964), *Jean Epstein*, Paris: Pierre Seghers.

Rancière, Jacques (2010), *Dissensus: On Politics and Aesthetics*, London: Continuum.

Singer, Ben (2001), *Melodrama and Modernity: Early Sensational Cinema and Its Contexts*, Berkeley: University of California Press.

Vichi, Laura (2003), *Jean Epstein*, Milan: Editrice Il Castoro.

3

Technology, embodiment, and homosexuality

Modernity and technics

Over the 1880 to 1920 period, modern life in Western cities became exponentially enmeshed with a host of new technologies: automobiles, express trains, aeroplanes, electrical lighting, electrical conveyances (tramways, elevators, funiculars, moving sidewalks, etc.), telephone, wireless, and of course cinema. There were also less public innovations in industrial production and chemistry, in medicine (X-rays, pharmacology, dentistry, surgery, cosmetics, eyewear), and in destructive technologies of war such as machine guns, long-distance canons, grenades, chemical gas, anti-personnel mines, etc. Moreover, cities increasingly became giant organisms with vast delivery and circulation grids (electricity, mail, pneumatics, water, sewer, telephone, public and private transportation). Around the time of World War One – and independently from the traumas of that war – thinkers and chroniclers took stock of the possible ways these rapid changes were altering the very fabric of human life. Broadly speaking, their reactions fell in two camps.

On one side were the technophobes whose evaluation of the new age of the machine was by and large negative, while on the opposite side were technophiles who celebrated the utopian horizons opened up by modernity's ever multiplying mechanical prowess. As is often the case, some of the more complex positions were to be found among intellectuals with a foot in both camps, such as Jules Romains (1885–1972) in France, Walter Benjamin (1892–1944) in Germany, and Lewis Mumford (1895–1990) in the US. What is striking, however, is how creatively technophobes, technophiles, and techno-critics alike responded to the massive intrusion of mechanics and systems in every facet of the human realm. Let us look quickly at two ardent technophobes, Henri Bergson (1859–1941) and Martin Heidegger (1889–1976), and two technophiles, Filippo Tommaso Marinetti (1876–1944) and Gaston de Pawlowski (1874–1933), before returning to Epstein.

If Gilles Deleuze starts from Henri Bergson in his diptych book on cinema, it is because Bergson was the first thinker to develop a philosophy in which cinema played a determinant role – albeit negative. The central concepts of Bergson, such as the qualitative time of inner duration, the complementariness of the virtual and the actual, and the importance of becoming, ultimately served to characterize human consciousness as embedded in and determined by the drive of organic life – a school of thought called Vitalism (Deleuze, 1986). Our sense of time and our inner development as time-immersed creatures, Bergson asserts, cannot be replicated by cinema for three reasons. First, cinema is made of discrete static images unlike duration, which flows; second, these images acquire movement only because of an illusion, hence it is not a true moving flow; and, third, cinema is but a translation of the temporal (actual motion) into the spatial (the film strip), thus bringing back what, for Bergson, is the major error of philosophy, the spatializing of time. We will see later what correctives Epstein brings to this selective understanding of cinema and the phenomenology of filmic perception. Yet for all of Bergson's technophobia – we can call it that since it is a wilfully partial account – cinema acts nonetheless as the precious litmus test that permits him to redefine what is specifically human. In a very concrete way then, Bergson finds in cinema the perfect contrast to restage humanism, to such an extent that we may wonder whether cinema does not become something like the Derridian supplement of Bergsonian duration.[1]

---

[1] A supplement, for Derrida, is the lesser opposite of a concept that, however, needs that lesser opposite to define itself. The classic example is the conceptual category of female, which in all of Western philosophy is considered the lesser opposite of the male category. But when it comes to defining the male category, lo and behold, all that can be said is that it is made of persons who are *not female*. Derrida points out that this makes female the logically dominant category since it is needed to define the male category. The term 'supplement' names the paradox of a logically dominant term (here, cinema, which serves to define duration) that remains conceptually inferior or excluded. See Derrida (1976: 144–56).

The case of Martin Heidegger's technophobia is broader than cinema, which he scarcely addresses at all. It has to do with a metaphysical issue regarding modern technology in general. In several texts, especially 'The Question Concerning Technology', Heidegger characterizes our modern technical attitude as amounting to taking the material world as a global reserve to be tapped, a gamut of resources to be extracted, and thus a heap of useless matter to be made into materials and consumables (Heidegger, 1993). Needless to say, he condemns such a profane view of the world. In contrast with such utilitarian–destructive approaches he outlines another, less invasive, that of philosophy, poetry and ancient Greece. It consists in letting things reveal themselves to our sense of being – letting things *produce* themselves to our attention but without having to transform them into *dead products*. For Heidegger what characterizes the human amounts ultimately to a certain relationship with the world that is based on our unique situation as mortals located in our personal time and our historical space. So even though he strongly disagreed with Bergson's spiritual vitalism, Heidegger ends up like him repudiating technology in the name of its essential incompatibility with a specifically human sense of death-bound temporality. This is the classical technophobic stance, but also its paradox. If technology disrupts or denatures our basic humanity, does it not also reveal what we take humanity to be? And how else could we realize what it is?

For those at the other end of the spectrum, technology is not merely of possible assistance to our understanding of what being human means, it directly impinges on our understanding and our humanity. That is the position of writer and poet Marinetti, the messiah of technophiles. His 1909 'Manifesto of Futurism' both launched the era of radical avant-gardes and made the question of technology central to twentieth-century thought. Published in France's leading newspaper of the time, *Le Figaro*, the Manifesto exults the present moment, masculinity, animalistic machines, speed and war, and bunches together and derides the past, women, knowledge, patience, and peace. 'Une automobile rugissante, qui a l'air de courir sur de la mitraille, est plus belle que la Victoire de Samothrace' ['A roaring automobile seemingly running on strewn bullets is more beautiful than the Victory at Samothrace [statue]', Marinetti writes (1909). Quite self-consciously, Marinetti qua provocateur mobilizes all that technophobes think is wrong with any extreme enthusiasm for technology:

a masculinist will to power and violence against tolerant parliamentary systems and social minorities. For technophobes, technophilia leads sooner or later to a military–industrial dictatorship, as progressively became the case when Marinetti joined Mussolini in 1919 and co-authored the Fascist Manifesto.

But there is a wide spectrum of technophilia. Misogynistic techno-fascism may be contrasted with other, much more democratic forms of techno-utopia, especially those involving a critique of excessive power. In fact, by the end of World War One this had become an established subgenre of science fiction in both literature and film. It can be found in Romain Rolland and Frans Masereel's illustrated film scenario, *La Révolte des machines* (1921), or in the films of Protazanov, *Aelita: Queen of Mars* (1924), and of course Fritz Lang, *Metropolis* (1927). Other strains of techno-utopia do not equate technological changes with necessary risks to the future of humanity. In Camille Flammarion's influential *La Fin du monde* (1894), nature itself provides the destructive power, in the form of an asteroid that threatens to destroy all life on Earth. And it is social progress – the astronomer who calculates the trajectory is a woman – technology harnessed for cosmic peace – friendly Martian astronomers quickly confirm the calculations – and global knowledge-based democracy – the Earth is ruled by a committee of wise scientists – that save the Earth. Abel Gance fully subscribed to such techno-utopia and adapted parts of the novel to the screen in 1931, in a film also entitled *La Fin du monde*, for which Epstein was one of the assistant directors.[2]

Another such techno-utopian was Gaston de Pawlowski. An early bicycle fanatic, among the first to write about it and create a biking association, he received a law degree in 1901. In this key year in France's Third Republic a new law was passed guaranteeing the right of free association, and in 1905 another law ensured the separation of church (i.e., the Vatican) from the state. France was thus at the height of its secular positivism. Pawlowski became a journalist, then the director of several weeklies (such as *Le Vélo*), and soon bought

---

2 Leprohon (1964: 51). The online ciné-ressources service of the Cinémathèque française lists Jean Epstein, Walter Rüttmann, and Marcel Sauvage as assistant directors: http://cinema.encyclopedie.films.bifi.fr/index.php?pk=48675 (consulted on 25/09/2011). Abel Gance is a less than perfect example, however, since letters he sent to Leni Riefenstahl in August 1940 have surfaced (Dallet, 2000: 63).

the newspaper *Comœdia*, which he transformed into a daily for all the arts in 1907. Starting in 1908, he published sections of a work that became a popular success as a book in 1912: *Voyage au pays de la quatrième dimension* (Pawlowski, 2004). In 1916, he penned another popular book, a burlesque collection *Nouvelles inventions et dernières nouveautés*. These range from hilarious (a funnel-shaped keyhole for drunk people) to starkly prescient (an electric pinpoint light mounted on rifles).

The reason to bring up this relatively unknown author to understand Epstein's technophilia is twofold. On the one hand, *Voyage au pays de la quatrième dimension* is mentioned by Marcel Duchamp as a direct source for his *Grand Verre*, one of the key artworks in the twentieth century (Clair, 2004: 11–12). Other artists in the 1910s such as poet Apollinaire and painter de Zayas were equally drawn to new notions of time taken as the fourth dimension that emerged at the intersection of H.G. Wells's *Time Machine*, Bergson's temporality and Einstein's relativity theory.[3] On the other hand, the very same disparate elements that Pawlowski was weaving together in his first-person sci-fi narrative – a utopian fourth dimension, pulp sensibility, and the cinema apparatus as prototypical machinery for overcoming our 3D world – figure prominently in Epstein's techno-philosophy of the cinema.

L'Intelligence d'une machine (1946)

There is indeed a remarkable convergence of views between Pawlowski's book and Epstein's texts regarding the fourth dimension. The former writes for instance:

> La conscience dont l'écran semblait s'opposer jadis aux sensations à trois dimensions, ne fut plus que la quatrième dimension opérant la synthèse définitive du monde, permettant à l'esprit de saisir d'un seul coup, sans l'intermédiaire d'aucune notion accessoire de temps et d'espace, la substance même des phénomènes.[4]

---

3 For the fourth dimension in the avant-garde, see Bohn (2002: 7–28).
4 'Consciousness, whose screen was seemingly the opposite of three-dimensional sensations, became but the fourth dimension operating the definitive synthesis of the world, allowing the mind to capture at once, without any intermediary notion of time and space, the very substance of phenomena' (Pawlowski, 2004: 236).

The fusion between a 3D Cartesian world and a Cartesian mind that is set in front of it like a screen occurs through a new mode of simultaneity and mobility akin to the cinematic. Pawlowski mentions cinema several times, in particular the close-up '*grossissement*' (*ibid.*: 162), and a new machine for seeing the invisible called the 'aphanoscope' (*ibid.*: 170). In *L'Intelligence d'une machine*, Epstein shares both the idea that reality has four dimensions, and that cinema is a prosthetic machine facilitating four-dimensional perception and investigation:

> Ainsi, la quatrième dimension, en même temps qu'elle oriente, du passé au présent et du présent au futur, tout le continu dans lequel se meut la pensée confère à ce cadre un sens causal, imprime à la rationalisation une marche vectorielle univoque.[5]

And while the fourth dimension appears causally directed, cinema's representation of it renders causality more fluid:

> De par sa construction, de façon innée et inéluctable, le cinématographe représente l'univers comme une continuité perpétuellement et partout mobile, bien plus continue, plus fluide et plus agile que la continuité directement sensible.[6]

Cinema does more justice to the time–space continuum than do our sensations, and it also reveals the directional fourth dimension to be at the very core of our thinking. If directionality is so important here it is because it allows Epstein to reopen the debate of Bergson against cinema by raising an issue the latter had glossed: reverse motion. For Epstein, reverse motion is a native property of cinema that precisely distinguishes it from nature since it inverts cause and effect, and thus displays another logic – an antilogic, in the same way we speak of anti-gravity: 'De cette antilogique ... le cinéma est le seul appareil qui nous présente un aspect visuel complet et rigoureusement exact' ['Regarding this anti-logic ... cinema is the only apparatus that gives us a complete and rigorously exact visual representation of it'] (*ibid.*: 322). For Epstein, cinema's unique and superhuman 'intelligence' thus lies in its power to alter the time's arrow of Bergsonian duration,

---

[5] 'Hence, the fourth dimension, at the same time that it orients – from past to present and present to future – the whole continuum in which thought moves, confers to this framework a causal direction, impressing upon rationality a unidirectional vector' (Epstein, 1921a: 321).

[6] 'In its very construction, innately and unavoidably, cinema represents the universe as a perpetually and everywhere mobile continuum – much more continuous, fluid and agile than the directly perceptible continuum' (Epstein, 1974: 323).

so as to present us with another face of our sensible experience of the world.

Epstein considers that there are four fundamentally unique aspects in cinema: accelerated motion, slow motion, rapid editing, and the close-up. All complicate Bergson's inner duration. Accelerated motion contracts it, slow motion stretches it, rapid editing disjoints it and presents it as part of a rhythmic patterning, and the close-up divulges a kind of *outer* duration resulting from our perceptual immersion in things or sights. Before Deleuze, Epstein might then be said to have used Bergson against himself to refine and show the materialist side of the spiritual energy of duration. And this complication comes entirely from the '*sui generis* sensibility' and the 'sorte d'activité psychique' ['kind of psychic activity'] that the cinema apparatus displays (*ibid.*: 332). These traits of the apparatus then intersect with and enrich 'our sensibility', thus transforming cinema into 'un dispositif expérimental, qui construit, c'est-à-dire qui pense, une image de l'univers' ['an experimental apparatus that builds, that is, that thinks, an image of the universe', against which we can for the first time measure our own 'appareil pensant' ['thinking apparatus'] (*ibid.*: 333).[7] Hence cinema is not a device of prosthetic perception, nor an illusion or a wholly virtual or mimetic realm of images, because it is 'un cerveau-robot qui n'a pas été intentionnellement et strictement réglé pour accomplir un travail identique à celui de l'organe vivant' ['a robot-brain that has not been intentionally and strictly built to accomplish a work identical to that of a living organ'] (*ibid.*: 331). A telescope or a microscope is a prosthesis in that it merely and only expands the reach of human vision. Epstein will never tire of pointing out the contrastive hybrid nature of the cinema apparatus, which is more than a mechanical prosthesis, since it reveals perceptual and conceptual domains beyond our psycho-physiological range that may then be annexed to human sensibility and intelligence.

In his last posthumous and ironically entitled book, *Alcool et cinéma*, Epstein takes this hybridity to run against phenomenology, since it exceeds natural phenomena, and its emergence threatens various philosophical systems with a problematic form of abject or heretic materialism (Epstein, 1976: 175–81, 205–10). Already in *L'Intelligence d'une machine*, he is concerned with how cinema invites

7 This *dispositif* may well be the first use of the word comprising an agency that completes human cognition, thus announcing its later use by Foucault and now poets and artists.

us to redraw the line between the human and the machine. To find this line, subjectivity and sensibility – the departure points respectively for Descartes and Hegel – are of little use. So, what criterion might be invoked instead? Epstein's answer is surprising:

> [La réalité substantielle], aucun être ne peut la rencontrer ailleurs que dans sa propre passion de vivre. Il manque, à la philosophie mécanisée du cinématographe, de pouvoir être, à sa source et sans intermédiaire, avalisée par l'indispensable douleur qui réalise la seule objectivité incontestable à l'état absolument subjectif.[8]

This dense passage suggests that with cinema neither the Cartesian cogito nor the Hegelian sense certainty are of help anymore, since cinema 'thinks' and 'senses' too. But it does not feel pain, which must then become the new borderland between humans and technology. Only the coenaesthesis of pain, as an affect that we undergo bodily, can serve to differentiate the human from the machine. It is not, Epstein suggests deftly, a matter of human subjectivity vs. mechanical objectivity, because the cinema has its own 'subjective' POV and in any case our own subjectivity has been hybridized with machines at least since the invention of the clock (according to Lewis Mumford, see Mumford, 1934: 13–17). But in making our capacity to suffer the ultimate test of our humanity, vis-à-vis an apparatus he never ceased admiring and indeed loving, Epstein sets up a clear ethical and political framework for cinephilia: cinema must be used as a sensitive tool measured through and against human suffering. This accords with his earliest analyses in *La Poésie d'aujourd'hui*, which is informed by the real problem of affective fatigue among urban workers. In other words, Epstein's technophilia nowhere implies a lesser commitment to the other, to social dignity or to an ethics of respect. Jean Rouch, the pioneer of modern ethnographic filmmaking, indicates in the homage to Jean Epstein after his death, that the only book he took with him to Niger in 1946 was *L'Intelligence d'une machine* (Douek and Krauss, 1998). It as if Epstein's reflections on the otherness of cinema and its hybrid mind paved the way for the cross-cultural work Rouch was contemplating.

8 'No being can encounter [the reality of substance] elsewhere than in its own passion for life. The mechanized philosophy of the cinema lacks the capacity of being, at its very source and without mediation, confirmed by pain, which is indispensable, in that it renders real the only incontestable objectivity within an absolutely subjective state' (Epstein, 1974: 332).

Epstein's corporeal technology

From Greek tragedy to serial melodramas, pain and suffering have always functioned as sensational catalysts for empathy and identification. As we have seen, however, Epstein is much more interested in the sensorial than the sensational although we can hardly dismiss the ties between these two words. In his first full-length feature, the docufiction *Pasteur* (1922), Epstein presents for instance a much less sensationalistic account of Pasteur's cure of Joseph Meister, the 9-year-old bitten by a rabid dog, than either Sacha Guitry's *Pasteur* (1935) or *The Story of Pasteur* (1936) directed by William Dieterle. Epstein even complicates empathy by showing a long documentary sequence of a live rabbit whose skull is drilled, thus exposing the brain, so that rabies can be injected directly into it before the incision is sutured shut (see Plate 7). Taking place only a few minutes before an amateurish reconstruction of how the child Meister was attacked by a rabid dog, this sequence provides a visceral antecedent for experiencing as more than fictive the painful intrusion of the deadly virus into the child's body. Only the technology of cinema can allow such splicing of fiction and actual vivisection to evince a new vicarious sense of the pain of the other – here a hybrid of the actual rabbit, the historical Meister, and the child actor (see Plate 8a).

Epstein's MCU of the unconscious child in the arms of the peasant who saves him is followed by a counter-shot CU of the peasant's face looking lovingly down at the swooned boy's face (see Plate 8b). In these two shots, pain, empathy, and altruism imperceptibly segue into a fleeting glance of homoerotic desire, as they do in a subsequent shot that represents the child's sculptural face in Pasteur's imagination, his tears beckoning him to find a cure (see Plate 8c). The sensational and the sensorial are also linked to sexual sensibility. As we have seen in the introduction, Epstein was gay and stayed in the closet. Yet it appears that for him homosexuality was nonetheless part of a broader mode of corporeality involving modern art and literature, the recognition of inner affects and sensations, whether normal or abnormal (coenaesthesis), and cinema as a unique apparatus for their disclosure. Epstein concludes la *Poésie d'aujourd'hui* on an almost Foucauldian note dismissing the notion of normative embodiment:

> Si vous voulez, oui, nous sommes tous malades. Mais qu'est-ce qu'une maladie dont l'univers vit, qui construit l'univers, à quoi personne

n'échappe? C'est UNE santé. La santé n'existe pas, mais il y a des santés, santés successives, qui sont des fragments de maladies, des équilibres instables sur les frontières de la pathologie.[9]

In this statement, the plural of *santés* embraces explicitly sensation and coenaesthesis, affects and addictions, and implicitly the whole spectrum from hetero to queer sexuality. In this, Epstein belongs to a continuous strain of sensorial holism in modern French thought and literature that runs roughly from Baudelaire to Proust and Genet.

Before examining homosexuality more closely below, let us note that Epstein makes use of sick bodies in many of his best films, such as *Cœur fidèle* (Marie's child), *La Chute de la maison Usher* (Roderick is attended to by a physician) *Finis Terræ* (life-threatening infection), *L'Affiche* (the ill baby dies), *Six et demi onze* (Mary is cared for by one of the protagonists who is a doctor), even *Le Tempestaire*, in which the ocean is said to be in need of a '*guérisseur*'. Sick or ill bodies tend to mobilize the coenaesthesis of viewers and create strong affect alignments with the sufferer and/or the caregivers. Illness is also the pretext for technical experimentation, as in Abel Gance's 1915 *La Folie du docteur Tube*, in which optical deformation objectifies the black protagonist's perceptual warp caused by a mysterious powder, and Germaine Dulac's 1921 *La Mort du soleil*, in which the movie seeks optical equivalents to a scientist's sight recovering from temporary blindness. Illness in Epstein's films acts therefore as a way of straining norms, expanding our sensorial range, and triggering correlative innovations.

The films of Gance and Dulac suggest moreover a direct link via illness between techno-science and formal filmic experimentation. In contrast to his contemporaries, Epstein would appear to make very little use of spectacular machinery or techno-scientific conceits, if we think of the paralysing ray in René Clair's *Paris qui dort* (1924), the efficiency of architectural modernism in Marcel L'Herbier's *L'Inhumaine* (1924) or the conceit of space travel in Jean Renoir's *Charleston* (1927). The lesson of *Pasteur* (see chapter 5) is that what interests Epstein are pedestrian technologies, in particular the telephone, photography, trains, electrified lighthouses and most especially, automobiles, as

---

9 'You might say we are all sick. But what is a sickness keeping the universe alive, creating the universe, from which no one escapes? It is A health. Health does not exist, only healths, successive healths that are fragments of illness, unstable equilibriums on the frontiers of pathology' (Epstein, 1921a: 212).

we will see below. Not only are these technologies numerous and unremarkable, they also share a very unique trait: each may be used as a partial and figural approximation of the cinema apparatus, and it is in this capacity that they often take an active part in the narrative. The four movies of Epstein we will examine now combine explorations of the holistic sensibility that encompasses illness and queerness, together with the operative role of devices, in particular automobiles and photography, both acting as partial proxies for cinema.

La Glace à trois faces (1927)

> Quelquefois, comme vous passez rapidement dans un hall d'hôtel, un double ou triple jeu de miroirs vous procure une étrange et inopinée rencontre avec vous-même.[10]

Considered among the best films of Epstein, *La Glace à trois faces* adapts a laconic short story by Paul Morand with the same title. It was shot in 1927, after *Six et demi onze* (1927) and before *La Chute de la maison Usher* (1928). We might do well to keep their closeness in mind since the title of the former is derived from the Kodak format 6 ½ × 11 centimetres (see below) and the latter centres on Roderick's act of painting his wife Madeline. *The Three-Sided Mirror* – more aptly translated as *The Mirror with Three Faces* – represents the middle panel of a triptych addressing representations of the human face on three visual supports – photography, mirror, painting – each of which accentuates a particular aspect of cinema, and a particular problem in social and sexual bonding.

Morand's story opens a 1925 collection entitled *L'Europe galante* that mixes autobiography, travel, politics, and the sexual mores of the inter-war period (Morand, 1925). In 'La Glace à trois faces', an unnamed male narrator discusses with each of three separate women their respective male lover. At the end of the story, he discovers that the three lovers were not only one and the same person, but a friend of his, whom, moreover, he chances upon, fatally wounded in a car accident, and who asks him to tell the three women of his death. The conceit of an absent protagonist and/or a third-party account is fairly common,

---

10 'Sometimes, as you walk hurriedly through a hotel foyer, a double or triple play of mirrors causes you to have an odd and unexpected encounter with yourself' (Epstein, 1974: 128).

for instance, in *A Letter to Three Wives* (1949) by Joseph Mankiewicz, or *Rashomon* (1951) by Akira Kurosawa. Morand's short story points to such postmodern recognition of our reliance on others for social identity – Sartre's famous 'hell is other people' – and, like these two films, it does so via an enigma about the identity and motivation of the narrator. In fact, readers can hardly suspend disbelief and accept that the narrator just *happened* upon each of these women, each of whom *happened* to have his very friend as lover, before himself *happening* upon the dying narrator. Either the narrator is a mere pretext for the literary purpose of a curio vignette about a polyamorous protagonist, or else, the story is surreptitiously meant to foreground the narrator himself. It would then be about the narrator's obsession to track his friend's love life, and ultimately to follow the friend himself, since why else would he be present at the accident? Just as in Joseph Conrad's short story 'The Secret Sharer', we are likely dealing here with cryptic homosexuality, the intersection of same-sex attraction with secrecy or unknowing. Two other stories of Morand in the same collection deal precisely with queerness and visibility, respectively a nocturnal sexual encounter between two men in a garden – a would-be assassin and his would-be victim – and the loss of aesthetic pleasure felt by an old lesbian marquise faced with two younger lesbians who cannot be bothered with encrypting their attraction for each other.[11]

Epstein's movie follows the arc of the short story rather closely. It keeps on title cards Morand's numbered parts (1, 2, and 3), each of which deals with the male protagonist's involvement with, and ultimate rejection of one of the three women: Pearl, Athalia, Lucie. The film differs in two singular ways. First, there is no narrator. Erasing this crucial narrative mediation might seem to cancel the conceit of homosexual desire altogether, which in turn would fit well with Epstein's closeted homosexuality. Second, the movie ends in a long ominous driving sequence in which the shots become shorter the more the car speeds up until a bird hits the protagonist's head. This ending emphasizes speed and the fateful accident over the suicidal fugue, so that the two major differences with Morand's short story appear to conceal its homosexual subtext.

Things turn out, however, to be more complex. We first need to be reminded that while French standards for censorship of homosexuality

---

11 See 'Lorenzaccio ou le retour du proscrit' and 'Éloge de la marquise' in Morand (1925).

in literature were very loose – Proust's novel published between 1914 and 1922 concerns itself very frankly with gay and lesbian themes and scenes – the exact opposite was true of the movies. In Marcel L'Herbier's *L'Homme du large* (1921), a quick shot featuring two women dancing together in a bar was targeted by censors and removed, even though the film had nothing to do with homosexuality.[12] Hence while twentieth-century French censors accepted the argument that literature could treat homosexuality openly (as did Gide, Proust, and Colette), they objected to pretty much anything that might be taken to depict same-sex desire on-screen.

It seems very likely that Epstein was interested in Morand's story precisely because of its cryptic homoeroticism, and more particularly, the paradoxical imperative of displaying cryptic homoeroticism on-screen *as such*, as a way to elude censorship. In 1924, in *Le Lion des Mogols*, Epstein resorted to a trick that strongly suggests a wilful wink at the censors of L'Herbier's scene. He features two women dancing together in a bar, quite conspicuously, right smack in the middle of an HA LS (see Plate 9). Why was it not censored? Because he skilfully diverted the viewer's focus by superimposing on them a fantasy CU portrait of Anna, the male narrator's love interest. In so doing, Epstein hides homosexuality in plain sight, as it were, with the help of an overlaid heterosexual fantasy vignette. That, in the end, the narrator of *Le Lion des Mogols* proves to be his paramour's brother ironically thwarts the heterosexual fantasy so conspicuously represented. So while I am not proposing that featuring homosexuality was Epstein's central preoccupation in the films we analyse here, I believe there are sufficient elements to suggest that part of his general programme of corporeal *photogénie* included weaving homoeroticism within heterosexual melodramas.

In *La Glace à trois faces*, Epstein finds two techniques to do so. In the first instance, he grafts the homoerotic desires of Morand's narrator onto the camera itself, instilling a queer eye to '*l'œil de verre*' of the camera, as Epstein calls it, and by extension, to viewers themselves. At the end of part two which concerns sculptor Athalia Rabinowich's insistent courting of the male protagonist, the latter uses his car to escape both her attentions and Paris. He arrives in a small village where he writes to her, and we see the following sequence:

12 Marcel L'Herbier, *L'homme du large* and *El Dorado*, DVD, Gaumont, 2009, brochure.

1. MS: old woman at produce cart cutting off lettuce.
2. Cut to rear-lighted LS from inside a café: in the background, protagonist exits his car and enters the café towards camera.
3. MS slight HA: protagonist writing a letter at a table on the terrace, smiling.
4. Dissolve to VLS: cars driving on a tree-covered country road.
5. Cut to MS: Athalia in her studio perorating with guests around her.
6. Cut to MS HA: the display of vegetables.
7. Cut to dolly LS: subjective camera of protagonist driving.
8. Cut to 3.
9. Cut to ECU of letter being written.
10. VLS: in the background across a plaza, the protagonist exits the café, framed by the vegetable cart, and gets in his car (see Plate 10).

Three cross-cut actions are going on jointly. First, the protagonist arrives at a café and writes to Athalia, and second he daydreams about racing his car in the countryside. Yet a third action is surreptitiously taking place: the camera was waiting for him in the café, it lingers on his backlit profile, and it spies him across the plaza when he leaves. The final shot of the sequence ties back to the first as if the POV was that of the lettuce seller (who plays no narrative part). We must conclude that Epstein wants to defamiliarize the neutral placement of the camera, in order to suggest an active viewing or voyeuring on the part of a third party, hiding in the café or behind the vegetable cart, identified with none of the protagonists. Hence while Epstein erases the narrator from Morand's tale at the diegetic level, his cinematography and découpage seem to involve us as participating onlookers. In other words, the camera and us, viewers and queer voyeurs, have become the equivalent of the vanished narrator of the short story. The narrator was stalking the protagonist, as we have established, probably to confirm the latter's failing at heterosexual romances, hence rendering him available for a queer affair. It seems very likely, then, that we are dealing here with a variation on the glass closet, with mirroring effects (see Plate 11).

The 'glass closet' is an expression from Eve Sedgwick pointing out the fact that a good deal of literature (and more generally narrative forms such as film) rather than simply evacuating and closeting homosexuality, insistently makes it a visible part of heterosexual construction.

In straight romances especially from the nineteenth century onwards, same-sex desire is evoked, addressed, mocked, rejected, displayed, alluded to, envied, euphemized, etc., but almost never ignored, hushed or erased. Straight love becomes in fact so dependent on supposedly tangential figures of homosexuals that Sedgwick calls this interdependence the glass closet, a particularly visual form of open secret within heteronormativity. Not only does Epstein seem to me to understand very well how the glass closet functions, but he also signals to us that we do too – that we already know and can recognize it.[13]

Behind its pseudo-libertine melodrama, *La Glace à trois faces* is, as its title suggests, a deep meditation on seeing, queering sight, and mirroring the glass closet back to the viewer. The opening sequence exemplifies keenly the problem of sight, and the multiple fractures between heterosexual genders. After the credits, a title card sets up the riddle: 'Trois femmes / aimaient un homme / mais en aimait-il une?' ['Three women / loved a man / but did he love one of them?']. The heterosexual fantasy quandary evinced by this question was of course that of the Greek hero Paris who, queried and courted and threatened by three goddesses, chose Aphrodite. By contrast, Morand's and Epstein's protagonist is progressively shown to refuse the choice itself, ultimately answering a final 'no' by killing himself. By parsing 'loved a man [*aimaient un homme*]' into a single verse, Epstein provided a tacit answer *within* the question: no, he did not love one of the women ... he loved men. Morand's title, *La Glace à trois faces*, draws our attention to such word choices by featuring an inner rhyme (*glace/face*), and the bizarre vocalic string *a-a-a-oua-a* resembling a shout. This might be a signal, with the film, to scrutinize appearances and signifiers beyond the stated narrative logic of the plot.

For instance, after its odd title and opening riddle, the film truly begins with the following sequence:

1 Title card '1'.
2 Very short LS sideway from a car, exterior night: a theatre or nightclub with the word 'entrée' above the door.
3 Cut to MS, exterior day: 2 then 3 male waiters peering over a hedge and laughing at something we cannot see.

---

13 The glass closet is then also a literary figure and an epistemological structure of homosexuality as Derridian supplement to heterosexuality (see note 1 above). Ultimately this is what makes *La Glace à trois faces* an iteration of this intertwining of homosexuality with heterosexuality, see Sedgwick (1990).

4 Cut to very short VLS, exterior night: a car on an empty street driving straight at the camera.
5 Cut to 3, with now 4 waiters peeking before a maître d' disperses them.
6 Title card: 'NERFS / LARMES' ['NERVES / TEARS'].
7 LS, then jump-cut to MS, exterior day: young woman with jewels crying while walking towards the camera (located across a street); she walks past a chauffeured car waiting for her; a car crosses quickly in front of her left to right.
8 Title card: 'PEARL'.

This opening sequence clearly breaks with rules of exposition and continuity already well in place in the late 1920s. While beginnings *in media res* are not rare, Epstein here cross-cuts between no fewer than three POVs. We understand that the waiters were watching a break-up scene or its aftermath, likely involving the woman whose name is Pearl. In so doing, we retrospectively match the men's eye line to the female object of their gaze and ridicule – which, by the way, recalls another central motif in heterosexual mythology: males spying on female bathers. Let us note that Epstein does not directly splice shots of gazing men and the gazed-at woman, and thus circumvents at once the shot–counter-shot idiom, and the heterosexual suturing of men and women.

But what about the third POV: those quick night shots taken from a car, and of a car? No indication is either provided or suggested to help us to place them within the budding narrative. Throughout the film, the protagonist fetishizes his automobile in an inverse ratio to his plummeting interest in women, before using it as an instrument of suicide. Let us open the question whether automobiles in Epstein's movie – and movies – might not partake of the glass closet, as a polyvalent technology of contact, cruising, stealth, and escape.

Even after this unorthodox opening sequence, narrative continuity hardly establishes itself. We see Pearl accosted by an older man whom she does not know, then shots of an outdoor restaurant she may have just left, and an LS and MLS of a man throwing a tantrum in an indoor restaurant. Only then do we finally discover the male protagonist. He is dressed in tuxedo and top hat and walks sternly among parked automobiles towards the low-angle camera that almost seems to be lying in wait, spying on him. We see nothing else but him and cars. As we follow him, an LS shoots him through the large windows of a car, which he then enters, sitting in it to read the paper. It is as if he had penetrated into an automotive glass enclosure/closet, to which the diegesis had become suspended: it appears indeed that the shot goes on only to show other cars driving by reflected on his window.

In both the opening and the vegetable cart sequences, if Epstein deploys a triple POV, it is because it adds one more point of view to the classic shot–counter-shot suture that defines heteronormative cinema and defines shot–counter-shot cinema as heteronormative. We are now in a position to address the most famous sequence of the film, a long take spiral pan shot from inside the sports car as the protagonist drives down the ramp of a parking garage, and which recalls the 'ghost ride' *vues* of the Lumière brothers, filmed from trains or cars. This shot triggers uniquely visceral and vertiginous reactions from its viewers by alternating in a distinctive rhythm sharp 180-degree turns on the flat with straighter downward movements. As such, it clearly indexes the direct tie between *photogénie* and coenaesthesis. But we can also read the bravura shot as a dialogue with the multiple 360-degree pans in *Cœur fidèle*'s merry-go-round scenes. In our reading of that film we had suggested a connection between circular shots and problematic heterosexuality, as the two couples facing the camera (Petit-Paul and Marie, then later Jean and Marie) are respectively under the sway of impending sexual violence and the difficulty of joyful love in its aftermath. The spiral shot of *La Glace*, by comparison, is structured as an escape from the heterosexual 'merry-go-round'. Since it is shot from the shotgun seat, it implies that two people are present – technically, the driver and the cameraman – although diegetically the protagonist is alone in the car. Yet the subjective POV in the spiral pan suggests the ghostly presence of an invisible companion or, say, a concealed narrator. This may be the ultimate way Epstein found to adapt and encode the glass closet of Morand's story. In French, the seat next to the driver is called '*la place du mort*' – the dead man's seat – a fitting term for a film that connects the silent closet to an automobile suicide.

Six et demi onze (1927) and *L'Homme à l'Hispano* (1932)

In the films that Epstein made both before and after *La Glace* (1927), we find a similar convergence of motifs of suicide with foreclosed homosexuality and a displaced attachment to automobile as well as other machines refracting the film apparatus. In *Six et demi onze* (1927), the younger and more saturnine of two orphan brothers, Jean (played by androgynous-looking Nino Costantini), falls in love with a cabaret singer, Mary Winter (see Plate 12). Yet Jean seems truly happy with Mary only when technology intervenes: the telephone, the automobile in which he ecstatically drives her, and foremost the Kodak camera he buys to take pictures of her. All this makes Mary cold – as her surname suggests – and she becomes attracted to a man whose surname evokes the warm glitter she yearns for, Harry Gold. Rather than confronting her or winning her back, Jean falls into a melancholy tailspin that leads him to kill himself. Epstein stages the suicide in front of a mirror, Jean shooting at his own reflection while holding the camera in the other hand, before turning the gun against himself (see Plate 13). (Perhaps Rossellini cites Epstein's film when Edmund shoots at his own shadow before his fatal fall in *Germany Year Zero* (1945); and perhaps Gaëtan de Clérambault, Lacan's teacher, did too when he similarly shot himself in front of a mirror.) As Jean is dying in MS, Epstein superimposes three ECUs of the Kodak camera lens – another figure of three-facedness – and after each of the lenses dissolves in turns, Jean dies. It is a curious composite shot that evokes Epstein's comments about the glassy gaze from the lens of the film camera such as: 'c'est un œil sans préjugés, sans morale'] ['It is an eye without preconceptions, without mores'] (Epstein, 974: 136–7). An eye that registers without judging.

Soon after Jean's death, his brother Jérôme, who is a doctor, meets Mary and they fall in love. She quickly realizes that he is Jean's brother when she sees Jean's photo in his flat, but she keeps it secret. She is with Jérôme, however, when he recovers a trunk of Jean's things. In the trunk is the camera, and Jérôme undertakes to develop the film, which, of course, reveals pictures of Mary (see Plate 14). Pointedly, Epstein shows CUs of Mary photographed by Jean in a long strip of negatives that resembles a film strip, all the more as Jérôme moves the film up and down as though to put it in motion. Later, as despondent Jérôme, sitting in a patio, looks at other photos of Jean in a booklet, in cross-cut we see Mary walking on a beach, wracked with guilt, pounded on by the sun and increasingly agitated. Ultimately she's struck by a grand mal epileptic breakdown. We never see the photos Jérôme looks at. Yet the cross-cutting is such that we get the odd sense that he is somehow remotely witnessing or even directing

Mary's delirium on the beach, as if the book of photos was a sort of telepathic screen or even a camera. (It is difficult to gauge this crucial sequence, however, because the film is a reconstitution rather than a fully preserved copy, so the splicing may not be Epstein's.) At minimum, it suggests that the photographic medium plays an important part in both brothers' psychosexuality. Nor can we ignore the fact that the protagonist who killed himself is named Jean and is played by Nino Costantini, whom Epstein films with an unmistakably homoerotic aura. In the end, while *Six et demi onze* is even less explicitly about homosexuality than *La Glace*, it is certainly a component of Epstein's stealthy queer deconstruction of heterosexuality. Mary's seizure, cross-cut with Jérôme's occult action – is he watching photos of his dead brother or telepathically triggering Mary's crisis? – clearly takes place in lieu of the traditional climax or denouement. The heterosexual matrix of the melodrama, upset by the queer death of Jean, cannot quite right itself through Jérôme and Mary.

L'Homme à l'Hispano (1932), a talkie, reprises the foreclosure of heterosexuality in relation to technologies of reproduction and locomotion explored in *La Glace à trois faces* and *Six et demi onze*. Georges, whose parents have just died, receives a small inheritance from a family friend lawyer. His plan is to go to Senegal to leverage his inheritance into a fortune, as he explains to a misanthropic and misogynistic British lord he meets on the train to Bordeaux, and who takes to him only because Georges professes to have no interest whatsoever in the fair sex. In the port of Bordeaux Georges meets an old rich friend, Deléone, who convinces him that, instead of waiting for the ship (that is being repaired), he should drive a car to Biarritz. It is the car Deléone has bought for his mistress and which he can't drive himself since both his wife and mistress are vacationing there. Georges accepts and when he arrives in Biarritz, he is taken for a rich man with his luxury Hispano convertible. A love affair develops quickly with Lady Oswill, who turns out to be the wife of the British lord he'd met on the train. She is French and her first name is the masculine Stéphane. They move in together in a luxury flat in Paris but Georges's money quickly runs out. The melodramatic imbroglio climaxes when Lord Oswill, who knows Georges has no money, confronts him with a devilish bargain: he will either give him a small fortune to disappear, or else he will divorce his wife but then Georges must tell her that he has lied about being rich. Georges is as unwilling as Jean in *Six et demi onze* to compromise with a picture-perfect fantasy of heterosexual coupling, and he drowns himself to avoid facing either Stéphane, social realities, or his own lies.

'Vous êtes trop tendre, trop sensible' ['you are too soft, too sensitive'] the kind old lawyer tells him in the first few minutes, without explaining what the issue is: too soft and sensitive for what? While the motif of the lure of the wealthy woman, and/or the woman requiring wealth and driving a man of a lower social caste to death, recurs in French cinema of the 1930s – Duvivier's *Pépé le Moko* (1936) is a prime example – Epstein's movie does not partake of poetic realism's nostalgia for heterosexual freedom outside of social and class constraints. Georges's masculinity is anti-heroic, unlike Gabin's tough-guy persona. Rather than committing suicide out of an insurmountable pang for his love object (as Pépé does), it feels more like he has just fallen back on the queer melancholy solitude the old lawyer pointed out at the onset. *L'Homme à l'Hispano* makes only faint references to homosexuality, as when the wife of Deléone wearing a tie and a flat hairdo holds the hands of Lady Oswill in pearls, with a clear wink at their butch/femme outfits. As for the film's title, '*l'hispano*' may mean a Spaniard and recalls the use of '*un hidalgo*' in French to mean a (pure) Spaniard, and thus is grammatically structured as 'the man with the man'. In the 1930s, however, Hispano-Suiza was a famous brand of sports cars that would make the title rather unproblematic (see Plate 15).

On the other hand, we have seen that automobiles for Epstein seem insistently related to the glass closet or, at the very least, to subverting the heterosexual matrix. When Georges and Stéphane decide to elope and drive to Paris, Epstein does not show their amorous closeness. In fact, instead of showing them at all, he weaves a beautiful rhythmic sequence of MSs and CUs of reflections of the moving trees and sky on every part of the car body. We can read this at minimum as a queer poetic distance Epstein maintains with the heterosexual engine of Pierre Frondaie's eponymous novel, whose adaptation Epstein took over from his colleague Feyder, largely because he was broke. But more than that, in those shots Epstein substitutes the body of the car to heterosexual bodies, as if the automobile could refract queer forms of embodiment. Such a substitution of car body to human body has always interested Epstein, who analyses a verse of Cendrars – 'J'ai des pommettes électriques au bout de mes nerfs' ['I have electrical cheekbones at my nerve endings'] (Epstein, 1921a: 58–9) – as based on sensations of speed making a driver feel at one with his convertible, which the spiral pan and death ride of *La Glace* neatly echoes. Let us note also that the shiny 'skin' of the car body becomes a mirror or even a screen showing the sky and trees. Thus if the automobile serves as a literal diversion from the heterosexual path, it is also because it is akin to cinema in its capacity to mirror other desires, and render sensible other modes of embodiment.

Epstein's queer œuvre: 'Le bel agonisant', *Ganymède*, and *Le Double amour* (1925)

In the previous chapter and in previous sections of this chapter, we have tried to suggest how some of Epstein's concerns with *photogénie*, melodrama, and embodiment dovetail with queer motifs. Here we will address Epstein's explicitly homosexual œuvre found in several of his written and film works. Homoeroticism is quite overt at the very beginning of Epstein's career, as in this passage from *Bonjour cinéma*:

Je vous ai vus
Je vous ai vus ô éphémères
ô visages inaccessibles
            cibles
où bondit le désir cloîtré
Je vous ai vus galerie préméditée et pathétique
derrière des vitres pures
satisfaites de vous exclure

...
Visages gantés de verre
luxe vivant où je me mire
            mon désir

...
Visages hâlés
des mécaniciens dans le vent de leur machine
et des garçons de la marine
qui furent tendres pour leurs aînés
Visages poudrés
Visages déguisés[14]

14 'I have seen you / I have seen you O ephemerals / O inaccessible faces / targets

Queer motifs encountered in his films were first explored in writing: the cloistering/closeting behind glass, the inaccessibility of the target of desire, the conceit of disguise, and the word '*tendre*' of *L'Homme à l'Hispano* as euphemism for non-straight. The following year, 1922, Epstein published in a Yugoslav journal the first part of a text whose second part appeared in his own journal *Le Promenoir* (1922b) (which might well be translated *The Cruiser*). The text is entitled 'Le bel agonisant' ['The handsome male in agony'], which may refer to Michelangelo's *Captive Slave* sculpture in the Louvre. It reads:

> Ma première Sodome bien trop chaste fut enfant de chœur entre deux messes. L'abbé m'embrassait au front. Des rhétoriciens en flanelle parfumée de tennis m'assuraient dans les escaliers d'une bien tendre camaraderie. J'aimais leurs beaux mouchoirs de soie et cette confiance que je prenais en eux. Innocent, c'est tout juste si je connus des lèvres, à côté des miennes, comme un dérivatif.
>
> Il y a de si belles odeurs, parfums mâles.
>
> Alonzo. Alonzo, la promenade en mer, les cadeaux, le chapeau avec un ruban dont la couleur était une erreur. Tu n'étais pas triste. Nous ne nous sommes pas embrassés. Une femme ne peut jamais devenir un homme. Mais toi je t'ai façonné selon mon dieu.[15]

To my knowledge, this text has never been referred to nor cited by Epstein scholars, even though Leprohon lists both the *Le Promenoir* and the *Zenith* source in his book (1964: 183). Epstein thus turns out to have outed himself in 1921–22, ostensibly distancing himself over the years from this public gesture, since no overt or public expression of his queerness ensued after *Le Double amour* in 1925. However, among his papers can be found an unpublished book manuscript of nearly 300 pages, which he wrote under the pseudonym Alfred Kléber in

---

/ in which cloistered desire leaps / I have seen you premeditated and pathetic gallery / behind pure glass / satisfied with excluding you / ... / Faces gloved with glass / living luxury in which I mirror my desire / ... / Tanned faces / of mechanics downwind from their engine / and of marine boys / who were tender to their elders / Powdered faces / Disguised faces (Epstein: 1921b: 53–4).

15 'My first, much too chaste, Sodom was as a choirboy in between two masses. The priest kissed my forehead. Rhetoricians in tennis-perfumed flannel assured me on the stairs of their very tender comradeship. I loved their beautiful silk handkerchiefs and the confidence I had in them. Innocent, barely did I know lips, besides mine, as derivative. / There are such beautiful odours, male scents. / Alonzo. Alonzo, the tour at sea, the gifts, the hat with the ribbon whose colour was a mistake. You were not sad. We did not kiss. A woman can never become a man. But you I fashioned you after my god' (Epstein, 1922a: 29).

the 1930s or 1940s. It is entitled *Ganymède, Essai sur l'éthique homosexuelle masculine* [*Ganymede: An Essay on Male Homosexual Ethics*]. Epstein clearly never stopped considering himself gay. Yet scholars of French silent cinema have contented themselves with a version of Epstein's queerness as *un secret de Polichinelle* (an open secret). In a radio programme on *La Chute de la maison Usher*, Jacques Aumont calls Epstein 'un homosexuel refoulé ou non-avoué', which he clearly was not.[16] It is well known that several key filmmakers of the French narrative avant-garde were gay. Germaine Dulac, for instance, another central figure in the *photogénie* movement, co-founded a film production with her lover and scriptwriter Irène Hillel-Erlanger in 1915, so it could be said that non-straight sexuality directly contributed to alternative structures, here the first film production company created by women. Marcel L'Herbier was also a 'known' homosexual, although little reliable information or critical work on homosexuality or queerness in French silent cinema exists, while the topic has been studied in the US for almost thirty-odd years.[17]

The *Ganymède* essay is therefore an important and unique document to begin the recovery of this queer memory. In it, Epstein takes up the project that Marcel Proust had toyed with when preparing *In Search of Lost Time*, namely, an essay on homosexuality. Unlike Cocteau's autobiographical and novelistic *Livre blanc* (1928), however, Epstein's treatise carefully resists queer auto-fiction to sketch a more general theory of male homosexuality. Note that the qualifier 'male' makes implicit room for female homosexuality by tacitly suggesting that it might be different – in and of itself a notable ethical gesture. The essay spells out clearly the fact that Epstein's closetedness or re-closeting was due to social pressure alone:

> En effet, le suicide, la limitation conceptionnelle [sic], l'homosexualité sont des découvertes de même classe, et nous dirons de la plus haute ... dans l'acception de la primauté des essentiels droits individuels sur certaines exigences collectives.[18]

16 'A repressed or unconfessed homosexual' ('*La Chute de la Maison Usher* de Jean Epstein', Ciné Club, France Culture, 30/06/1999, Institut National de l'Audiovisuel).
17 For general evidentiary problems, see Slide (1999), Porter (2001) and Russo (1981).
18 'Suicide, contraception, and homosexuality are discoveries of a similar, and I will say, highest order ... [in terms of] the acceptance of the priority of essential individual rights over certain collective imperatives' (Epstein, 1930–40: 28).

Epstein unambiguously asserts homosexuality as the right of disposing of one's self over and above the homophobia of established mores and laws. He would certainly have been on the side of today's mainstreamed recognition of the need to secure equal rights for gay and queer citizens.

Throughout *Ganymède*, Epstein surprises us again and again with his clear thinking and prescience. He asserts for instance that, 'depuis quelques décades déjà les esprits moins prévenus se ralliaient à la conception de l'homosexualité comme disposition innée', 'for a few decades the least prejudiced minds have rallied around the conception that homosexuality is an innate disposition' (Epstein, 1930–40: 44), and he ends the treatise on a call for homoparental rights through *in vitro* reproduction (*ibid*.: 288) (Plate 16). In between these two positions that are still largely controversial at the beginning of the third millennium, Epstein reviews every known aspect of male homosexuality, arguing against the model of inversion and the default notion of heterosexual norm (*ibid*.: 53), while recognizing the bisexual coexistence in individuals of same and opposite sex desire (*ibid*.: 51). After systematically debunking arguments against homosexuality (whether associated with nature, reproduction, heterosexual masquerade, or social order), Epstein argues in favour of homosexuality on a historical basis that includes the birth of democracy (*ibid*.: 69, 117). He presents various configurations of male homosexual couples, focusing on couples with a large age difference in which the attributes of youth are exchanged for those of experience, arguing for the social and educational benefit of such arrangements. Moreover, while heterosexual unions are based on reciprocated love, Epstein finds that homosexual unions accept unidirectional love between the lover and the beloved, with 'amitié' ['friendship'], going from the beloved to the lover. Indeed, the Greek figure of Ganymede is associated with the younger, passive role of beloved in a male–male relationship in which the active lover mirrors the powerful lust of Zeus. Rejecting 'la détermination anatomique et physiologique de l'homosexuel' ['anatomical and physiological determinations of the homosexual'] (*ibid*.: 41), Epstein ultimately steers clear of essentializing or defining fixed aspects of homosexual sensibility. It may therefore be more exact to speak of his ethics and aesthetics as queer, that is, as a broad rejection of heteronormativity based on the recognition of same-sex desire.

From the purview of film studies, Epstein's queerness manifests itself, against the grain of mainstream cinema, through his *double amour*, his equal interest for female and male bodies. In *Bonjour cinéma* (1921b) he celebrates eroticism in a Whitmanian vein: 'sensuel comme une hanche de femme ou de jeune homme' ['sensual like the hip of a woman or a young man'] (*ibid.*: 43). Sections on male stars may also be read through a more homoerotic lens, while titles such as 'Amour de Charlot' and 'Amour de Sessue', might read as either 'Lovely X', 'Love for X', or even 'Loved by X'. Such queer fandom provides an important answer to the crisis of masculinity and male embodiment that followed World War One, and which, some critics argue, marks the French cinema of the late 1910s and 1920s.[19] Epsteinian *photogénie*, in connecting male viewers and male actors' bodily affects, invites film studies to rethink the notion of queer visibility in the post-war and silent periods. As Epstein puts it, 'Tout fait humain est une triade indivisible: anatomique, physiologique et psychologique. L'étude de l'homosexualité doit aussi coordonner ces trois aspects de la connaissance'] ['Every human fact is an indivisible triad: anatomical, physiological and psychological. The study of homosexuality must also coordinate these three aspects of knowledge'] (1930–40: 42). In relying on both physiological and psychological 'facts', *photogénie* theory maintains a close affinity with such a queer perspective on filmic embodiment.

The most queer of his movies is most certainly *Le Double amour* (1925), whose very title hints at the possibility of desire within 'un couple du même sexe' ['a couple of the same sex'] (*ibid.*: 281). The melodrama opens at a fashionable casino in Biarritz where it turns out that the money Laure Maresco collected from her rich friends for charity purposes was lost by her young gambling lover, Jacques Prémont-Solène, the scion of an automobile manufacturer. Laure sends Jacques away to protect him, facing the situation by herself, giving up all her belongings and even her station to repay his debt. Meanwhile, Jacques's father sends him to the US to straighten him out. Alone and poor, Laure almost throws herself into the ocean, when we suddenly learn that she is pregnant: 'Mais déjà palpite en sa chair / La promesse d'une vie nouvelle ' ['Already, there beats within her

19 Ruby Rich opened with this keen comment the first US retrospective on Dulac, entitled 'Duty, Deviance, Desire: The Films of Germaine Dulac' (14 September 2003, University of California at Berkeley).

flesh / The promise of a new life']. So she opts for life out of maternal love, this acceptable form of 'double love'. Thus far, the story remains within a rather plain heterosexual matrix. Laure then becomes a cabaret singer who meets quick success, is feted and soon wealthy again, and her son also named Jacques (played by Pierre Batcheff, later the lead in *Un Chien andalou*) grows up without want. Only, he too turns out to be a gambler who proceeds to lose all her money. Already, the critique of heterosexuality is biting: men are leeches to good hard-working women willing to sacrifice everything for them.

In the meantime the elder Jacques, having made his fortune overseas as a responsible and bachelor businessman, returns to France somewhat nostalgically. Playing in a casino for the first time in twenty years, Jacques unknowingly sits at the same card table as his son. Jacques Jr. has just stolen a batch of chips from the casino, which he promptly loses to his father, now a very serene player. Jacques Jr. is accused, and Jacques Sr. is called upon to serve as witness for the casino. When the group of men arrive to Jacques Jr.'s house, Jacques Sr. discovers that his mother is Laure, and she tells him he is his son. Jacques Sr. ungentlemanly responds, 'Mon fils? / Ou celui d'un autre?' ['My son? / Or that of another?']. But then Laure retorts: 'As-tu regardé ses mains / filles des tiennes! / ... et qui ont agi comme / les tiennes autrefois!' ['Have you seen his hands / They are the daughters of yours! / ... and they acted as / yours did once!']. In French, the hand is feminine, which ostensibly explains the daughter simile. But the synecdoche is quite striking in pointing to a resemblance of father and son through a body part not merely feminized but anthropomorphized as a daughter. Moreover, gambling is here clearly euphemistic, since it is presented neither as a moral failure, nor as a weakness of the will, or even a psychological addiction, but purely as an *innate bodily disposition passed on from father to son*. Gambling – whose equivalent in French is the much broader 'jeu' – would seem to be the surface or transferred impulse concealing and coding homosexuality. At the narrative level, let us not forget, Jacques Sr.'s 'gambling' directly competed with his love for Laure.

In national film industries permeated by repertory theatre, as is the case in France, the appearance of male actors heavily made-up (face powder, eye shadow, and lipstick) may strike us today as much more gender-bending then it did to contemporaries (see Plate 12). Hence the encounter of the main protagonist early on in *La Glace à trois faces* with a powdered-face and lipstick-wearing 'fâcheux', or 'bore', in the restaurant where he eats with Pearl, should probably not be read as a queer encounter, in spite of a series of quizzical glances between the two men. Given such strictures of context, to return to *Le Double amour*, we find two scenes that present Jacques Jr. plainly as a homosexual. The first takes place after the movie establishes that Jacques Jr. is afflicted with the same dilettantism as his father. After Laure promises to bail him out, she takes him in her arms on his bed, and both keep one languid hand on their chest: Pierre Batcheff's vulnerable face and bare neck facing the camera, their parallel feminine gesture – with the *hand* again – reads very much as though son and mother had just acknowledged to each other that he was gay. It cannot be excluded that this very touching moment had biographical resonances for Epstein.

The second scene takes place after Jacques Jr. enters his jail cell: it contains probably the most overt depiction of a gay encounter in silent French cinema. As he steps in, Jacques Jr. realizes with palpable discomfort that the cell is occupied by a young hoodlum, who would be referred to as *un Apache* (originally someone living in la Zone outside Paris). The latter's first glance at Jacques Jr. conspicuously goes from head to toe. The *Apache* is dressed in a close-fitting suit with a high collar, a sailor's cap, and a large blond curl between his temple and cheek. As Jacques Jr. stares at him, the Apache takes out a white mouse from under his coat (*une souris*, in French, is slang for a sexually promiscuous woman), and he begins strumming an air guitar while smiling and staring at the new resident. Epstein then creates a composite shot with a CU on Batcheff's face and superimpressions of a large feather fan moving up and down, a viola rotating upon itself, and three men circling slowly around each other (among whom we recognize one of Jacques Jr.'s friends) (see Plates 17a and 17b). No intertitle is provided during the whole sequence. We might interpret it as the visual equivalent to a bawdy pick-up song the Apache is singing at Jacques Jr., mocking his glass (and class) closet. If so, the Apache's function would be that of 'outing' the homosexuality the movie has carefully coded and euphemized as gambling, with the alibi that the Apache is an outlaw anyway, thus outside of and condemned by proper bourgeois purview.

Epstein skilfully concludes the narrative on two bifurcated levels. To satisfy the demands of the straight melodrama, Jacques Sr., Laure, and Jacques Jr. are reunited in the perfect nuclear family in the end. For viewers attuned to the association gambling–gayness, the resolution concerns Laure's understanding, through her son, that the original problem with his father – her lover – had been that he, like their son, was queer. It is noteworthy that Laure and Jacques Sr. do not kiss: their new union is based less on rekindled love/sex than on the admission of parental responsibility by the latter as well as mutual friendship.

The title of the movie leaves it open whether *Le Double amour* points to Laure's steadfast love for both her lover and son, or whether it labels the queer swerve of desire between opposite and same sex running through both father and son, via the euphemism of gambling addiction in French: *l'amour du jeu*. Since in all of Epstein's queer-themed productions narcissism is a central motif, it is not excluded that this last expression echoed with *l'amour du je*.

Certainly, more work is needed to determine to what extent the experimental research of the French narrative avant-garde was motivated by the wish to find cinematic techniques capable of depicting psychological and sensorial states from non-straight perspectives. While there is little work on the topic of queer aesthetics among directors who were the predecessors or contemporaries of Jean Epstein, new studies are coming out regarding directors who were influenced by him. For instance, Steven Dillon has explored thematic and aesthetic similarities between the films and the writings of Jean Cocteau and Derek Jarman, and his queer criticism seems to me to apply strikingly well to the films and writings of Jean Epstein. To take but one example, Dillon (2004) considers that in both Cocteau and Jarman two queer motifs play an operative role: the mirror and the sea. The tension between the two, that is, roughly between the narcissism of self-exploration on the one hand, and the dissolution or sublimation of the ego within a broader embodied engagement with reality, on the other, traverses some of their most important work. The same can be said of Jean Esptein. Stuart Liebman (1998) has drawn attention to the paradigmatic role of mirrors and self-visualization in *Le Cinématographe vu de l'Etna*, and in the next chapter we will see that next to melodramas and documentaries, the most important group of works by Epstein were his Breton films in which the ocean is in many ways the main protagonist. Some of Epstein's philosophical formulations of the self also belong to this queer continuum between the hard images of self-reflection and the fluid contours of self-dissolution:

> L'individualité est un complexe mobile, que chacun, plus ou moins consciemment, doit se choisir et se construire, puis réaménager sans cesse, à partir d'une diversité d'aspects qui, eux-mêmes, sont fort loin d'être simples ou permanents, et dans la masse desquels, quand ils sont trop nombreux, l'individu parvient difficilement à se désigner et à se conserver une forme nette. Alors, la supposée personnalité devient un être diffus, d'un polymorphisme qui tend vers l'amorphe et qui se dissout dans le courant des eaux-mères.[20]

In this densely poetic passage, Epstein brings together the sea, moving water, and fluidity – here with a figurally maternal dimension – to suggest how the material sensorial register of *photogénie* conjoins visual mobility and coenaesthesis to redefine (queer) individuality. Elsewhere he writes: 'Le monde de l'écran ... constitue le domaine par excellence du malléable, du visqueux, du liquide' ['The world of the screen ... constitutes the privileged domain of the malleable, the viscous, and the liquid'] (Epstein, 1974: 347). In haptic vision, the eye feels as though it were alighting upon distant things, but the contact remains at the surface. Epstein's *photogénie* is decidedly a fleshier intersection of technology with coenaesthesis, kinaesthesia, and synaesthesia, in which seeing pierces the surface, letting itself be engulfed by the subjacent currents animating matter and bodies alike, and rendering identity malleable.

---

20 'Individuality is a mobile complex, that each of us, more or less consciously, must choose and construct for himself, then rearrange ceaselessly, through a diversity of aspects which, themselves, are far from being simple or permanent, and within the mass of which, when too numerous, the individual succeeds with great difficulty in keeping clear form. Then, so-called personality becomes a diffuse self, whose polymorphism tends towards the amorphous and dissolves itself in the watery current of motherly depths' (Epstein, 1974: 394).

References

Clair, Jean (2004), 'Introduction', in Gaston de Pawlowski, *Voyage au pays de la quatrième dimension*, Paris: Éditions images modernes, 11–27.

Dallet, Sylvie (2000), 'Boîter avec toute l'humanité ou la filmographie gancienne et son golem', *1895*, vol. 31, October, 53–80.

Deleuze, Gilles (1986), *Cinema 1: The Movement Image*, Hugh Tomlinson and Barbara Habberjam (trans.), Minneapolis: University of Minnesota Press.

Derrida, Jacques (1976), *Of Grammatology*, Gayatri Chakravorty Spivak (trans.), Baltimore and London: Johns Hopkins University Press.

Dillon, Steven (2004), *Derek Jarman and Lyric Film: The Mirror and the Sea*, Austin: University of Texas Press.

Douek, Simone and Mireille Krauss (1998), 'Jean Epstein, Les mardis du cinéma' (radio programme aired on 19 April, Institut National de l'Audiovisuel).

Epstein, Jean (1921a), *La Poésie d'aujourd'hui, un nouvel état d'intelligence*, Paris: Éditions de la Sirène.

— (1921b), *Bonjour cinéma*, Paris: Éditions de la Sirène.

— (1922a) 'Le Bel Agonisant', *Zenith* 14 [Zagreb], 28–9 May.

— (1922b) 'Le Bel Agonisant', *Le Promenoir* 6, 9 June.

— (1930–40) (Alfred Kléber), *Ganymède, essai sur l'éthique homosexuelle masculine* (28), Fonds Epstein, Collection Cinémathèque française, BiFi, 227 B 60.

— (1974), *Écrits sur le cinéma*, vol. 1, Paris: Éditions Seghers.

Flammarion, Camille (1894), *La Fin du monde*, Paris: Ernest Flammarion.

Heidegger, Martin (1993), 'The Question Concerning Technology', in David Farrell Krell (ed.), *Martin Heidegger: Basic Writings from 'Being and Time' (1927) to 'The Task of Thinking' (1964)*, rev. edn, New York: HarperCollins, 307–41.

Leprohon, Pierre (1964), *Jean Epstein*, Paris: Éditions Seghers.

Liebman, Stuart (1999), 'Sublime et désublimation dans la théorie cinématographique de Jean Epstein: *Le Cinématographe vu de l'Etna*', in Jacques Aumont (ed.), *Jean Epstein: cinéaste, poète, philosophe*, Paris: Cinémathèque française, 125–37.

Marinetti, Filippo (1909), 'Le Futurisme', *Le Figaro* (Saturday, 20 February), www.gallica.bnf.fr.

Morand, Paul (1925), *L'Europe galante*, Paris: Grasset.

Mumford, Lewis (1934), *Technics and Civilization*, New York: Harcourt, Brace.

Pawlowski, Gaston de (2004 [1912]), *Voyage au pays de la quatrième dimension*, Paris: Éditions images modernes.

Porter, Darwin (2001) *Hollywood's Silent Closet*, New York: Blue Moon Press.

Rolland, Romain and Franz Masereel (1921), *La Révolte des machines, ou la pensée déchaînée*, Paris: Le Sablier.

Russo, Vito (1981), *The Celluloid Closet*, New York: Harper & Row.

Sedgwick, Eve (1990), *Epistemology of the Closet*, Berkeley: University of California Press.

Slide, Anthony (1999), 'The Silent Closet', *Film Quarterly* 52(4) (summer), 24–32.

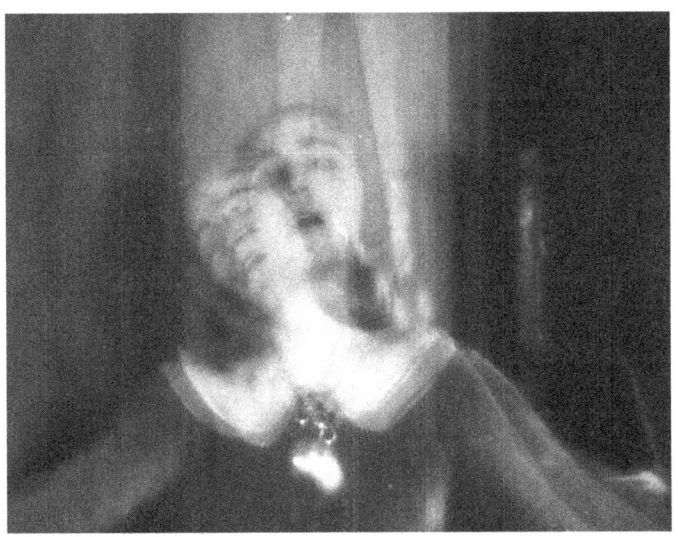

1a Composite shot of Madeline, *La Chute de la maison Usher* (1928)

1b A montage of stills of the Russian actress Alla Nazimowa in Epstein's *Bonjour cinéma* (1921)

2 Shivering curtain, *La Chute de la maison Usher* (1928)

3 Funeral procession with its hand-held 'heaving' shot, *La Chute de la maison Usher* (1928)

4 Jean (Léon Mathot) the melancholy dockworker, *Cœur fidèle* (1923)

5 Marie (Gina Manès) and Petit-Paul (Edmond van Daële) on the first merry-go-round sequence, *Cœur fidèle* (1923)

6 Third shot to last in the epilogue, *Cœur fidèle* (1923)

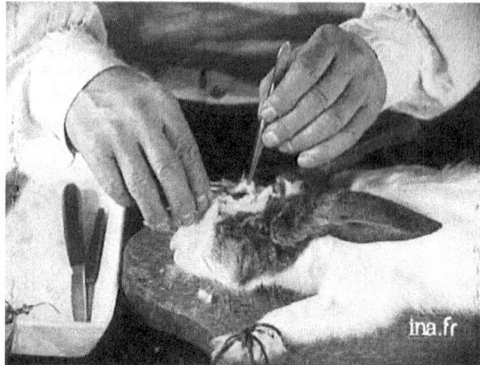

7 Still from the vivisection scene of the inoculation of rabies in a rabbit, *Pasteur* (1922)

8a Peasant holding boy bit by a rabid dog, *Pasteur* (1922)

 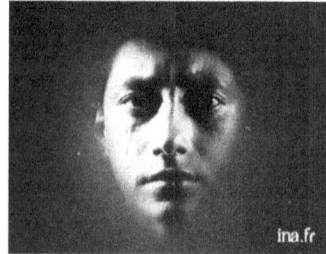

8b [*left*] Counter-shot of swooned boy's face, *Pasteur* (1922)
8c [*right*] Boy's crying face in Pasteur's imagination, *Pasteur* (1922)

9 Two women dancing together, with a superimpression of Anna, *Le Lion des Mogols* (1924)

10 Protagonist getting in his car, shot through a vegetable cart, *La Glace à trois faces* (1927)

11 Protagonist in his automobile glass closet, *La Glace à trois faces* (1927)

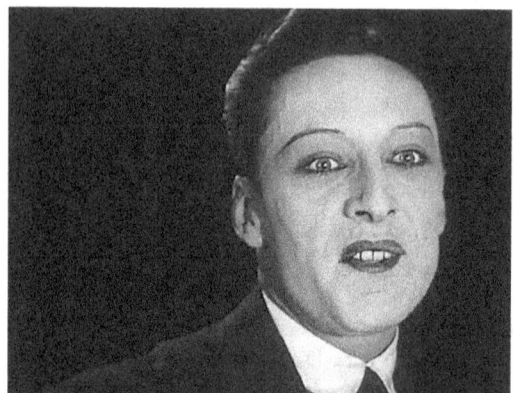

12 Androgynous Jean (Nino Constantini), *Six et demi onze* (1927)

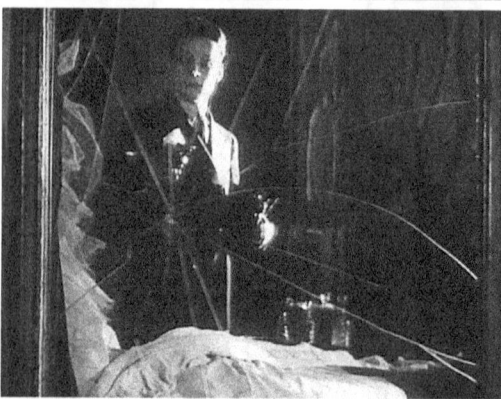

13 Jean shoots at the mirror, holding a camera, before killing himself, *Six et demi onze* (1927)

14 Photo strip from Jean's camera, dangling in front of Jérôme's eyes, *Six et demi onze* (1927)

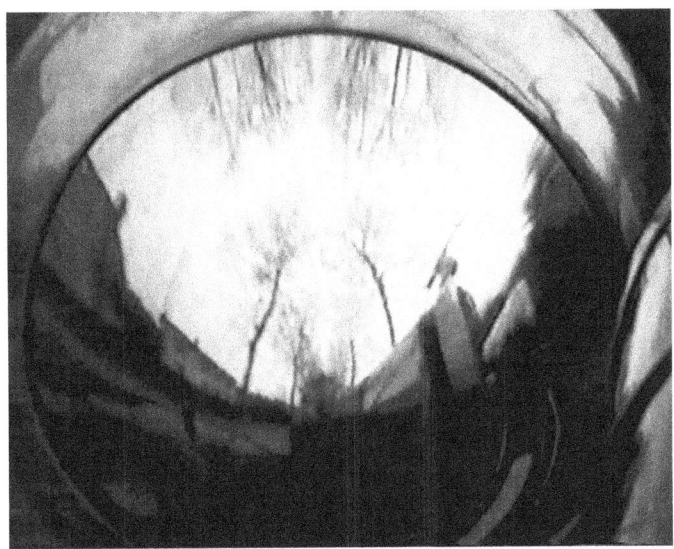

15 Reflections on the Hispano-Suiza car, *L'Homme à l'Hispano* (1932)

16 Pierre Batcheff in his mother's arms, *Le Double amour* (1925)

17a Composite shot of Pierre Batcheff, the singing 'Apache' (faint, top left), the lute, and feather fan, *Le Double amour* (1925)

17b With three men circling each other, *Le Double amour* (1925)

18a Ambroise, *Finis Terræ* (1929)

18b Jean-Marie, *Finis Terræ* (1929)

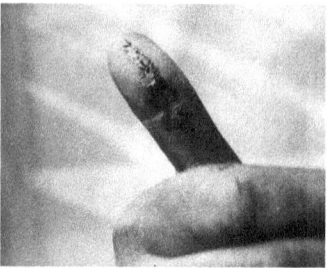

19 [*left*] Broken bottle with two small daisies, *Finis Terræ* (1929)
20 [*right*] Ambroise's injured thumb, *Finis Terræ* (1929)

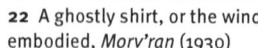

21 Example of intertitle verse, *Morv'ran* (1930)

22 A ghostly shirt, or the wind embodied, *Morv'ran* (1930)

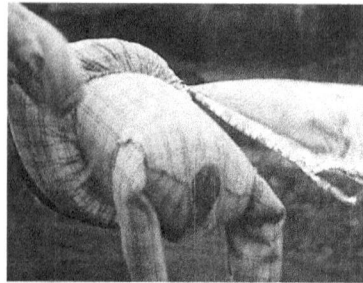

23 Lighthouse keeper behind the lens, *Morv'ran* (1930)

24a Soizic showing her shy beauty to Rémy, *L'Or des mers* (1932)

24b Soizic trapped in quicksand, *L'Or des mers* (1932)

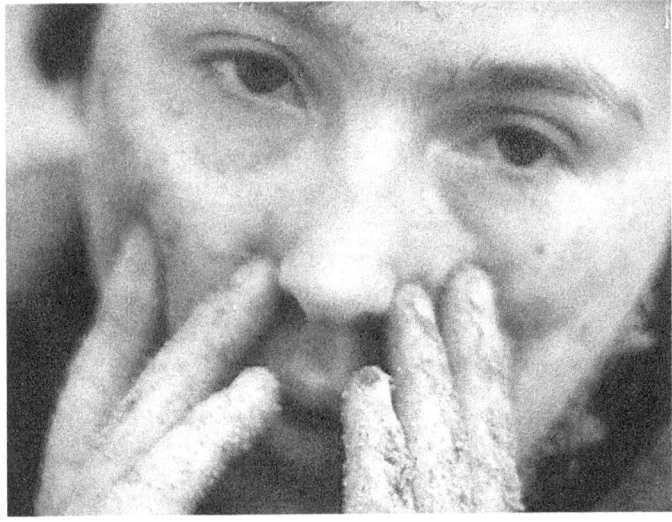

25 'Zip-line' shot of the quarry, found in both *La Bourgogne* (1936) and *Les Bâtisseurs* (1938)

26 Two masons working on a cathedral, *Les Bâtisseurs* (1938)

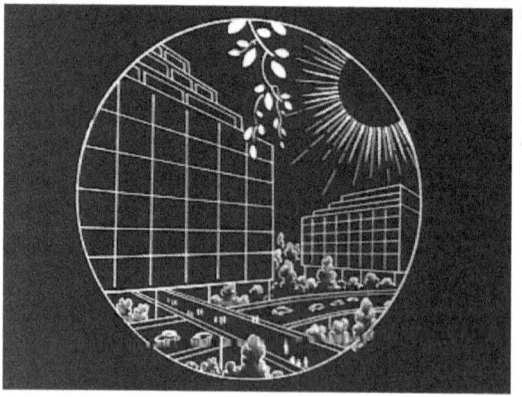

27 Animated cartoon depicting Le Corbusier's utopian social housing, *Les Bâtisseurs* (1938)

4

Brittany, the edge of the modern world

A sudden shift that has never been fully explained took place in Epstein's œuvre in late 1927. Turning his back on melodramas that had been his mainstay since 1923, whether through social themes or critiques of heterosexual mores or both, Epstein discovered in himself a sudden and overwhelming passion for Brittany.[1] This passion came with the refocusing of his filmmaking on a minor and semi-documentary genre, the so-called Breton film, thereby amplifying the documentary tendency present in his work since his 1922 docufiction on Pasteur (see chapter 5).

This shift involved leaving behind at once the comfort of the studio, the financial structure of the French production system, and immediate concerns with the cultural and intellectual brokers of Paris. The shooting of *La Chute de la maison Usher* in 1928 had caused open rifts with Antonin Artaud and Luis Buñuel, exacerbating the conflict of the narrative avant-garde's work with the Surrealist group, then at the apex of its sway over the French intelligentsia.[2] This episode certainly contributed to what must have been, however, a much deeper artistic and professional crisis. Both Pierre Leprohon and Marie Epstein suggest that the studio atmosphere itself had become stifling for Jean, although neither elaborates on specifics. We know that in 1926 Epstein had set out to adapt for the screen a novel by Swiss writer Charles-Ferdinand Ramuz about alpine peasantry and the power of the natural world (Leprohon, 1964: 46; Guigeno,

1 For this whole chapter, see Guigueno (2003).
2 The final straw would be the Surrealist group's negative reception of Germaine Dulac's *The Seashell and the Clergyman* (1928), after a scenario by Artaud; see Virmaux and Virmaux (1999).

2003: 24). This ultimately unsuccessful project belies nonetheless an increased appeal for on-location shooting among remote populations at the edges of the Hexagon. Another likely factor for severing ties with the studios was economic. The meagre ticket receipts for Epstein's 1927 films probably did little to entice financial backers to support his future projects. Moreover, some of Epstein's bigger-budget movies, such as the 1926 six-episode adaptation of George Sand's *Mauprat*, often came with demands from producers that Epstein – like many other filmmakers – found intrusive, even though it too was largely shot on location. We may conjecture that setting off with a skeleton crew to the coastal wilderness of Brittany represented a radical way to regain at least a modicum of creative independence, not to mention some degree of popular realism.

But why Brittany? In the late 1920s this north-western region of France was still a wild frontier where Breton was spoken and which therefore belonged more to the old Celtic coastal world of Gaels, Scots, and Welsh, than with Paris-centred France proper. Although Epstein had known Brittany first-hand at least since he and his mother and sister came there for vacation in 1908, his movies until then had taken place in the south – Biarritz, Marseille, and Nice – or central France – Sologne, Indre, and Burgundy. We might note that these locations involve bodies of water, whether ocean and sea, rivers or marshes. If we recall that *La Belle Nivernaise* was set on a barge and the rhythms of canal life, and that the lost 1923 documentary *La Montagne infidèle* centred on the lava flows of Mount Etna, we might consider the visual and physical sensations of fluidity, with which we ended the last chapter, as an increasingly important aesthetic and philosophical subject matter for Epstein's maturing work.

In a section entitled 'Towards Another State of Perception: Liquid Perception', Gilles Deleuze keenly notes that many experimental filmmakers in the 1920s were drawn to water as a unique perceptual element:

> A considerable part of Epstein's and Grémillon's work forms a sort of Breton school, which realizes the cinematographic dream of a drama without characters, or at least which would move from Nature to man. Why does water seem to correspond to all the requirements of this French school: abstract aesthetic requirement, social documentary requirement, narrative dramatic requirement? (1986: 77)

After addressing water as almost pure movement, Deleuze goes on to say that films exploring the boundary between earth and water take up the problem of

> a drama where there is a confrontation between, on one hand, attachments to the land and, on the other, mooring-ropes, tug-ropes, free and mobile ropes ... The drama was that it was necessary to break the links with the earth, of father with son, husband with wife and mistress, woman with lover, children with parents; to retreat into solitude to achieve human solidarity, class solidarity. (*ibid.*: 78)

For Deleuze, a fluid practice derived from the thought of water implies unbinding and motion, in contrast to the prevalence of stable binds on land. This accords well with our reading of Epstein's earlier films as critiques of heterosexual strictures. It also explains, for instance, the compositional role of the rhythmic shots of water in *La Chute de la maison Usher*, at a point where both the narrative and the protagonist appear to have reached a standstill. The movie ends on the fiery destruction of the castle – which casts its imposingly static shadow in so many shots – leaving Roderick, Madeline, and the doctor unhurt, albeit utterly exposed to smoke, wind, and sky. In a way, the three characters reach Deleuze's perceptual horizon whose fluidity makes them sever or loosen or free the social ties that had encircled them – and us viewers too. We can hardly miss the fact that the fall of a building signals at minimum a new relationship to the elements – an unmooring that precipitates a more nomadic life. Epstein's turn to Brittany films represents similarly a radical unmooring of cinema from rigid formulae, in order to expand *photogénie*'s potential for reaching and transforming viewers. To melodramatic plots that unfold *narrative affects* along *private spaces of interiority*, albeit across social classes, Epstein came to substitute docudramas of survival pitting *generic human affects* against the *exterior forces of nature*. While Epstein's early *photogénie* had relied on close-ups of well-rehearsed melodramatic stars like Gina Manès or Nino Costantini to mobilize affect responses, in this second phase, *photogénie* centred on non-professional actors' much less theatrical faces, counting on shots of raging sea and wind to evoke new dynamic correlates with more naturalistic human affects.

We may enlarge the 'Breton school' alluded to by Deleuze to include other coastal Celtic populations that became the focus of important movies such as Robert Flaherty's *Man of Aran* (1934) for Gaelic fishing villages and Michael Powell and Emeric Pressburger's *The*

Edge of the World (1937) for Scottish islanders. The film that probably most inspired Epstein is Jacques de Baroncelli's adaptation of a Pierre Loti 1886 novel, *Pêcheur d'Islande* (1924). Produced by Albatros, with whom Epstein worked in 1924–25, the movie was shot on Brittany's northern Côtes d'Armor with professional lead actors Charles Vanel and Sandra Milowanoff – each playing lead roles in subsequent Epstein movies – while using both local extras and stock footage of cod fisheries. Loti's narrative is structured around the seasonal cycle of fishing campaigns with the separation between male and female villagers, and their hopes and fears. Epstein's *Le Tempestaire* (1947) largely follows the same template. André Antoine's *Les Travailleurs de la mer* (1918), a naturalist adaptation from Victor Hugo shot in the Finistère region, was probably a less accessible predecessor. Why such simple and 'reality-based' Breton stories appealed to filmmakers of the 1920s and 1930s – notably Grémillon in his well-known *Gardiens de phare* (1929) – has to do with several factors.

Certainly, the 1917 Russian Revolution had renewed interest in proletarian and peasant life, not least of all because peasantry was often profoundly traditional and anti-revolutionary, and city-grown social progressives set out to circumvent their resistances to political change. This is for instance the ambiguous theme of Alexander Dovzhenko's film *Earth* (1930). The 1920s and 1930s also heralded the start of a conservation mindset given the quick modernization – and already globalization – of world cultures, languages, and local traditions. Anthropologists went around recording disappearing languages, folklores, and oral literatures, and museums overlapped colonial and scientific imperatives in collecting vanishing data while illegitimately obtaining artefacts or human remains. Recent scholars have also demonstrated that modernist thinkers saw no contradictions in embracing together the technological and socio-aesthetic leaps of the inter-war period, and the crafts of so-called primitive populations as an inspirational counterweight to modernization: Pablo Picasso, Jean Cocteau, or Antonin Artaud are cases in point. Finally, we should add that the documentary movement beginning in the 1930s rests on social, political, and cultural interests on the part of filmmakers, but also on more commercially driven demands by exhibitors and distributors for films with a mixture of educational, touristic, and nationalistic themes.[3]

---

3 This is clearly the double aspiration of the documentary work of Jean-Benoit Lévy for instance, Vignaux (2007). For the development of documentary in the

Certainly, we can trace such concerns within Epstein's six fiction or fictionalized movies about Brittany, as well as the three documentaries he shot there (for these, see chapter 5). However, his two undisputable Breton masterpieces – *Finis Terræ* and *Le Tempestaire* – should be approached within a much more metaphysical sensibility, linking them to such poetic works as Poe's *The Narrative of Arthur Gordon Pym*, Melville's *Moby Dick* and Victor Hugo's *Les Travailleurs de la mer*. This isn't to say that all these works are somehow abstract and abstruse – quite the contrary. The sea with its drama of human communities striving for survival against the overpowering elements is indeed an answer to what may be called 'dry land' metaphysics, which takes place in more urban and protected environments, and involves often the very overcoming of material issues – *meta*-physics. Oceanic metaphysics is always situated at the forceful convergence of moving matter, temporal uncertainty, corporeal limits, and death. Murder and especially suicide figure in just about every melodramatic plot of Epstein's, and so do they in the Breton cycle, for instance, as *Chanson d'Armor*'s double suicide or the near death of the daughter in *L'Or des mers*. But while in city bourgeois melodramas, suicide or social injustice bring about death as an unwanted scandal, in the Breton cycle, death and life are everywhere interwoven: in the inhuman energy of water and sky, in the rocky and barren landscapes that nonetheless holds hidden life (such as the crabs that the daughter offers the empty-handed hunter in *L'Or des mers*), in the body that suddenly takes ill, and in the small villages overshadowed by imposing cemeteries that hold the many empty graves of the sailors lost at sea. It is therefore an immediate, material, and ecological metaphysics that is enacted on-screen, rather than delayed, theoretical, and non-situated metaphysical atmospheres such as those of poetic realism or film noir. Epstein is not drawn to the former metaphysics just out of his particular sensibility, but as a filmmaker, because it appears to him in deep symbiosis with the cinema itself. This is clearly illustrated by the film that opened the cycle, *Finis Terræ*.

1920s, see Gauthier (2004: 52–72).

Finis Terræ (1929)

In an interview for a local newspaper, Epstein insists at the outset that '*Finis Terræ* is not a documentary'. He adds that 'this film comprises a precise and studied dramatic action. By collecting several local accounts, writing down a few facts, I wanted to compose a reality with the help of a certain number of true elements' (Guigeno, 2003: 30). Using only non-professional actors and weaving local stories into a fiction of lived reality, Epstein became de facto, as Pierre Leprohon claimed, 'the pioneer of neo-realism' (Leprohon, 1964: 47). But Epstein was seeking much more than a blank slate on which to create the 'reality effect' of coastal villagers' lives. Roland Barthes calls 'reality effect' the efforts and means deployed to generate an impression of reality where there is no reality, only concerted artificiality. Epstein is not at all concerned with the inherent problem of realist filmmaking, that between reality vs. fiction and naturalism vs. aestheticism. Rather than banging his head against such absolute oppositions, he considers that his film reflects a unique collaboration between real people and cinema: 'Le film est prêt à naître comme l'empreinte de cette personnalité collective ou individuelle, devenue enfin apparente' ['The film is ready to be born as the imprint of a collective or individual personality that has finally become apparent'], Epstein writes, adding further on that 'Ouessant tout entière vivait et jouait avec moi à faire le film' ['the whole of Ouessant [island] lived and played with me at making a movie'] (Epstein, 1974: 207, 222). If Epstein indeed pioneered a form of neo-realism with his first Breton films, he also initiated a more collective version of auteurism, one in which a film is the record of a creative encounter between a professional director and the non-professional actors who actually make the film come to life. For both *Finis Terræ* and *L'Or des mers*, Epstein asserts that he prepared no découpage before the shooting.[4]

When Epstein and crew arrived on Ouessant, they were initially viewed with great suspicion, and gaining the confidence of the inhabitants was part of the cultural and human challenge of the film. It was shot on both Ouessant itself and on two small islands where, during the summer months, kelp was harvested and burnt into ash to make fertilizer. The plot revolves around the islet of Bannec where 'four

---

4 P. Leprohon, *Cinémonde* 184 (1932), cited by V. Guigueno in www.melvan.org/epstein-or-des-mers.htm (consulted 07/08/11).

men, two teams', work the whole summer long in the combined heat of the huge kelp fires and sunny weather. The focus is on two young hands and close friends, the wilder Ambroise and the more grounded Jean-Marie, each of whom works as assistant to an older man (see Plates 18a and 18b). While clowning around, Ambroise breaks one of the last bottles of wine that Jean-Marie was going to share with him. As nerves are running thin at summer's end, Jean-Marie explodes with rancour, accusing Ambroise of stealing his pocket knife as well. Ambroise cut himself on the broken glass of the bottle, and the cut becomes infected, partly due to a lack of drinking water (there is a drought). But Ambroise's illness and indeed increasingly delirious state go unnoticed by his companions: the older worker merely condemns his laziness for bringing the entire crew to a halt. Jean-Marie ultimately finds his knife and understands that Ambroise is dangerously ill. He takes him by boat on the windless passage and rows towards Ouessant. Meanwhile people on the island had noticed the lack of smoke and thus became alarmed, and the long estranged mothers of the two boys suddenly reconciled to convince the rector (the island's administrator) to dispatch the doctor to Bannec. The two boats meet, despite a dense fog and scarce wind, and the movie ends with Ambroise saved, comfortably ensconced in bed.

Richard Abel provides a keen description of the generic, diegetic, and rhythmic particularities of the movie (Abel, 1984: 500–7). Hence, after the thumb cut and the fight between the two friends, the film veers towards the documentary, with only a few CUs on various utensils and objects to side-shadow the drama. Then as the illness intensifies, Abel notes, the movie adopts the POV of Ambroise, displaying some remarkable uses of variable slow motion to impart on viewers the effect of perception altered by illness. This sensorial involvement – indeed optical contamination – of the viewer caused by the subtle alteration of filmic duration, and combined with the dusky silvery contrasts of the cinematography and film stock, makes the first part of the movie disarmingly beautiful. The second half follows the drama through an alternating structure, with series of rhythmically adjusted cross-cuts between Bannec and the main island of Ouessant, between the sea and the boys' two mothers, and finally between the two boats seeking each other through a still fog. For Abel, Epstein's shooting and editing rhetoric consists in this heavily rhythmic and dramatic patterning being placed in dialogue with another, much less obvious. Abel calls it a '"submerging" of the narrative'. It consists in shots/sequences that are neither literal nor symbolically transparent. Abel describes a comparatively long sequence during which a bowl, ostensibly left in shallow water to be washed, is shot in CUs as waves progressively crash against and submerge it. Another such shot is described by Abel as 'a miniature still life – the ECU of a glass fragment framing a tiny daisy among the rocks' (*ibid.*: 503). It is not immediately clear how we are meant to understand such sequences, and thus Abel's choice of the term 'submerged' seems felicitous. We might note, however, that both sequences deal with receptacles that no longer fulfil their function: a half-sunken bowl and a broken bottle (see Plate 19). Moreover, the daisy sequence would be more precisely described as CUs and an ECU of not one but *two* daisies ringed (rather than framed) by what's left of the bottle's cylinder. The symbolic encoding of love is difficult to miss: two youthful flowers grown side by side on an inhospitable rock, united by a circle both symbolic and severed. Combined with the dented bowl churned by the ebb, the submerged part of the narrative might point to a 'broken up' amorous relation between the two friends. What's more, Ambroise's injured thumb and Jean-Marie's lost pocket knife both represent rather conspicuous phallic injuries (Plate 20).

This is not to say that the movie becomes a cryptic tale of homosexual love: like in his other movies Epstein depicts here same-sex attraction as part of complex queer desires foreclosed or redirected or tangent. For instance, we cannot ignore the joy of Jean-Marie at finding his fiancée after he lands on Ouessant. Nonetheless, Epstein was very interested in his treatise on homosexuality by how same-sex attraction can flourish given environmental circumstances such as incarceration, enrolment in the military, or indeed any lengthy situation of gender segregation. I believe the implied narrative of the movie is that during summer camps on kelp-gathering islands young Breton men may discover sex together, given the strict gender segregation before marriage. Perhaps the submerged drama is that Ambroise – who carries and breaks the wine bottle and whose name echoes *ambrosia*, the divine drink of immortality – becomes ill because he revels excessively in their joint discovery of sex. In other words, he transforms a homosocial ritual between straight-men-to-be into a queerer pleasure. When he washes his wound with water, an intertitle has Jean-Marie complain, 'Tu crois qu'on va te laisser faire la fille ici?' ['You think we'll let you behave like a girl here?']. Ostensibly addressed to the way Ambroise squanders precious drinking water, this ambiguous comment might also serve to recall Ambroise to his straight identity. As often with Epstein, the ultimate focalizer of knowledge, that is, the POV from which the film views a situation, might end up being the doctor, since an intertitle near the end of the film reads: 'The devoted Doctor Lesenn, in spite of his 67 years, is the best comrade of the young islanders'. In a position to understand better than anyone else the psychosexual development of the young men, the doctor might well be the submerged figure of Epstein himself. After all, his life philosophy was that 'there is not a single health but plural healths', which means that Ambroise's illness might well veil healthy queer desire. We might then reread the plot, from the purview of the doctor's understanding, as the evolution of psychosexual entanglement between the two protagonists. At first, Jean-Marie erroneously accuses Ambroise of stealing his pocket knife, symbolically meaning that the latter is misusing the intimacy stemming from their shared discovery of sex. Ambroise's illness would then be a depressive reaction to Jean-Marie's rejection of Ambroise's queerness. The movie's central dramatic turn would consist touchingly in Jean-Marie recognizing and accepting the root of Ambroise's illness, thus overcoming his own initial phobic reaction to queerness. This reversal might also echo in the sub-plot of their mothers hating each other – as a sort of negative of the potential love between the two boys? – yet reconciling when both appear in danger. In a way, then, this film would be the polar opposite of *La Glace à trois faces*, since in that movie the glass closet was fatal to queerness. Here, the glass closet, the structural but coded co-embedding of queerness and heterosexuality, leads to acceptance and friendship. Of course, unlike Jean-Marie, Ambroise is left with no available love object at the movie's end: but as the non-professional actor playing him seems incapable of melancholy, we might read the large smile he wears as a convalescent as a positive omen for queer identity.

Yet for all the importance of the amorous motif between the two male protagonists, let us remember Epstein's words in the epigraph of this book: '[In cinema] there are no stories. There are only situations'. A plot or sub-plot does not a movie make. If *Finis Terræ*, as its title indicates, reaches a kind of extreme – the edge of the abyss – in Epstein's œuvre, it is because of its admirable synthetic quality.

Its emplotment closely and almost organically blends dramatic action, social realities, the body, coenaesthesis, the four Aristotelian elements (earth, air, fire, water), and cinematographic technique. We see for instance a long sequence five minutes into the movie in which Ambroise and an older worker burn kelp among barren rocks. Ambroise's body goes in and out of the thick smoke which acts as the fluid medium of the scene and as such mirrors the flux of filmic images. It is a mini-ode to the compact of film, elements, and bodies. Right at the end of this sequence we segue into the first signs of Ambroise's illness, before a cut shows us the bowl stirred by waves. The bowl is so well integrated a quasi-symbol that it does not appear symbolic at all, even though it recalls a ship sinking in miniature. Rather, it constitutes an elliptical expression of waywardness or sullenness that does not clearly 'belong' to Ambroise, or the sea, the plot, the camera eye, or ourselves as viewers. This mysterious porosity between the physical and the psychic wasn't lost on contemporary viewers. Film critic Harry Potamkin writes in *Close-Up* in 1929:

> The best instance of the pictorial mind rightly applied is Jean Epstein. He insists upon the image, lingers over it, penetrates it. What does it matter that *Finis Terræ* is slow? What does it mean that it does not satisfy those who wanted the subject treated *physically* instead of *psychically*? Epstein has shown how the physical material may be rendered psychical by persisting in the examination of the physical image. (1929: 61)

We might contrast such seamless expressionistic sequences with Hitchcock's brilliantly jarring use of objects as symbols meant to seem incongruous, uncanny, or excessively self-reflective: the spooled thread entangling dancers in *The Man Who Knew Too Much* (1934); the tea label stuck to the outside of the train window in *The Lady Vanishes* (1938); the film canisters with a bomb inside carried by the boy in *Sabotage* (1936), etc. Whereas all such devices partake of a kitsch *sensationalism* (again, absolutely brilliant) Epstein favours a plainer *sensorialism*. Further on in *Finis Terræ*, when the two mothers anxiously await the boats, an LS shows them lodged among the rocks at the edge of the sea, while in counter-shot the raging spray blanks out the screen, a discrete echo of and rhyme with the smoke enveloping Ambroise on Bannec. They too are exposed to the fury of the elements, uncomfortably beholden both to their fluid unbinding and to their steadfast love for their sons. When Epstein intersperses in that sequence an MCU of the lighthouse's lens, it takes a second or two to note how uncanny a reference it is to the camera and the human gaze – the mothers' but ours too – so entirely canny is any recourse to the lighthouse in this situation. But that is precisely how Freud characterizes the *Unheimlich*: the familiar rendered unfamiliar, and all at once the reverse.

The varied and subtle shooting and editing techniques Epstein deploys in *Finis Terræ* can only be sketched here and would warrant a much more detailed study. Ambroise's sickness, as we mentioned earlier, is traduced in very slight slow motion: enough to feel a slowing down, an impairment of 'normal' cadence, but not enough for us to enter consciously into slow-mo perception. The result is a unique teeter in which our identification with Ambroise's *situation* seems both accrued and lessened, as we mentally gauge the slow-mo effect and thus come out of immersive viewing, before realizing that it also forces us deeper into the image, into the actor's embodied condition. Certainly, Epstein's care in crafting viewers' reactions reaches a summit. He not only chose exactly the right film stock to optimize generally luscious contrasts with light conditions beyond his control, he also paid the most sustained attention to framing seemingly mundane shots into strikingly controlled yet airy compositions. The horizon line and horizontality in particular are closely attended to throughout the film: variations of low or high horizon, low and high angle shots, as well as canted camera shots, all contribute to accentuating our bodily reactions towards gravity, and thus our sensorial identification with Ambroise's illness. To mention just one example, Ambroise's fever culminates in a sequence that intercuts very high angle MSs of Ambroise lying down and very low angle LSs of the sun and the lighthouse of Ouessant. In doing so, Epstein shows the teenager to be powerlessly stuck to the ground, pounded by the harsh gaze of the sun, and entirely dependent on the transmission of (optical!) solidarity between the islet and the main island. When we watch the film, we do not need to put words on such transitions. Film lexicon would call them 'elliptical transitions' ostensibly because narrative continuity is not strictly obeyed. Yet such ellipses do not complicate or distract from the narrative, they simply rely on preconscious perceptual understanding that is one step ahead of words. Epstein was always aware when he began directing movies that filmic idioms age quickly over a span of five to ten years (Epstein, 1974: 110,

126–8). Indeed, several of his movies feel incurably dated. Yet with *Finis Terræ*, he crafted a masterpiece whose visual grain and rhythm have lost nothing of their freshness and precision. One can even venture to say that it will long remain for our post-digital era a model achievement of argentic film stock cinema.

Morv'ran (La Mer des corbeaux) (1930), *L'Or des mers* (1932), *Chanson d'Armor* (1934)

Epstein shot six other fiction (or rather semi-fiction) films in Brittany: the three listed in the heading just above, and *La Femme du bout du monde* (1937), *Le Tempestaire* (1947), and *Les Feux de la mer* (1948). *Morv'ran*, which means cormoran or literally 'sea raven' in Breton, is the only other silent Breton film apart from *Finis Terræ*. It was shot on l'île de Sein, south of Ouessant along the Atlantic coast. At 900 meters, or about 25 minutes, it is a short resembling a modern geographic documentary in that the text on the intertitle cards fashions a didactic narrative tying together hardship, death, and occasional celebrations in order to introduce urban viewers to the lived reality of the island. Interestingly, the intertitles are written in what might be called *intertitle verse*, such as the following:

Ouessant, 'île d'épouvante',	[Ouessant, 'scary island'
reine de l'archipel,	queen of the archipelago
la plus accueillante	the most welcoming
et riche.	and wealthy.
Les moutons innombrables	Innumerable sheep
divaguent	meander
à l'état sauvage.	gone wild.]

This is a mini-poem, with actual rhymes (épouvante / accueillante) and near-rhymes (**archi**pel/**rich**e; innomb**ra**bles, diva**gu**ent, état sau**vage**) (see Plate 21). There are also keen plays on words since 'moutons' means both sheep and foaming waves, and 'divaguer' contains the word for wave (vague). It is as if the sheep on land 'rhymed' visually and cognitively with the foaming waves. Epstein revels in filming the moving sea, the stormy coasts, and the barren country with two of its three cemeteries entirely dedicated, another card tells us, to fishermen who have drowned. Although Epstein does not belabour the point, this means the cemeteries hold only empty caskets and graves – the real cemetery being the ocean. Epstein points to this obliquely with the haunting shot of a shirt inflated by the strong wind, and resembling nothing so much as a phantom (see Plate 22). Another ghost is shown when Epstein films the silhouette of the lighthouse keeper behind the huge ridged lens of the lighthouse (already present in *Finis Terræ*, but without the 'ghost') (see Plate 23). The ominously deformed shapes that seem inhuman evoke the way the cinema deforms and reforms both the human body and our 'natural' vision. Epstein is always reminding us that cinema is not just an artifice or a machine, but a new way of perceiving the real that is both as 'unnatural' as all human artefacts and as 'natural' as all non-human phenomena. *Morvr'an* takes pains to show that deformations of perception and imagination, and the haunting of the dead, do not take away from collective joy, and in fact ground it as a vital necessity. The games everyone plays during a festival are nonetheless segregated among men, women, and children, unlike a similar festival Epstein shot close to Paris in *La Glace à trois faces* where everyone revels together. This segregation is of course at the very heart of *Finis Terræ*, and in his two other Breton full-features, Epstein ventures to dramatize it directly.

In 1932, he wrote a novel entitled *L'Or des mers*, and shot a film with the same title on the island of Hoedick with only non-professional islanders. The two stories are both based on the ramifications of the discovery of a treasure by villagers, but they are otherwise distinct (Epstein, 1995). The movie opens on a whimsical credit sequence: the names are written on glass plates that a hand manipulates inside a small fish tank with fish swimming about awkwardly. The first diegetic shots show a simple village of dirt streets with houses made of stone and thatched roofs, through which an old man meanders in search of food. He bangs at windows and shouts at people who peer at him through shutters and dirty glass panes. Malnutrition, poverty, and precariousness give the film an urgent quality at a time when the French government wasn't doing much to assist these small communities apart from providing them with free wine (as a later scene in the cantina makes clear). The plot revolves around this bitter and selfish unnamed old man, as he stumbles on a box containing shiny objects he takes to be jewels. He was seen with the box before burying it at the edge of the sea, so now all the villagers assume he is rich and they offer him food, drink, and tobacco. The portrait of the community Epstein depicts is far from flattering: to the lack of resources and solidarity are added hypocrisy and self-interest. In a particularly realistic scene where the old man shouts at his daughter and breaks a plate – in a way that makes us physically wary that a scene of abuse is about to unfold – Epstein shoots him in a low angle MS to put the viewer in the position of the daughter who sits near the fireplace. Throughout, the implications of beating, perhaps even sexual abuse, are quite strong. It is rather remarkable then that the locals as a whole accepted the plot and particulars of the movie as a faithful rendering of what goes on in the island.

The narrative develops as a love story between the daughter, Soizic, and a young man, Rémy, as the two exchange the scarce foods they find: crabs and shellfish. The old man ultimately dies, struck while standing in front of a huge standing stone symbolizing the Celtic world, with a tiny Catholic cross in the background signalling the thin overlay of Christian religiosity. Before dying, he tells Soizic the location of the box, in the quicksand. Rémy's father will allow his son to marry Soizic on one condition: she must produce the box as part of her dowry. She goes to retrieve the box on her own and finds it, but gets caught in the quicksand. Rémy saves her when all seemed lost. Of course, the box contains only trinkets that the deluded old man took to be riches. Throughout this simple tale, Epstein finds ways to intersperse beautiful shots of both landscapes and close-ups. For instance, there is a CU of Soizic's face beaming and shyly hiding behind her hands, as she is in the presence of Rémy (see Plate 24a). A few minutes later, almost the same CU is shown, but with Soizic's hands and face covered with sand as she is in an all-too literal pit of despair (see Plate 24b). Filmmaker Robert Bresson famously insisted on working with non-professionals he called 'models' so he could reveal their raw potential for unexaggerated expressivity. Epstein does this in both this film and *Finis Terræ*, and just when the story seems predictable and perhaps not very compelling, one such CU is enough to reidentify strongly with Adelina le Gurin, a waitress who lent her real emotions to the fictive character. This explains the lyricism behind Leprohon's description of these two shots:

> Je ne connais pas – et je le dis en pesant mes mots – de gros plan de visage plus émouvant que celui de l'héroïne de ce film – interprété par une servante d'auberge de Quiberon – découvrant le bonheur d'être aimée. De plus émouvant, d'aussi pudique que celui-ci où le visage s'éclaire d'un demi-sourire et que deux mains, ces deux mains

courtes et grasses de fille du peuple, remontant de la bouche au front, viennent lentement cacher comme si l'amoureuse voulait enfermer en elle son bonheur. Mais avant que les mains n'atteignent et n'effacent le regard, Epstein – ainsi le fera Fellini trente ans plus tard dans les *Nuits de Cabiria* – Epstein nous livre le regard – face à la caméra – de son héroïne. La complicité s'établit entre elle et nous, comme une confidence faite. Et c'est proprement bouleversant !

Ce visage, nous le retrouvons à la fin du film, ravagé par l'angoisse, trituré par les gestes de la peur, sali de boue marine, le regard perdu, quand la jeune fille jambes et jupe happées par le sable, sent venir la mort dans la solitude familière.[5] (1964: 91–2)

Leprohon suggests very aptly a bit later that the 'lenteur calculée' ['calculated slowness'] of the gestures of Soizic and Rémy in the quicksand lets out 'la réalité animale des humains' ['the animal reality of humans'] shine forth (*ibid.*: 93). This slowness results from the *mise en scène* – the acting within the shot – as much as from the editing tempo, and both contribute to expressing in a unique way the raw, animal-like affectivity of bodies that Epstein calls coenaesthesis. Although the film was shot as a silent (in fact, the film was shot twice, the first negative having been damaged by water), it came out in 1933 when sound films had become the new norm. Light dialogues were added by dubbing, as Epstein had planned, but a grandiloquent soundtrack was also imposed by the producers in spite of Epstein fighting mightily to retain the spare aesthetics he had envisaged (*ibid.*: 54). It is very likely that *Le Tempestaire* (1947), with even sparer dialogues, was meant as a corrective to the sonic defacement suffered by *L'Or des mers*.

While the drama of social and affective ties, to return to Deleuze's remark, was happily resolved in *L'Or des mers*, it is the exact opposite

---

5 'I know not – and I weigh my words carefully – a more moving close-up of a face than that of the heroin of this film – played by a waitress from Quiberon – uncovering her joy at being loved. More moving, and more modest than that moment when her face shines with a half-smile as her two hands, these two squat and round working-class hands, going up from her mouth to her forehead, come to hide her as if, beloved, she wanted to enclose that happiness within herself. But before her hands reach and erase her smile, Epstein – as Fellini would too thirty years later in *The Nights of Cabiria* – Epstein delivers the gaze – facing the camera – of her heroin. Complicity sets between her and us, as if in confidence. And it is truly affecting! / This face, we find it again at the end of the film, stressed with anxiety, worked over by the gestures of fear, smeared with sea mud, her gaze lost, when the young woman with her legs and garments swallowed by the sand, feels the arrival of death against a solitude with which she is familiar.'

in *Chanson d'Armor*, which ends on a double suicide. Jean-Marie and Rozen are in love. Jean-Marie is a high-school graduate from a modest family of fishermen, and he plans to attend the seminary to receive an education. Rozen is the daughter of a modern and wealthy Breton businessman who lives in a castle. Jean-Marie is a singer and a lover of tradition, and Rozen is attracted to him in part as a rejection of the modern cosmopolitan lifestyle of her father's circle. When they meet they speak in Breton, and the absence of subtitles is noteworthy – as though our lack of literacy in Breton granted them an intimacy Epstein refused to violate. After her father tries ending their relationship, Jean-Marie goes off on a fishing boat to try to forget her. There is no wind and a sailor falls to his death, and Jean-Marie, perhaps in reminiscence of Melville's *Billy Budd*, is scapegoated as bringing bad luck with his lovelorn singing. Rozen, in despair over her father's prohibition, throws herself off a cliff. In a closing scene meant to be symbolic more than diegetic, Jean-Marie is shown singing next to her Ophelia-like body covered in seaweed. We understand that he too killed himself to be with her in death.

The diegesis is cross-cut with often long documentary scenes of markets, religious processions, and Breton sporting events. Financing was secured by one of France's most powerful regional newspapers at the time, the liberal *Ouest-Éclair*, which wanted to counter an anti-Brittany campaign that was turning away tourists. In parallel with the movie, which was released to very little local acclaim, Epstein shot a documentary on the newspaper that is in many ways more successful, as we'll see in the next chapter. One can wonder to what extent the propagandistic nature of the commission pressured Epstein into making a film that over-aggrandizes folklore and constrains *photogénie*. Perhaps in inserting the oddest character in the film – a vagabond played by François Viguier who barks like a rabid dog, chases Rozen through the forest, and howls with joy when the lovers must separate – Epstein was making a parody not just of the wild and dumb Breton caricatured in some quarters, but of himself forced once again into telling a story rather than making a film.

We will examine *Le Tempestaire* (1947) and *Les Feux de la mer* (1948) in the next chapter, since they are best approached as sound documentary works. The last Breton fiction film of Epstein we will address is *L'île perdue* (1937), generally referred by the title of the novel from which it is adapted, *La Femme du bout du monde*. We might say that at one end of the world, there are the ambiguous ties between two boys in *Finis Terræ*, and at the other *bout du monde*, there is a woman, perhaps Woman, depicted as a siren not because she is dangerous, but because men's Homeric competition to get her renders *them* dangerous.

The story has a group of men embark for a South Sea island – in actuality, Ouessant – to find *pitchblende*, which contains uranium and radium ore. Epstein closely followed the work of physicists such as the Curie and Joliot-Curie, and this may be the first film with an atomic theme, eight years before the atomic bomb was invented. The expedition finds no minerals but instead stumbles on an inn kept by Anna, a Breton woman from Roscoff, with a husband who does not utter a word and their young child. She is indeed *la* femme, the only woman, and strife quickly ensues among the male protagonists, even a state of quasi-war when a British crew puts in and enters the inn.

The two male protagonists are Robert, a naval lieutenant played by a young Jean-Pierre Aumont, and Durc, a ship mechanic played by middle-aged Charles Vanel. Anna is 40-year-old Germaine Rouer who played the female lead in André Antoine's famous adaptation of Zola's *La Terre* (1921). At the beginning of the film, Robert's fiancée appears to be close to leaving him, while separately Durc mentions 'la Marzo', a woman he misses and may have killed. Hence we begin again with a double crisis of heterosexuality. After the crew stumble upon Anna – who first appears then disappears like a chimera or siren among the rocks of the island – both Robert and Durc project on her their fears and fantasies, especially when she proves to be a singer, performing with ease in front of throngs of sailors. In fact, Anna is not a Marlene Dietrich-like *femme fatale*, or even a vamp, and has truly no interest in men other than her silent husband. Rendered half mad with desire and isolation, Robert ends up attempting to force himself on Anna, who bites him to defend herself, while Durc kills a man after being prevented from similarly assaulting her. In the end the ship departs with no mineral, leaving Anna and her child happily alone on the shoreline. Upon arriving back in France, Robert realizes his fiancée did love him after all, and Durc vanishes to escape punishment.

Leprohon, who was a friend of Epstein, wrote a measured but largely negative review of the film, to which the latter apparently took exception. Leprohon then asserted – with relief it seems – that no copies of the film had survived, which proved untrue (*ibid.*: 57). Certainly, the film is by and large too strained and belaboured to be successful, and some of its devices – rip dissolves shaped like a star, a chequerboard, a lightning bolt, etc. – seem contrived. Nevertheless, within the frame of a queer reflection on heterosexuality, it is far from devoid of interest. For instance, when Robert confronts his fiancée at the opening of the film, her blank stare gazes as if past him and above the camera, breaking the shot–counter-shot edit which is the heart of heterosexual cinema. When the captain and the shipowner want to see Anna for themselves to understand why such mayhem is caused around her, the same happens: she gazes *through* them, indifferent to their sexualizing stare and straight male desire. That this transparency is subtly thematized by Epstein is illustrated in a remarkable shot that echoes *Le Double amour*. The mute husband strums a wooden viola when the crew enters the inn, but suddenly, in a low angle MS, the viola is shown to be *transparent* as we see the hand playing through it. This striking correspondence between music, speechlessness, and vision reminds us of the manifesto of synaesthesia of *La Chute de la maison Usher*, while pointedly reversing that narrative's obsession with capturing and freezing female identity and desire. The husband is not a male intent on asserting his desires through domination of the female other. He is on the side of the transparency sought by Anna and Robert's fiancée, on the side of music rather than words, on the side of passion and patience rather than the kind of phallic hyperaction that poisons the straight male protagonists.

The critique of the masculine will-to-capture female desire finds another expression in the ship's boy, angelically blond and also lovestruck by Anna. Disastrously, he misreads the maternal tenderness she bestows on him for the adult love all men are vying for, and his soul is destroyed when the ship anchors away. As it leaves, the boy is shown alone at the poop deck in a low angle MS. His eyes are lost in the sea below, upon which, in a counter-shot, a superimposed MS of Anna appears, while we hear the sound of her voice in a clear siren motif. Anna and the boy are directly superimposed, but they significantly look away from each other. This signals non-reciprocation, a breakdown in the shot–counter-shot structure that enacts the myth of heterosexual reciprocity. This composite shot is followed by an LA MS/MCU of the boy slowly falling towards the camera, before a top-to-bottom vertical swipe transitions to an LS of the ship's poop deck moving away from the camera, with the POV at the place where the boy fell in the water. We are meant to understand that the boy slipped into the sea and drowned – a literal rendering of falling for a precocious straight phantasm. Interestingly, the blond boy displays the same uneasy mixture of sullenness, distraction, and frustration as the blond Bruno in *Germany Year Zero*: indeed, it seems very likely that Bruno's final plunge is a direct reminiscence by Rosselini of Epstein's closing sequence.

One conclusion we can come to regarding the Brittany films of Epstein is that they both do and do not constitute a 'cycle'. The pre-eminence of elemental sensations animating human protagonists and the translation of the grand agency of the landscape into semi-narrative filmic images bring a certain degree of unity to them. Filmmaking with a skeletal crew and non-professional actors also suggests their collective importance for the history of neo-realism and auteurism. Yet in spite of short footage that Epstein recycled from one to the other, the Breton films are very distinct projects, amalgamating fiction and documentary in different ways, indeed in part because they devolve from differing purviews on authorship; from literary adaptation (*L'île perdue*), to more auteuristic works (*Finis Terræ*; *Le Tempestaire*), geo-documentary genre (*Morv'ran*), and non-auteurist storytelling and acting (*Finis Terræ*; *L'Or des mers*). Epstein's Breton films do stand as a whole as one of the most original adventures of cinema outside the studio and the studio system.

References

Abel, Richard (1984), *French Cinema: The First Wave, 1915–1929*, Princeton: Princeton University Press.
Deleuze, Gilles (1986), *Cinema 1: The Movement Image*, Hugh Tomlinson and Barbara Habberjam (trans.), Minneapolis: University of Minnesota Press.
Epstein, Jean (1974), *Écrits sur le cinéma*, vol. 1, Paris: Éditions Seghers.
— (1995) *L'Or des mers*, Quimperlé: La Digitale.
Gauthier (2004), *Un siècle de documentaire français*, Paris: Armand Collin.
Guigueno, Vincent (2003), *Jean Epstein, cinéaste des îles*, Paris: Jean-Michel Place.
Leprohon, Pierre (1964), *Jean Epstein*, Paris: Pierre Seghers.
Potamkin, Harry (1929), 'The French Cinema', *Close-Up* 5(1) (July), 57–64.
Vignaux, Valérie (2007), *Jean Benoit-Lévy ou le corps comme utopie: une histoire du cinéma éducateur dans l'entre-deux-guerres en France*, Paris: AFRHC.
Virmaux, Alain and Odette Virmaux (1999), *Artaud–Dulac:* La coquille et le clergyman, *essai d'élucidation d'une querelle mythique*, Paris: Paris expérimental.

5

Documentaries and sound films

Epstein's filmography contains roughly an equal number of films that can be labelled fiction and documentary – a little over twenty in each category. This will likely come as a surprise to the many cinephiles who know him only as the filmmaker of *La Glace à trois faces* and *La Chute de la maison Usher*. Unfortunately, only two of Epstein's documentaries are accessible outside of archives, and very little critical attention has been devoted to this substantial part of his œuvre.[1] Indeed, in-depth research on the documentary work of French narrative avant-garde directors such as Germaine Dulac and Epstein, or for that matter of pre-World War Two French directors of poetic realism or other schools, remains entirely to be done.[2]

A further complication comes from Epstein's consistent loosening of the difference between fiction and documentary. A good half of his 'fiction' films could be more precisely described as dramas thinly overlaying a deep interest for documenting real life, while conversely a large portion of his documentaries might be best approached as docudramas and even, in the case of his 'chansons filmées', docu-poems. When we get to his sound œuvre we encounter similar paradoxes. To begin with, Epstein is mostly known as a silent-era filmmaker, when in point of fact exactly half of his production is made of post-1930 talkies. More problematic yet, apart from his few clearly mercenary mainstream efforts – *La Femme du bout du monde*,

---

1 *Les Bâtisseurs* (1938) was recently posted online by the archives of the Parti Communiste Français, at www.cinearchives.org/Catalogue_general-62-53-0-0.html (consulted 26/10/11), while *Pasteur* (1922) can be streamed via the website of the Institut National de l'Audiovisuel.
2 For a cursory overview, see Reynolds (2000).

La Châtelaine du Liban (1933) (a film he disavowed), *Marius et Olive* – some of Epstein's sound films attempt to work on the aural in a way that is analogical to the way *photogénie* 'works' on the visual. Epstein himself calls this experimental approach to sound cinema *phonogénie* to underline the connection with *photogénie*, experimentalism, and an aesthetic that belongs, paradoxically again, to the pre-talkies era. As we have suggested in the introduction, Epstein explored the intersections of disparate genres and technical possibilities, the better to put in question boundaries and accepted oppositions. In this chapter, we will further examine this radical aim in his documentaries and sound work, which led him to undertake bold attempts at undoing some of the fundamental categorical divides in cinema historiography: reality vs. fiction, visual sense vs. verbal meaning, and corporeal impressions/expressions vs. language systems.

Epstein and the origins of French documentary cinema

Behind the reality vs. fiction dichotomy just mentioned, it is easy to recognize the alternative of Lumière vs. Méliès promulgated by historians such as Georges Sadoul as structural for understanding the heydays of cinema. According to this view, cinema history offers itself as forked at its inception: either it is a sober tool for documenting reality with some kind of ultimate political lucidity, as the news and ethno-touristic *vues* of the Lumières attest, or else it functions as an alluring toy for entertainment, fantasy, and magic as in the famous trick-films of Georges Méliès that blazed the way for special-effect blockbusters (Sadoul, 1985). The problem with this distinction is that the Lumière catalogue contains hundreds of comic and trick-films, while Méliès shot numerous *actualités* and historical reconstructions, some of which are highly committed such as *L'Affaire Dreyfus* (1899), arguably among the very first activist political films. Neither in catalogues nor in performances or journalistic accounts was there a clear difference in how early films were treated by spectators, projectionists, producers, or commentators. So it would appear that the division was extremely porous between fiction and documentary, and not perceived to be central at all. Cinema historians such as Tom Gunning and André Gaudreault began reconceptualizing early cinema in large part because they realized how subsidiary notions of genre or the imperative of realism were to the lively and mechanical dimensions of the experience of the projected show – what they called the 'cinema of attractions'.[3]

As the recently published *Encyclopedia of Early Cinema* edited by Richard Abel attests, since there is no entry for 'documentary', the division documentary vs. fiction film comes rather late, if not retrospectively, to cinema historiography.[4] Instead, we find such entries as *actualités*, newsreels, industrial films, sports film, scientific films or Pathé-journal (1908), the first regular journalistic service delivered to theatres (Abel, 2005: 477–8). Around 1908, we also witness the first microscopic films, such as Jean Comandon's *La Circulation du sang dans une petite veine de la queue d'un têtard de grenouille*, in which sensationalism, novelty, and science intersect. Such films do not, however, constitute a new genre since they took over the niche formerly occupied by conferences with magic lantern slides that helped to disseminate instruction at the height of the Third Republic (Gauthier, 2004: 27). Only around 1911, did the term 'documentaire' appear in a catalogue of Gaumont shorts, and it applied equally to education, travel, and science films (*ibid.*: 40).

Several factors hastened the rise of what we term documentaries in the course and aftermath of World War One. The initiatives came largely from the government, concerned with ways of using cinema for educational, civic, and nation-building purposes in a time of war. In 1915, the Section cinématographique de l'armée française was created (later renamed Service cinématographique des armées) with a mission that is all at once historical and military documentation, and nationalistic propaganda. A parallel section was created for civilian affairs in 1916 by a commission of the Ministère de l'instruction publique et des beaux-arts, with a very broad mandate. This official embrace of cinema directly opened the door to the development of a new variety of non-fiction movies. After the end of the war, the military and civilian aims merged when cinema figures in the early discussions of the League of Nations as an international vehicle for

---

3 For a recent reappraisal, see Strauven (2006).
4 While it is well-known that 'silent cinema' or 'cinéma muet' are labels invented after the fact (for a kind of cinema that was by and large neither silent nor mute, since it involved musical accompaniment and live commentary), it is less obvious that the same goes for 'documentary' which isolates the documenting function of certain films that are often every bit as constructed as fiction films.

peace and cooperation.⁵ The transformation of cinema is then almost complete: from what was considered in pre-war conservative circles a mindless entertainment potentially sapping culture and civilization, cinema becomes in the early 1920s a new means for states and non-governmental organizations (NGOs) to reach, train, educate, and inform national citizens as well as shape world opinion. Add to this the release of new super-light cameras by Pathé in 1922 (the 9.5 mm Pathé-Paby), Bell & Howell in 1923 (the 16 mm Filmo) and 1925 (the 35 mm Filmo which Epstein used), and documenting private and public life while using cinema as a utensil for knowledge quickly became part and parcel of the cultural landscape of the inter-war.

The crucial surname in the birth of the French documentary is Benoit-Lévy. First came Edmond Benoit-Lévy (1858–1929), an Alsatian Jewish lawyer and civil rights advocate who turned to cinema after the Dreyfus affair. In 1905, he launched the first professional trade journal about movies (*Phono-Ciné-Gazette*), then opened the Pathé-Omnia in 1907, the first luxury movie palace of Paris, in collaboration with Pathé. The son of a schoolteacher from Strasbourg, he was among the first to insist publicly that cinema had a promising educational potential (Abel, 2005: 65–6; Vignaux, 2007: 16). But it was his nephew, Jean Benoit-Lévy (1888–1959), who must be considered the pioneer of French documentary as such. A member of the civilian commissions on cinema during World War One, he created a film company in 1922 dedicated to the production and distribution of instructional movies. In the course of his career as a filmmaker himself, he shot dozens of films about health, hygiene, pregnancy and related social issues, agriculture, labour training for both men and women, industrial production and techniques, etc. His recent biographer Valérie Vignaux has underlined the imperative of caring for the body – both individual and social – as a key motivation in the development of the documentary in the post-war period. He also directed several fiction films, some in collaboration with Marie Epstein, such as *La Maternelle* (1933).

Benoit-Lévy's office, as we indicated in the introduction, happened to have been next door to that of the Éditions de La Sirène where Epstein came to work as secretary after leaving his position with Auguste Lumière in Lyon. When Benoit-Lévy thought about making a film commemorating the centenary of the birth of Louis Pasteur he

---

5 For World War One and its aftermath, see Vignaux (2007: 15–27).

decided to ask his new friend. This was a bit of a gamble since Epstein had only cursory experience as assistant director to Louis Delluc on *Le Tonnerre* (1921) and as general assistant on Abel Gance's *La Roue* (1922). On the plus side, his medical training guaranteed that he would not misrepresent Pasteur's pioneering work.

Pasteur (1922)

To say that it is Epstein's first film would be simplifying things a bit. The credits indicate it was 'réalisé' (directed) by Epstein, after a scenario by Edmond Épardaud, 'cinégraphié' (filmed) by Edmond Floury, 'sous la direction' of Jean Benoit-Lévy, and 'sous le contrôle artistique' of a representative of the Ministère de l'éducation, with most of the scenes coming from a book by René Vallery-Radot. 'Two thousand and three collaborations encircle us like a jail', Epstein wrote about 'his' film (1974: 113), although he duly admitted that Floury advised him tirelessly about camera-work. He indicates also that he had to vie against another project, proposed by an equally inexperienced director and pushed by the powerful Institut Pasteur and Pasteur's heirs (*ibid.*: 49–56). In spite of the epigram by Vallery-Radot that Pasteur was 'a citizen of the whole world', the project was close to the nation's heart, and at some point the yellow press reported that Epstein had either German or 'vague' – read: Jewish – origins. Such attention certainly put even more pressure on the first-time director. During editing he worried that there were so many high angle shots the film might seem to be looking at Pasteur 'from a balloon', and his overall assessment what that the film ended up being 'unremarkable' but 'honest' (*ibid.*: 55–7).

Although French critics by and large lauded the film's skilful and faithful re-enactment, Epstein must have been right. To our eyes, however, the movie is rather peculiar in just how many different kinds of footage it manages to mix together. We see laboratory sequences showing microscopes and beakers and actual manipulations by lab technicians. There are 'touristic' sequences of some of the actual locations in Pasteur's life, and of farming locales illustrating his work on agricultural epidemics. Both kinds are documentary in the robust sense. A third kind of footage consists in *mise en scène* sequences recreating various episodes in Pasteur's life, and played by professional actors. This is the dramatic and fictionalized part of the film. As if to bridge reality and fiction, there are finally a few shots whose status remains liminal and unclear. Around the 3-minute mark, we see an exterior night LS of a single lit window surrounded by darkness, with snow falling in front of it, right after a card stating that Pasteur was born 27 December 1822. Are we to believe this is the exact bedroom where he was born? Or is it just any window meant to suggest that unique bedroom? This matters little of course, for the shot displays both a documenting effect (to adapt Roland Barthes's famous 'effet de réel') and the staged pathos of drama. Epstein explains that verisimilitude is less important than the necessity for 'spectators to see something in a test tube which they have never before seen in it' (*ibid*.: 53). So the documentary ethos of dedication to a transparent depiction of the real seems far from being of central concern for Epstein in 1922.

This is not to say that that ethos does not inform the film. One clear example is a two-minute sequence showing every stage of the inoculation of the rabies virus to a rabbit, from attaching its legs to a wood plank, slicing open the skin of its head, drilling the skull, driving the needle into brain matter to inject the virus, then sewing back the skin, all without any apparent anaesthetic (see Plate 7). What makes this sequence remarkable is that the precise but indifferent gestures of the technician appear to our contemporary sensibility so brutal that no laboratory today would allow them to be filmed, and no audience could watch them without profound discomfort. As mentioned in chapter 3, this very long sequence displaces the actuality of the inoculation from the historical past to the present animal, while our visceral reaction to vivisection is itself metaphorically transferred back onto the child actor. In a sense, Epstein suggests that there is no difference between animal and human bodies, while simultaneously reasserting the humanist order whereby animals are sacrificed for the good of humans.

What Epstein noted, once *Pasteur* was finished, was at once simple and deep. He had become a filmmaker. Or perhaps, we might say, he was now addicted to the spell of filmmaking, to the virtual films whose possibility he began foreseeing in the very interstices of *Pasteur*. In a short text of 1923, he explains that he discovered in the final version of his first movie, 'that the great cinematographic silence was interspersed with secondary silences like deep syncopes'. These puzzling moments of rhythmic suspension weave, he suddenly saw, a different story and a different film within the film: 'Je voudrais qu'on sût lire dans la transparence des images de film leur envers le plus secret' ['I would like it if one could read through the transparency of a film's images their most secret other side'], and he adds that 'Cette autre face, la seule qui compte, de la petite histoire, s'appelle sujet' ['this other face – the only one that matters – of a simple story, is called a subject'] (*ibid.*: 114). Together with the negative vocabulary of 'ineffable' and 'ne pas comprendre' ['not understanding'], (*ibid.*), Epstein describes this other mysterious face of cinema positively as a new language: 'Le cinéma qui n'est qu'un langage ...' ['Cinema, which is nothing but a language ...'] (*ibid.*); or, in another text on *Pasteur*, he addresses 'le plus cruel des mutismes du film: langue étrangère, sonnant fluide à nos oreilles ... la plus vivante et la plus rapide des langues ...' ['the most cruel speechlessness of the film: a foreign tongue, resounding fluidly to our ears ... the liveliest and quickest of languages ...'] (*ibid.*: 113).[6] In the same way that Pasteur learned how to think microscopically, by discovering and understanding the microbes that inhabit all vegetal and animal creatures, Epstein was learning how to think cinematographically, by discovering and understanding in each shot the powerful charge of sensorial meaning that, as cinema alone revealed, inhabits every aspect of the real. He writes that what he discovered from filming at the Pasteur Institute was 'the not yet well-known beauty of so-called inanimate objects, all of which are prodigiously alive' (*ibid.*: 112). So, in the end, it might be less the hybrid character of the docudrama that mattered to Epstein, than the way its 'subject', Louis Pasteur's unique fascination for microscopic agents, brought about a kind of oblique revelation in Epstein concerning the nature of cinema's agency as a medium. This is what he soon articulated theoretically as *photogénie*, while endeavouring to create new possibilities of filmic expression in *Cœur fidèle*. Within the gaps and 'transparency' of this documentary film about a scientist, Epstein found the formal inspiration for his next fiction film, while continuing to translate in his own idiomatic way (as he had done in his early books) science and sensibility into new possibilities for art.

6 Let us note in passing that in distinguishing between two faces of a film along the distinction of prosaic story vs. latent 'subject', Epstein anticipates one of the fundamental dichotomies of Russian Formalism between *fabula* (the story as mere sequence of events) and *suyzhet* (the order and way in which these events are recounted). See Albera (1996).

La Montagne infidèle (1923)

Epstein's second documentary was just such a project mixing science and aesthetics, volcanology and cinema's affinity for registering the sheer spectacle of fluid states. Epstein took a small crew to the 1923 eruption of Mount Etna and descended inside the summit rim to shoot the lava flows surrounded by swirling clouds of gas and smoke. Sadly, no copy of this film has been located since its initial release, and there is little trace of this film in the contemporary press. Nonetheless, this documentary on Mount Etna was probably another key revelation for Epstein. He published a short book entitled *Le Cinématographe vu de l'Etna* (1926) that opens with an essay relating some of his experiences of filming on the volcano, in turn using these accounts to rethink cinema. As he climbs up the volcano, Epstein witnesses the lava flow, 'ce mur de braise avançait par écroulements successifs' ['this wall of embers advanced by crumbling over and over'] (*ibid.*: 131) – as if swallowing and transforming everything in its wake. This wall reminds us of the famous 1896 film of the Lumières, *Démolition d'un mur*, which viewers begged to see projected forwards and backwards, to see the wall crumble over and over.[7] For Epstein, who invokes Ricciotto Canudo, 'l'une des plus grandes puissances du cinéma est son animisme' ['One of the greatest powers of cinema is its animism'] (*ibid.*: 134). Like a volcano, cinema has the unique power of swallowing all things to make them appear, albeit for a fraction of a second, alive and sentient. The trip to the volcano and Sicily also took on a personal dimension, as Epstein encountered not just nature as an overwhelming force, but also as a refraction of his own subconscious. Walking down a hotel stairway covered with mirrors, Epstein is uncannily confronted with images of himself he does not recognize or accept: 'Chacun de ces miroirs me présentait une perversion de moi, une inexactitude de l'espoir que j'avais en moi' ['Each of these mirrors presented to my eyes a perversion of myself, an inexact version of what I hoped for myself'] (*ibid.*: 136). For Epstein, there lays the ethic and aesthetic agency of cinema, in proposing 'un œil doué de propriétés analytiques inhumaines' ['an eye endowed with inhuman analytical properties'], which Apollinaire called 'surréel' ['surreal'], in that it convinced artists and thinkers that, 'tout était à recommencer'

---

7 In *Esprit de cinéma* (1955), Epstein begins the section 'Art and technique' with a mind experiment about simply filming a wall (1976: 76–9).

['Everything was to be started anew'] (ibid.: 136). *Le Cinématographe vu de l'Etna* (1926) collects a number of conferences and key essays by Epstein on *photogénie*, language, and the avant-garde, as well as two lyrical sections of homage to Chaplin and Hayakawa in which he tries accounting for his attraction to the two male stars.

To return briefly to the film, we might wonder about its title, *La Montagne infidèle*, particularly since it seems to relate more or less explicitly to his other film of 1923, *Cœur fidèle*. What is the nature of this tacit opposition? Is the notion of fidelity, central to the documentary with its ethos of transparent or faithful translation, shown paradoxically to lie more on the side of fiction? Is Epstein telling us that reality, like a volcano, is not something still that can be documented, but is rather an unforeseeable eruption, a sudden surge, the very movement of something intruding into our sense and senses? Epstein in fact says as much in a 1947 text concerning the documentary in general, which he calls the 'vériste' and 'véridique' genre:

> La conséquence capitale de cette recherche de la vérité est que celle-ci ouvre et rouvre la porte au hasard, à l'imprévu, à l'insolite, lesquels se trouvent rigoureusement exclus du programme de travail d'un film ordinaire de studio et d'acteurs professionnels.[8]

This passage may represent not only the best encapsulation of what drives Epstein to the documentary, but also what informs his Breton films as well.

The question of fidelity, faithfulness, and translation remained present in Epstein's later philosophical work where he argues in favour of cinema as restoring a pre-linguistic contact with meaning. For him, the problem with language is that its logic of representing the world seduces us into an excessive rationalism of reduction, which in turns isolates us from the real world, as in the philosophical systems of Descartes and Kant:

> *Fidèle ou infidèle* à son objet, mais pratiquement suffisante, la représentation rationnelle parut à ses découvreurs et paraît encore à l'échelle humaine une merveille de précision et de sécurité, une grâce divine.[9]

8 'The crucial consequence of this search for truth is that it opens or reopens the door of chance, the unexpected, the oddity, which were rigorously excluded from the work program of an ordinary studio film with professional actors' (*ibid.*: 84).
9 '*Whether faithful or unfaithful* to its object, but sufficient in practice, rational representation appeared to its discoverers and still appears, at the human scale, to be a marvel of precision and safety, a divine grace' (*ibid.*: 190, my emphasis).

Rational representation is a kind of magical instrument that filters out affects imprinted on us from the real, and chance as well, to deliver instead a purified and safe model of the real. This rational representationalism never questions itself, nor does it try to explore what forces might motivate it – as Nietzsche and Freud pointed out in their revolutionary ways. Hence, the documentary, with its veridical contingency effects – the lava flows are unforeseeable in their shape and direction, as are angle shots and moments of excitement or fear – offers an exit to rationalism, the opportunity for discoveries unfaithful to reason.

Epstein and sound cinema

> Le cinématographe visuel, en noir et blanc, a gagné sa vraie place, compris son rôle: d'opposer, de réunir de très simples images selon des rythmes, des recoupements, des répétitions, des chevauchements qui signifient. Le rôle du film sonore me paraît être également dans l'écriture de telles évolutions des sons, de leurs groupements significatifs, de leurs successions spécialement éloquentes, de leurs compositions et parentés, de leurs scissions et filiations.[10]

The arrival of sound in France in 1929–30 was an unmitigated disaster for filmmakers on the experimental fringe of the mainstream. French cinema as a whole entered into a deep crisis of identity since the changes brought about by the synchronous soundtrack system were orchestrated by the American and German film industries. Throughout the 1930s, the production of French full-feature fictions steadily dropped, even though the Popular Front triggered a renewal of short subjects and documentaries. Thus not only technical but organizational and financial realignments tolled the bell of what Léon Moussinac called simply 'the death of the avant-garde' (Abel, 1988: xviii). Nonetheless, while many French artists and film personalities such as Antonin Artaud and Germaine Dulac strenuously argued against the sound revolution, which in many ways put an end to their

10 'The visual cinematograph in black and white has earned its true place, understood its role: to oppose and unite very simple images according to certain signifying rhythms, criss-crossing contacts, repetitions, and overlaps. The role of sound film seems to me to be similarly in the writing of such evolutions of sounds, of their signifying regroupings, their particularly eloquent successions, their compositions and relatedness, theirs scissions and filiations' (Epstein 1974 [1929]: 204).

fiction film career, others such as Gance, Epstein, or Cocteau saw in the talkies an unavoidable leap, soon to be followed by colour and 3D technologies – or so they thought, in the spirit of utopia of the technocritics that they were (see chapter 2).

Epstein's sound production throughout the 1930s reflects these profound changes in French cinema. The feature films he directed, both *films parlants* and *films sonores*, tended to be very much mainstream dramas, often with stars or rising stars of the likes of Madeleine Renaud and Charles Vanel.[11] As for the shorts and documentaries he directed, they varied greatly in subject, scope, and originality. They range from documentaries for national fairs such as *La Bretagne* and *La Bourgogne*, to corporate commissions like *La Vie d'un grand journal*, and truly experimental genres such as the *chanson filmée*, a new kind of artistic short for which Epstein hoped there would be a new demand. In the second part of the 1930s, Epstein collaborated with NGOs from the left and new Front Populaire-sponsored social networks such as trade unions, youth hostels, or the French section of the New York International Fair. Finally, after World War Two, he directed but two sound films: one for the UN on lighthouses, and the other constituting his artistic testament, *Le Tempestaire*, in which he applied his theories of *phonogénie*.

Chansons filmées

In 1931 and 1932, Epstein shot five short sound films subtitled 'chanson filmée' that attempt to combine the rhythm of filmic images with that of lyrics and their melody. In *La Chanson des peupliers*, Epstein takes a popular nostalgic poem of the same title written by a Belgian Communard, Camille Soubise (an alias of Alphonse Vanden Camp), in which the song of the poplars is simply the wind. Of course, it is easy in French to hear in the title, *la chanson des peuples* ['the song of the people'], so a collective political subtext blows through it. The soundtrack of the archival copy I consulted at the Archives Françaises du Film appears to me to include the actual sound of

---

11 The term 'film parlant' was used for direct synchronous recording of sound together with images (the default in the French industry), by opposition to 'film sonore' whose soundtrack was recorded post-synchronously (Hollywood's preference), see O'Brien (2005: 68–72).

the wind, besides the sung lyrics. But this might be only scratches from the aged strip, and I have not found documented confirmation (even though Epstein played explicitly with the sound of the wind in *Le Tempestaire*). The opening shot, a slightly canted LS of poplars with the moon above, in a slight fish-eye and gauzy lens, recalls *La Chute de la maison Usher* – whose poem-like sequences, as we have seen, accompany the (inaudible) singing of Roderick on his guitar. *La Chanson des peupliers* makes use of both dynamic superimpositions (pans of poplars overlaid with two series of clouds going in different directions) and static ones (fixed LS of poplars overlaid on MS of the shimmery surface of a pond). Some of the cuts between shots follow pauses in the song, but not always, so parallelism appears to be only an intermittent goal. Several intriguing still shots show subtle variations, within the shot, in the focus and lighting of the foliage, as if the operator tried a slight rake-focus or waited for clouds to alter the light and shade of the poplars. It is likely such improvised rhythmic dialogue between the singing and the contingent plasticity of the foliage was what Epstein wanted to propose to viewers.

Another *chanson filmée*, *Le Cor*, subtitled 'L'évocation cinégraphique du célèbre poème d'Alfred de Vigny', similarly plays with superimpositions (of deer and forest landscapes), focus changes (a shiny object is shown in a completely out-of-focus ECU), slow-motion of horseback hunters, and manipulations such as fish-eye and irises. Epstein's affection for the forest world of *Mauprat* and *L'Arbre ou le pas de la mule* (1930), his last silent documentary on woodcutters – much more so than hunting, especially the aristocratic *chasse à courre* – seems to be motivating this short. His inspiration comes from popular culture and the tradition of performing visual illustrations of well-known songs, which dates back at least to magic lantern slide shows, and includes movies made during the so-called silent era and projected with synchronous songs on phonograph cylinders or gramophone cylinders or discs: Alice Guy Blaché directed hundreds of these between 1902 and 1913 (McMahan, 2003: 43–77).

The popular nature of the 'chanson filmée' is plain in *La Villanelle des rubans*, which is based on the popular song 'Les rubans de la vie', sung by Junka, a French crooner of the 1910s. This short features non-professional actors celebrating important moments of life, illustrating concretely the theme of the song with shots of ribbons accompanying every event from birth to death. Epstein multiplies superimpositions of footage of ribbons in the wind with footage of a river's flowing water, and of gathered and celebrating people in MSs or MCUs. Interestingly, 'un ruban' is a term that was often used in early French cinema interchangeably with 'une vue' to denote a reel of film. The passing of time, rendered visually by both the river's flowing waters and the serpentine ribbons floating in the wind, is thus meant to reflect the passing of the *ruban* itself through the projector, i.e. this very moment of the viewer's enjoyment of the short lyrical film. The poetic form of the *villanelle* involves the playful recurrence of two verses from the previous stanza within each subsequent stanza. In so doing it almost precludes a continuous narrative in favour of a patterned refrain or weave, again bringing focus on situations rather than forming a cohesive story. With the 'chanson filmée', Epstein was marking the transition from the metaphor of the 'book of life', implying narrative continuity, chapters, beginning, and end, to a life feted as a stream of contingent images and moments – a poem made of the filmed *rubans* of our lives.

Perhaps the most successful 'chanson filmée' is *Les Berceaux*, the adaptation of a short *Lied* by the first Nobel prize-winner for literature, Sully Prudhomme, with music by Gabriel Fauré. The metaphoric theme is simple, and recalls Deleuze's quip about the water element as severing ties in Epstein's Brittany cycle: cribs rocked by women are akin to ships rocked by the wind, so when men get on their ships they feel the blind tug of those cribs, and probably too, of the hands rocking them. Epstein presents the first images as stills of cribs and ships separated by iris fades (with an obvious wink at the rocking cradle of Walt Whitman cited in Griffith's 1916 *Intolerance*). We then see so-called phantom shots: facades of houses filmed from a ship gliding on a canal or a port channel, a literal illustration of the collective impersonality of the poem. These shots are intercut with a *mise en scène* of a man in MS at a front door, calling up to a window, where another MS shows a mother rocking a crib. The sequence ends with an MCU of the same man pulling at ropes on a ship. Epstein takes his cue from Prudhomme's non-narrative poem blending disconnected gestures and affects, united by the kinaesthetic analogy cradle–vessel, which alters the ancient static analogy crib–casket. Towards the end of the short, we find several shots that extrapolate an interpretation beyond the express content of the poem. A swirl of smoke is superimposed on a MCU of some kind of vegetal form, then a cut shows a Dutch angle MS of a cradle surmounted by gauze, its tear-shaped opening strongly lit, looking like a cocoon against an abstract background of sharp lines from doors and walls. By that point, the illustrative inspiration of Epstein's 'chanson filmée' morphs into a filmic variation on a theme, reaching a jazz-like improvised riffing that circles broadly around its thematic conceit. This short thus defines a rhythmic–abstract extreme in Epstein's work, on a par with the epilogue of *Cœur fidèle*, and the cross-cut of guitar strumming and natural imagery in *La Chute de la maison Usher*. Unfortunately, the 'chanson filmée' genre never took off, and after a couple more shorts, *Le vieux chaland* and *Le petit chemin de fer*, both from 1932 as well, this new experimental genre came to an end.

Men and women at work

The rest of Epstein's sound documentaries or quasi-documentaries (with minor staged scenes) may be gathered under the rubric of displaying people at work, workplaces, and settings and environments in which work is conducted. In both his regionalist and industrial films, Epstein's lens finds innumerable ways to tarry with agrarian and proletarian labour, at times with a tenuous link with the running commentary or the general topic of the film. Although he was never an outspoken Marxist, it is clear that throughout the 1930s Epstein's concerns, like those of his colleague Germaine Dulac, strongly gravitated towards an activist leftism, especially after the success of the unified Front Populaire at the 1936 elections. His posthumous *Alcool et cinéma*, from the late 1940s, contains a strong critique of workers' alienation verging on incarceration:

> Mais, en attendant de pouvoir transformer la terre en un paradis électrifié, ce glorieux planisme impose le travail à la chaîne, le minutage de la moindre distraction, la normalisation de chaque geste, la standardisation des individus, mille règlements, mille restrictions, mille contraintes, et tend à faire de l'homme, pendant les trois quarts de ses journées, un automate, un robot, en qui personnalité serait vice rédhibitoire, et fantaisie, péché mortel.[12]

12 'But while we wait for the earth to be transformed into an electrified paradise, this glorious planning spirit imposes assembly line work, the clocking of the slightest diversion, the normalization of every gesture, the standardization of

That a tangible aim of his filmmaking was to depict the working classes and make their work more visible and more valued was already obvious to a reviewer for the *Socialist Review* in England in 1929.[13] But Epstein has written very little on his documentary work (or else what existed was destroyed during the Occupation), so we can only surmise the nature of his political commitment or social inspiration. We might locate his interest in documenting work as a logical continuation of the sustained focus of his earlier melodramas on the social fate of working-class protagonists. So here too the generic and socio-political divides between fiction and non-fiction cinema prove to be rather unproductive. Moreover, unlike the propagandistic ethos of many Russian fiction films in the 1920s and 1930s, or French movies with a clear political agenda such as René Clair's *A nous la liberté* (1931) or Jean Renoir's *Le Crime de Monsieur Lange* (1934), in which working-class protagonists come out on top (unlike the protagonists of *Cœur fidèle*), Epstein's documentaries do not transform workers into emblems or figures, let alone heroes. It is workers' gestures, the absorption in their task, their dedication and physical efforts – more so than their alienation, even though Epstein has it present in mind, as we've seen – that he is first and foremost intent on documenting. In other words, real people take precedence over ideological militancy.

This bent is explicit even in his regionalist films on Burgundy and Brittany which were commissioned by the 1937 Exposition Internationale des Arts et Techniques dans la Vie Moderne [International Exposition dedicated to Art and Technology in Modern Life], and co-produced by the national railway company SNCF and Jean Benoit-Lévy. Both films contain establishing sequences that lead viewers into the region by dint of an automobile being stopped. In *La Bourgogne*, the car is waiting at a railroad crossing, while a driver stops to ask children for direction in *La Bretagne*. The urban or Parisian viewers, in their imaginary visit of a distant region begin, in a sense, by accepting to be hampered or even lost. Epstein uses this ploy not to show how friendly the natives are, nor does he segue with the usual displays of regional folklore and specialities. To the contrary, he turns to work.

---

individuals, a thousand rules, a thousand restrictions, a thousand constraints, and this tends to make of a person, for three-quarters of the day, an automaton, a robot, in whom personality is a sinful vice, and fantasy a mortal sin' (Epstein, 1976: 191).

13 Greenidge (1929: 264); the film is *Finis Terræ*.

Hence, the commentary explains, Burgundy's history rests on the trade routes criss-crossing its topography, and on trading tin, salt, stone, and wine – all materials, we should note, that require heavy human labour to extract, produce, or transport. Roughly halfway through the 23-minute short *La Bourgogne* hard work becomes the explicit focus when Epstein spends two full minutes documenting the back-breaking work of a stone quarry. One of the takes, which he recycles later in *Les Bâtisseurs*, is a long aerial LS taken from the cabin of a cable stone-lift as it slowly hovers over the quarry (see Plate 25). The camera films almost vertically, from several dozen feet above, the stoneworkers wrestling with pneumatic hammers and huge blocks of white granite. This shot presents an intriguing contrast with Leni Riefenstahl's famous aerial cable shots in her roughly contemporary *Olympia* (1936–38). While in Riefenstahl's film the aerial shots serve as a sublime all-seeing prop, an eagle-like POV swooping over an orderly mass of people in a stadium built to celebrate the Nazi state, in Epstein's film the footage is filmed from a real machine and documents the real back-breaking toil of workers.[14] From this point on, workers multiply in the documentary: Cistercian monks ploughing fields, fieldworkers harvesting grape, barrel-makers hammering, etc. Only after we understand the sheer amount of labour subtending the cultivated and built environment, and the social sphere at large, does Epstein show us some of the art treasures such as the tombs of the Dukes of Burgundy. By the time these artefacts appear, viewers have indeed come to approach everything, even art and architecture, not as inert cultural objects part of France's patrimony, but as remarkable concretions of the labour of real people.

In the Brittany documentary also, the conceit of regional tradition at a remove from Paris the capital of modernity quickly makes way to documenting the work of various segments of the Breton population. After the stopped car sequence, we see an establishing extreme LS of the old stone downtown of one of Brittany's oldest cities, Morlaix. But no sooner do we admire its historical architecture than a freight train appears on the high viaduct in the background, at once a signal of technological modernity and the movement of commodities within

---

14 Leni Riefenstahl may well have seen Epstein's film, which was shot in 1936. She appears to have been familiar enough with his work that she wrote to Abel Gance in a letter from 1937 that she is hoping to 'work with Jean Epstein' (Dallet, 2000: 60).

the landscape. A pan follows women wearing the traditional apron-and-hat white lace, but far from being folkloric models, they are leading cows to the market. Doing so, they pass in front of a modern car garage with busy mechanics, and the ethno-touristic gap between tradition and modernity is bridged by the commonality of men and women at work. Other activities follow in quick succession: woodworkers carving clogs and dishes; a cooperative where women sell their wares; a market which Epstein films in LS, de-emphasizing local colour and specialties in order to register the anarchic and crowded activities of busy sellers and buyers. Epstein does integrate the landscape of Brittany, which, as we have seen, exerted such a power upon his cinematography. But he does so here mostly in so far as the physical environment contextualizes work: we see boats in a port, then sardine and tuna fishermen unloading their catch; men sitting in a warehouse by the sea while making sails; and when we find again Breton women in traditional garb, they are now weaving fishnets and stuffing cans of pâté in a modern factory. Epstein's regionalist documentaries do not concentrate on narrowly vaunting the wealth and beauty of France's varied provinces. Rather, they subtly shift the focus from the macroscopically inert dimension of landscape and traditions to the actual conditions of singularized workers.

The left newspaper *Ouest-France* had commissioned both *La Chanson d'Armor* (1934) and a documentary entitled *La Presse Moderne, Comment se fait un grand régional* (1934). It depicts almost in its entirety men and women working at breakneck pace. The opening sequence shows an aeroplane landing, with reporters jumping out of it onto a motorcycle to bring the latest news of a bicycle race to the newsroom. In a bit of meta-journalism, Epstein shoots parts of the race itself, including a caravan of trucks with advertising, and spectators at the finish line who then metamorphose into hungry readers waiting outside the newspaper warehouse for the latest edition. There is a discrete political dimension in displaying the commercial underpinnings of the race, on the one hand, and the relationship of mutual reliance between the newspaper and the public on the other hand. The bulk of the documentary shows the news-making workflow, starting with the reporter's camera and desk, then his handing the sheets to be typeset. A 25-second long dolly shot behind the row of typesetters suggests that the centre of gravity of manual labour and skill is to be found there, where words as ideas become block of steel letters. The camera then turns to sheet metal engravers making the clichés, female phone operators receiving news dispatches, female readers of pneumatic and telegraphed messages, and rotating-presses operators. It ends with throngs of paperboys wearing paper hats with *Ouest-Éclair* written on them. Of all of Epstein's documentaries it is the one that shows the tightest intertwining of technology, work, and bodies. Yet it manages to do so in the name of a collective and free spirit, using a bicycle race at the beginning, and parodying the 'bonnet d'âne' paper hat traditionally placed on the head of 'mauvais écoliers' in its finale. The newspaper thus stands for the free voice of the community, an institution that links commerce, labour, and recreation. The perspective, it should be added, is utopian and largely uncritical since there is no treatment of journalistic policy per se, nor of the place of the newspaper in local politics.

It comes as no surprise that Epstein's best-known documentary should be entitled *Les Bâtisseurs* (1938), the builders – since that word crystallizes the productive dimension of all manual labour. Commissioned by a building trade union that was part of the CGT (Confédération Générale des Travailleurs), France's most powerful union, the documentary opens with credits written in stone-shaped letters against a background of flat geometrical shapes. The soundtrack starts on a chorus of workers singing about trade union solidarity, the lyrics signed by Surrealist poet Robert Desnos. The song morphs into a religious hymn as images of a cathedral begin to unfold. Many viewers on the left – with its tradition of deep anti-clericalism – would no doubt have shown some alarm. A Gregorian chant? After a few shots of stained-glass windows with 'god rays', LA VLSs show the cathedral's belfry surrounded with scaffoldings, on which we distinguish the silhouette of two workers. The credits indicate that they are actual masons, unemployed at the time of the shooting. In an MS they discuss their work while finishing to install a gargoyle, as the soundtrack reverts to the workers' song. It is not the religious symbol or institution that is at issue here but, as the two workers explain, the cathedral as a *building*, and its construction as a collective enterprise involving massive labour. The conversation of the workers discloses the secular face of the cathedral, serving as '*une maison du peuple*', a community meeting-house akin to a trade union hall. Not only were cathedrals illustrated books telling illiterate lower classes the story of the Scriptures through images and sculptures, but, as the two masons point out, the workers also left their own marks in the form of counter-discourse; for instance, the devil sculpted in the likeness of a local bishop. (See Plate 26.)

The bulk of *Les Bâtisseurs* is avowedly a *film à thèse* about social housing. Its first thesis, rehearsed by the two masons, is that the working classes have built for everybody else along the ages – from kings, lords, and priests, to 'petit bourgeois' and the new middle classes under Haussmann and Napoleon III – but never for themselves. In the second section of the film, a voice-over narrates the story of the development of concrete and reinforced concrete. It pays homage to new architects such as the brothers Perret, Mallet-Stevens, Jeanneret, and Le Corbusier who developed a new style based on the possibilities of concrete and overcoming the lumbering spaces and gilded pretence of 'art nouveau' and architectural 'modernism'. Somewhat against the grain of the film's empowering the workers themselves, this and the following part provide a forum for cadres, namely the two architects, Léon Perret and Le Corbusier. Both explain in some detail their new theories of building and especially mass housing. Le Corbusier insists on a 'doctrine' of urban planning that is based on the distribution of sunlight, trees, and green spaces, which he illustrates with drawings on paper as he speaks. Earlier, the workers had voiced their desire for a house with windows and a little garden. The voice-over asks rhetorically: 'La question n'est-elle pas comment construire pour vivre pleinement dans la joie et la lumière?' ['Is not the question how to build so as to live fully with joy and with light?']. The answer provided in the banlieues after World War Two by state-sponsored developers who erected HLM known as 'cages à lapin' (rabbit cages) was of course a far cry from the social and utopian urbanism of Le Corbusier (see Plate 27).

The fourth segment comprises white-on-black animated drawings with a voice-over arguing against the slums in and around Paris, which contribute to bad health and high rate of mortality at birth. The voice-over discussion of the masons returns against images of slums, soup kitchens, and destitute workers. The argument in this part is aimed at the 1937 International Exhibition that demonstrated both how central French architectural ideas were to the modern world, how capable the French building trade is, yet concealed how little had been done to remedy the housing plight of French workers. This section ends ominously on a quasi shot–counter-shot sequence that alternates between the Nazi pavilion and the Soviet Union's Communist tower that face each other at the fair. Accordingly, the concluding part is both didactic and propagandistic: it shows in animation the flowchart of the union, staging a meeting of the CGT directorate with several reports and speeches calling for mass construction, intercut with documentary segments showing the difficult conditions of building trade workers digging the Paris Métro. The movie ends on still images of a mass demonstration reminding viewers to remain actively involved in supporting their unions in the name of class solidarity, while the song of Desnos comes back to celebrate 'les gars du bâtiment'.

Epstein shot an accompanying short film, also commissioned by the CGT: *La Relève*, 'Troop relief'. While it features the same two unemployed workers as in *Les Bâtisseurs*, *La Relève* (1938) is, by contrast, a direct political call aimed at the leftist government of the Front Populaire to come to the help of Spanish Republicans. It might be considered a documentary of the foreign policy branch of the CGT concerned with global solidarity, as compared with the domestic policy of *Les Bâtisseurs*. These two films bear a resemblance to the project of *La Vie est à nous* (1936), a similar effort that Jean Renoir oversaw for the PCF, and which he edited. Epstein also directed a documentary with a title that echoes Renoir's, *Vive la vie* (1937), which presents 'Auberges de jeunesse' in the south of France within the *ajiste* movement launched to provide vacation venues to working-class youth while reinforcing class solidarity.

A last documentary deserves to be mentioned, even though Epstein died before completing the shooting and editing – both finished by Edmond Floury, the the director of photography who had first trained Epstein on *Pasteur*. This 1953 film, *Efforts de productivité dans la fonderie*, might appear at first to be but a corporate vehicle commissioned by the Association française pour l'accroissement de la productivité (AFAP) with the aim of boosting post-war industrial productivity. We might thus wonder whether Epstein did not shift his political allegiance after the Liberation. In point of fact, the AFAP was created in 1950 by economist Jean Fourastié, who was then working with Jean Monnet, the *éminence grise* behind the reconstruction of Europe reshaping itself as an entity based on peace and solidarity, and serving as counterweight to the two polarized Cold War camps. In the early 1950s, the Marshall Plan administrators wanted evidence that France was actively modernizing its workforce and its industrial methods. Of course, with a recent history that included the Front Populaire, World War Two, Liberation and reconstruction in the short span of ten years, productivity was understood quite differently in France than in the Fordist corporations of the US boosted by the War Effort. As a recent critic puts it: 'The French changed the static definition of productivity into a social movement involving a rediscovery of humanism together with the latest findings in assembly or stocking' (cited in Boulat, 2008: 396–7).

This is exactly what the film demonstrates, thus in a sense picking up where the two masons had left off in the pre-war *Les Bâtisseurs* when they lent expertise and creativity to the cadres and intellectuals. Productivity is presented at first as a question to be debated among corporate management and assembly floor executives in a classroom environment. But quickly, discussions migrate towards workers themselves who know first-hand how to optimize the assembly stream while lessening their physical strain. Epstein shows that the initial difficulty is that management and workers must reconsider every aspect of the task to be ameliorated. Some of the top-down improvements result from mapping out better processes or flows of materials between assembly stations. But the more important improvements seem to come from the base of the pyramid, from workers themselves – at least, these are the ones Epstein documents at greater length. Workers readily take to finding better ways to optimize their task: one proposes for instance to stack in a different pattern metal sheets to be dried so as to allow more per tray; another redesigns a die cast to minimize the loss of raw material. Enhancing productivity thus means reforming the process by which tasks are envisioned, structured, and enacted. Workers are shown to be active participants in that reform, collaborating in improving their working conditions, profiting financially from improvements to the bottom line, and exercising a new kind of awareness and creativity vis-à-vis the tasks they carry out. Certainly, that is the bent of the documentary, and in the same way that HLMs were the perverted result of Le Corbusier's utopian urbanism, we can surmise that this active participation in redesigning the work flow resulted mainly in the end in the heightened alienation of assembly workers.

The signature of Epstein, in spite of his curtailed role in the film, consists again in pushing forward the gestures, creativity, and environment through which workers carry out their actual work. It is fitting that Epstein began in the 1920s with the fatigue and sensorial exhaustion of mass workers as the distinctive mark of modernity, only to end at a specific moment of utopia in worker–management relationship in late Marshall Plan France, when remedying or at least lessening such fatigue was seen, albeit flittingly, as an important goal for socially conscious reconstruction.

Le Tempestaire, *Les Feux de la mer*, and *phonogénie*

Epstein's cinematic œuvre culminates in a remarkably short 22-minute *film sonore* (post-synchronized) that counts among the most beautiful, powerful, and intriguing films ever made. I would wager that most viewers watching *Le Tempestaire* (1947) for the first time have no clear idea that it is so short – and in an important way that is exactly Epstein's point: cinema transports us into another dimension of time, and does so actually, not metaphorically. Perhaps the mysterious title, an old word rarely used in French, is a kind of formula announcing such mobility and reversibility: *Le temp[s] est aire*. Time is space. (We will see in the next chapter why this is such an anti-Bergsonian idea.)

The title of Epstein's last film also contains two opposites: *Les Feux de la mer*, the fires of the sea. It is a historical documentary about lighthouses as instruments of peace, since, as the voice-over tells us, even at the worst of Franco-British wars, the two countries joined forces for the upkeep of lighthouses around the Channel. Although it intriguingly embeds a 6-minute mini-fiction about a young lighthouse keeper in its last segment, there is little to say about this film as a whole: we will refer to it only in so far as it throws light on its immediate predecessor, *Le Tempestaire*, to which we return.

The story is utterly simple – the fragment of a narrative, we might say, or a 'situation' to return to Epstein's motto. A young woman fears for her fiancé when he joins his crew of sardine fishermen because a storm is approaching. She consults a retired storm-tamer who agrees to use his magical art one last time in order to stop the storm. But then she is surprised by her fiancé, who is already back. They walk away arm in arm. The end. Perhaps even less than a situation the film results from the kind of collective affective impetus that shapes a fable or a myth. The young woman is spinning yarn with her grandmother at the opening of the movie, so we might see the women as mimicking the activity of the Fates, the spinners of the thread of life. The young woman incarnates Clotho, the Fate who sets the time of birth, and her grandmother represents Lachesis, the Fate who measures the length of a life with her thread – while Atropos, the Fate who severs the thread of a life, is not present. We might also think of Penelope's weaving, since the movie, like Homer's epic, has to do with a sailor's uncertain return to his home island (in this case, Belle-Île in lower Brittany). But as in several of Epstein's fictions and documentaries that reference cinema figuratively, this activity of spinning a continuous string or strip using wheels must be thought of as pointing to projection – projection speed in particular.

Narrative sequences per se represent only about half the length of the movie, the other half consisting of footage of a windstorm on the coasts of Belle- Île. And in the same way that the Fates and Penelope play with the time of life (Penelope undoes each night her daily weaving to prevent time from elapsing after Ulysses' departure – in a way an early instance of reverse motion), Epstein manipulates our experience of duration, as if spinning the time of the film between his fingers. This alteration of duration is precisely what propels the narrative: the young woman projects to herself a fateful future, and projects herself into that future. But her fisherman fiancé, of necessity, inhabits the present of his work. In a way the crisis comes from the fact that they are not only separated in space, but also in time – as if thrown into two different regions of duration. That is why the storm-tamer's ultimate victory remains ambiguous: has he in fact silenced the storm, or did he act just when the storm was abating? Perhaps the desperate action of the young woman, and the reluctant acquiescing of the storm-tamer to reprise an art he said he had not practised for a long time, have strictly nothing to do with the return of the fiancé. When he finally stumbles upon her, the first thing he says is: 'Qu'est-ce que tu fais là? Je te cherche depuis une heure' ['What are you doing here? I've been looking for you for an hour']. Clearly, she has lost her sense of time by consulting an old wizard – who may exist only in her reverie as she spins. We too, in the same way, lose our own sense of the present by immersing ourselves in a filmic reverie, so we might be the ones saying to ourselves: 'Je te cherche depuis une heure'. After all, what we see in the crystal ball of the old wizard is nothing other than images from a silent film. So, the old wizard might turn out to be Epstein himself, who had not practised his art of filmmaking in a long time.

But again, it is less at the narrative than at the technical level that Epstein deploys his time-altering craft of 'tempestaire' – or timemaster. Just as soon as the film starts, credits unfold superimposed over disorienting and slightly underexposed dynamic pans: they are VLs of the Belle-Île coast, spliced in quick succession, panning quickly from both right to left and left to right, at 180 and 360 degrees, with the sound of the wind mixed with wind instruments on the nervous soundtrack. This credit sequence is quite ominous. All at once it generates tension, signals a reconnection with *photogénie* experiments such as the merry-go-round scenes in *Cœur fidèle*, and finally presents visually the central motif of the film: sensorial disorientation and temporal reversibility. Before the narrative even begins, the film has been foreshadowed for us through purely perceptual means.

The first segment begins on a panning VLS of low-tide mudflats with mirror-like water, then LSs of boats on the mud, and an MS of three old sailors perfectly immobile, looking at the sea. 'The old men are strangely immobile, frozen, on the wharf', reads Epstein's original scenario (reproduced in non-paginated illustrations in between pages of Epstein, 1976: 168–70). What is striking in this sequence of handheld pans and fixed shots, is that viewers have no clue whether they show still images (pans over a photo) or actual footage of extremely still scenes. The former seems to be the case, but the slightly trembling frame casts some doubt. In any case, the next few shots are real footage since a slight wind starts rustling the brush and rippling on the water. But then we see a definitely still image of the young and older women sitting and spinning yarn. They appear all the more suspended in magical sleep that their eyes look downwards and seem closed. As more wind shakes the brambles and agitates the sea, the same shot of the two women recurs, but this time in motion. Yet we notice after one or two seconds that it is not live motion but slow motion. We also wonder whether the soundtrack, including the slow ominous music to which we've been listening for half a minute may not also be artificially slowed down. The musical score is by Yves Baudrier (1906–88) who formed the musical movement 'Jeune France' in 1936 with three other composers including Olivier Messiaen. In 1945 he became co-director of IDHEC with Marcel L'Herbier. The affinity with Epstein was almost guaranteed by the fact that Baudrier loved

Brittany and, among his musical composition, had an *Eleonora* suite after Edgar Poe. With regard to the film's soundtrack, Epstein acknowledges only that he had indeed altered ambient sound: 'tout au long du *Tempestaire*, j'ai pu me servir de bruits de vent et de mer, réenregistrés à des vitesses variables, allant jusqu'au rapport quatre' ['throughout *Le Tempestaire*, I was able to use wind and sea noises, re-recorded at variable speeds up to a ratio of four'] (ibid.: 130). These first sequences thus suggest that the film may be about interstitial duration, the continuum of temporality that lies between stillness and normal movement, in both vision and audition.

Epstein had been thinking about manipulating sound since the very first years of sound cinema. 'Le propre d'un art est de créer, du nôtre son monde' ['What is proper to art is making its world out of ours'], he wrote in 1930, giving to sound more autonomy than that of mere handmaiden to images. He adds: 'nous voulons entendre ce que l'oreille n'entend pas. Comme nous voyons par le cinématographe ce qui échappe à l'œil' ['we want to hear what the human ear cannot hear, the same way we see through the cinema what escapes the eye']. This is what he calls 'phonogénie', and with it, 'on déroulera les cyclones en berceuses' ['we will stretch hurricanes into lullabies'] with the hope that 'les secrets de leur éloquence soient arrachés aux frondaisons et aux vagues' ['the secrets of the eloquence of foliage and waves might be wrenched from them'] and 'nous en reconstruisions des voix plus vraies que les naturelles !' ['we might reconstruct with them voices more true than the natural ones'] (ibid.: 227–8). In 1947, Epstein finally seized the chance to reprise his silent-era experiments in *photogénie* by expanding and translating them, as it were, into aural innovations. One of the most striking sequences in *Les Feux de la mer*, is a quick edit of shots of radios and lighthouses accompanied by a soundtrack that mixes international languages, male and female voices, Morse code, radio dial screeches and hisses, to form a frenetic hybrid of mad Lettrist performance and hallucinated speaking in tongues. The soundtrack seems here independent of the images.

We have to wait about two minutes into the *Tempestaire* for Epstein to offer us a shot in which the sound is synchronous with the image: an LA VLS of a luminous wave crashing far below on the sand of a steep gully. Cut to the two women looking up in slow motion almost straight at the camera, with a counter-shot of the door slowly creaking open. After another shot of laundry drying on a line, we're back to the same shot of the two women, but now finally moving at normal speed. 'C'est un signe ... Un mauvais signe' ['It's a sign, a bad sign'], the youngest says pointing at the door, launching the narrative of human fear, magic, and elemental power. We should note that the beginning of the movie consists of a progressive reconstruction of the historical cinema apparatus, going from the still/moving image ambiguity characteristic of the early cinema of attractions, to slow-motion shots without dialogue (but with sound and music, as occurred in early silent cinema), and finally to synchronous dialogue at regular speed. As a parenthesis, it is rather likely that Chris Marker remembered Epstein's experiment in the overall conception of his 1963 film *La Jetée*, made of stills (some of which include dissolves) with only one live-action shot.

'C'est un signe ... Un mauvais signe', the young woman utters, thinking about her lover at sea. The grandmother answers: 'Il ne faut pas croire aux signes. C'est défendu' ['Don't believe in signs, it is forbidden']. The prohibition is intriguing. Certainly, it applies to Celtic beliefs in prophecy forbidden by Catholicism. Thus official religion and rationalism see eye to eye in dismissing omens. By aligning us with the fear of the young woman, however, Epstein invites us to question this prohibition since it clearly concerns cinema's use of signs for prolepsis ('flash-forward'), but also as a new mode of signification.

The first chapter of one of Epstein's most important books, *L'Intelligence d'une machine* (1946) is entitled 'Signes', and addresses the way cinema's images constitute material signs that our understanding of time, cause, and effect, can be changed (Epstein, 1974: 255–334]. So cinema, for Epstein, makes an impact on the very way signs relate to what and how they signify. For us, who come after semiotics, a sign is a Saussurean entity made of an outward appearance (the signifier of four letters: TREE) linked arbitrarily to an abstract meaning (a signified, here, the general idea of trees). But the sign is not at all connected to trees as such, its referent, and it entails no presentation of a tree image (unlike a pictogram). It is this disincarnate and immaterial view of the language system that Epstein sought to overturn his entire life, since cinema demonstrates a new order of signs. In filmic images, the relationship between the signifier and its possible signifieds is almost never arbitrary, because the signified *is* the signifier *is* the referent. Thus the filmic image of a face (signifier) signifies that face (signified) through that very face (referent). On top of that image, we can graft an emotion, therefore a meaning, leading to a story. But that secondary layer is made of words, and ideas, and interpretations of filmic images: it is language on top of the substrate of signification of the filmic image. The problem with the talkies is that they make it seem as if that secondary layer were native to cinema.

To return to our film, the pared-down narrative of *Le Tempestaire* centres on what happens when someone – the young woman – *misreads* a creaking door as not signifying itself, but instead pointing to an obscure message, an abstract signified. In a way, this is what we do and perhaps must do as movie viewers: we misread filmic images that are, in Godard's words, not 'une image juste', only 'juste une image', and therefore we project ourselves in a world of linguistic signs. *Le Tempestaire* sets out to disclose and counter, both narratively and cinematically, our mania to slap linguistic meaning on what we experience visually and sensorially. When her fiancé asks the young woman 'what are you doing here?' at the end of the film, we can hear Epstein asking us what we're doing in our mental world of linguistic signs, asking what things mean, when we should begin by immersing ourselves in the primary layer of signification: the *photogénie* and *phonogénie* of the film.

The narrative turns against itself, we suggested, because when the young woman seeks a magician ostensibly to prevent the realization of the sign she fantasized, what he does, and what we see on-screen, is to enclose the filmic image back into a glass ball. Epstein hence forces us to view the film *en abyme* in the glass ball as the only meaning of the film!

As the storm-tamer blows on the ball, we see MCUs of the young woman's entranced face. This directly echoes the trance of Madeline in *La Chute de la maison Usher*, as she too is shown to us as a film *en abyme* when footage of her mesmerized likeness appears in the portrait's frame. Here again, Epstein short-circuits the viewers' quest for linguistic meaning by both doubling up (*mise en abyme*), interrupting, and altering the course of the narration. When the storm-chaser drops the glass ball, it shatters without a sound. Is it to indicate that, like the young woman, we too are entranced and fail to be in the present? Or is it because Epstein suggests a reversibility between the film (*Le Tempestaire*) and the film within the film (the storm in the ball that is silent)? Or is it another reminder of the surreptitious haunting of silent cinema within any talkie?

This open question leads us to the most famous sequence of the film: the waves crashing on the rocks, which suddenly reverse themselves. One of the Lumières' 1896 shorts shows us simple footage of children diving in the sea. But we know that this pedestrian film was primarily of interest when, projected backwards, the water seemed to spit out a child flying upwards and swallow its own splashes. Cocteau cites this reversibility in *Le sang d'un poète* when the poet comes out of the liquid mirror in reverse motion. The thick, almost creamy waves shot in slow motion strikingly resemble lava – possibly as a remembrance of Epstein's lost film on Mount Etna. Certainly, if there is a culmination in Epstein's fascination with fluidity as the intersection of *photogénie*, our bodily affects, and another system of signs, it is to be found in the stormy sea shots of *Le Tempestaire*. The storm-tamer is also called *le guérisseur de vent* by the young woman, as if stormy winds were particularly strong effluvia of nature's affections. We will recall, finally, that in defining *photogénie* Epstein pointed to a kind of anthropomorphism palpable in both natural and artificial objects. Towards the end of the film we see three quick cross-cuts between the waves in slow motion and a wall covered with radio dials. Besides the pointed reference to both radio waves and sea waves – in French also, *ondes* denotes both – it is hard to miss the face-like aspects of the dials, their *faciality* Deleuze would say, directly spliced onto the furious liquidity of the ocean. In spite – and because – of the simplicity of its narrative, *Le Tempestaire* is one among a handful of films that invites us to meditate on the crucial elements of cinema – time, fluidity, affect, duration, rhythm, material signs, reversibility, elementary forces, myth, and faces – without bringing our meditation to a set conclusion, that is, a linguistic meaning. As such, *Le Tempestaire* stands as a summation not only of Epstein's film work, but of his philosophy of the cinema, which we will now examine in a broad overview in the next chapter.

References

Abel, Richard (ed.) (1988), *French Film Theory and Criticism*, vol. 2, 1929–39, Princeton: Princeton University Press.
— (ed.) (2005), 'Newsreels', *Encyclopedia of Early Cinema*, London and New York: Routledge, 477–8.
Albera, François (1996), *Les Formalistes russes et le cinéma*, Paris: Nathan.
Boulat, Régis (2008), *Jean Fourastié, un expert en productivité*, Besançon: Presses universitaires de Franche-Comté.
Dallet, Sylvie (2000), 'Boîter avec toute l'humanité ou la filmographie gancienne et son golem', *1895*, vol. 31, October, 53–80.
Epstein, Jean (1926), *Le Cinématographe vu de l'Etna*, Paris, Les Écrivains réunis.
— (1974), *Écrits sur le cinéma*, vol. 1, Paris: Éditions Seghers.
— (1976), *Écrits sur le cinéma*, vol. 2, Paris: Éditions Seghers.
Gauthier (2004), *Un siècle de documentaire français*, Paris: Armand Collin.
Greenidge, Terrence (1929), 'Present-Day Tendencies in the Cinema', *Socialist Review* (November), 261–70.
Leprohon, Pierre (1964), *Jean Epstein*, Paris: Pierre Seghers.
McMahan, Alison (2003), *Alice Guy Blaché: Lost Visionary of the Cinema*, New York and London: Continuum.
O'Brien, Charles (2005), *Cinema's Conversion to Sound: Technology and Film Style in France and the US*, Bloomington: Indiana University Press.
Reynolds, Siân (2000), 'Germaine Dulac and French Documentary Film Making in the 1930s', in John Izod, R.W. Kilbon, Matthew Hibberd (eds.), *From Grierson to the Docu-Soap: Breaking the Boundaries*, Luton: University of Luton Press, 71–81.
Sadoul, Georges (1985), *Lumière et Méliès*, Paris: L'Herminier.
Strauven, Wanda (ed.) (2006), *The Cinema of Attractions Reloaded*, Amsterdam: Amsterdam University Press.
Vignaux, Valérie (2007), *Jean Benoit-Lévy ou le corps comme utopie: une histoire du cinéma éducateur dans l'entre-deux-guerres en France*, Paris: AFRHC.

6

'A young Spinoza': Epstein's philosophy of the cinema

Epstein and the emergence of film theory

By the early 1920s, film criticism and short movie reviews were firmly if eclectically established in France through industry publications, journals, or illustrated magazines for cinephiles, and a few articles in mainstream newspapers and journals. Similar to theatrical or musical reviews, film reviews became a part of the print context surrounding movies for general audiences. But the cine-club movement born at the end of World War One also produced a more specialized audience, through a broad context of dedicated theatres, lectures on cinema, conferences on the future of film, etc., which hastened the creation of an artistic and intellectual film press (Gauthier, 1999: 53–70). Hence journalists, producers, and writers alike launched a number of film journals during the late war and post-war periods: for instance, Henri-Diamant Berger created *Le Film* in 1916, Pierre Henry *Ciné pour tous* in 1919, and Louis Delluc *Cinéa* in 1921. Even journals more broadly devoted to the arts and letters progressively integrated columns and special issues on cinema, such as *Le Crapouillot*, a journal originally for soldiers at the front (Abel, 1988a: 95–107). The authors of these new critical pieces on cinema were either aficionados and theoreticians (Ricciotto Canudo, Émile Vuillermoz), directors or budding directors (Louis Delluc, Jean Renoir), reviewers and chroniclers (Lionel Landry), or young writers and artists improvising themselves critics (Colette, Léon Moussinac, Jean Cocteau, Marcel Gromaire, Fernand Léger).[1] Book-length treatises about the cinema were, however, few and far between. This is understandable if we recall that books and cinema

[1] See Abel (1988a, b), for a broad selection of these.

intersected mostly through the definitely lowbrow *ciné-romans*, that is, pulp adaptations of serial movies beginning in the 1910s. Cinema was still very much on the side of popular entertainment in spite of attempts by the Film d'art company and other production firms to craft more highbrow films. Still, the idea of writing a serious treatise about cinema seemed probably far-fetched to most. Accordingly, besides the large production of press articles around movie culture and films, we find only a handful of technical manuals and a few pamphlets before the end of World War One.

Yet as soon as the war was over, a new kind of book began trickling in almost immediately. French cinema had been decimated by the war, and the domestic market was taken over by Hollywood's first great export wave of films. The new books that soon came out offered synthetic and forward-looking views, with the more or less unstated aim of restarting an autonomous national cinema. This is the case with Henri Diamant-Berger's 1919 *Cinéma*, a collection of articles meant to serve as a broad guide for understanding recent changes in the industry. The real innovator, and in many ways the pioneer of French film theory, was Louis Delluc (1890–1924), a young novelist and playwright fascinated by the cinema, who became film critic and just as quickly filmmaker. He wrote three important books in three years: *Cinéma & cie: confidences d'un spectateur* (1919); *Photogénie* (1920b), perhaps the first attempt to theorize cinema's medium specificity; and *Charlot* (1920a), the first monograph on Chaplin, the very incarnation of Hollywood's superior craft and global reach.

Epstein clearly followed in Delluc's footsteps in the initial conception of his first book dedicated to film, *Bonjour cinéma* (1921b), which brings together some of the components Delluc had developed in his books: the central experience of the viewer, the specificity of cinema as *photogénie*, and the cult of Chaplin. While Epstein's book is far from systematic, and the verse and poetic sections would likely disqualify it in today's normative academic publishing as a serious theoretical work, there are good reasons to consider this book a threshold (see chapter 1 for an analysis of *Bonjour cinéma*). Before *Bonjour cinéma*, books about the movies aimed at understanding or legitimizing the new medium, always weary of the suspicious eyes of the intellectual public and, in France especially, of the pronouncements of cultural brokers and governmental institutions. By contrast, Epstein's book addresses an audience comprising both experimentalists of the avant-garde – including filmmakers, critics, poets and multimedia artists – and more technique-driven cinema professionals, aware of the stylistic originality of Hollywood's directors such as Griffith, Ince, and de Mille. Thus, one of the first books that may truly be considered to develop a new theoretical view of cinema is informed equally by the modernism of l'Esprit nouveau and Simultaneism (while taking its distance form Futurism and dada), and by the sense that a new syntax of cinematography, *mise en scène*, narrative rhythm and editing was now available. It is at this intersection of a broad artistic and literary viewpoint, a deep cinephilia, and professional considerations on apparatus and craft that a theory and philosophy of the cinema first arose in France. By placing cinema de facto at the highest cultural level, and without the need to legitimize this move, *Bonjour cinéma* undoubtedly ushers in the first mature era of film criticism that took place from the 1920s to World War Two.

Early influences and *La Lyrosophie*

Epstein came to writing about cinema, then to filmmaking, after having studied and linked together medicine, and more precisely psychophysiology, and literature, in particular modernist poetry (see chapter 1). These two early strata in his thought explain why his theoretical outlook on cinema was always informed by the corporeal and the aesthetic. What does cinema do to our bodily being-in-the-world? How might it find its own place among and besides the other arts? These are some of the central questions Epstein asks throughout his career as a film thinker. And, as he suggests, he was among the first to consider them from a philosophical as much as aesthetic viewpoint. 'A cet art si neuf qu'il n'en existait alors que le pressentiment, les mots, même aujourd'hui, manquent pour avoir trop servi à des images hélas inoubliées. Poésie et philosophie nouvelles' ['For this art so new that it existed then only as foreboding, words, even today, are lacking for having unfortunately served for unerasable images. New poetry and philosophy'] (Epstein, 1921b: 29). Although his subsequent book appears not to be explicitly concerned with the origins of cinema, it may be argued that the invented word in its title – *La Lyrosophie* (1922a) – compounds the 'new poetry and philosophy' that the thought of cinema requires.

La Lyrosophie is predicated on a single and broad thesis. Epstein proposes that certainty, evidence, reason, proof, and truth do not call solely for logic, science, and mathematics, as post-Enlightenment scientism takes for granted. Mathematical proof, Epstein argues, is predicated on a unique sensation and emotion that accompanies and perhaps guides demonstration. A mathematician will accept a proof only after it *feels* right, and may abandon certain paths that *intuitively* do not appear promising. But science has relentlessly attempted to leech affect from any and all its disciplines and procedures, and Epstein considers his treatise a corrective. By linking all affectivity to sexuality, and in this agreeing with Freud, Epstein insists that emotions represent both a separate realm of knowledge and a unique tool worth using to understand a new order of experience. Hence our daily life rests on a deep dichotomy: 'la connaissance de sentiment et la connaissance de science coexistent et sinon se tendent la main, au moins se côtoient et parfois rudement' ['knowledge from emotion and knowledge from science coexist, and if they do not hold hands, at least they are side by side, albeit at times roughing each other'] (*ibid.*: 39). And instead of pretending that we can lead logical and wilful lives solely or mostly with our inner 'knowledge from science', we would do well to reckon instead with our inner 'état lyrique' ['lyrical state'], corresponding to the subconscious, that is, affects, desires, and love, and especially aesthetic invention (*ibid.*: 46). It is precisely when he advocates for a different relationship between these two states of knowledge – the scientific and the lyrosophical – that Epstein invokes cinema. The two short examples he adduces in the book both claim that even though the viewer experiences a *fiction*, her experience is nonetheless *real*, and thus any reflection upon it also produces real knowledge. This is because cinema does not so much represent as *present*, or make present: 'Jamais même dans la kabbale, désigner ne fut si exactement nommer. Et, après cette création, je conserve le sentiment d'une réalité seconde et particulière, sui generis, cinématographique' ['Even in the Kabbalah, never was designating so strictly equivalent to creating. And after that creation, I preserve the feeling of a particular and second reality, *sui generis*, cinematographic'] (*ibid.*: 93).

Freud was just starting to be read in France, and together with André Breton, Jean Epstein was among the first to do so. Yet the thinker that suggested to him the importance of non-conscious sexual energy was Remy de Gourmont. His *Physique de l'amour: essai sur l'instinct sexuel* (1903), had reinscribed human sexuality within the broad spectrum of animal sex from which moralizing scientism had wrenched it. The book, which might have been entitled in a Jamesian way *The Varieties of Sexual Experience*, had a tremendous impact on the reappraisal of psychosexual life by modernist writers, in particular Blaise Cendrars, Georges Bataille, and Ezra Pound – who translated it into English. Epstein examines other works of de Gourmont's in *La Poésie d'aujourd'hui* and 'Le Phénomène littéraire', but *Physique de l'amour* represents a clear prototype to *La Lyrosophie*'s thesis. De Gourmont writes for instance, 'Il n'y a donc pas lieu de tenir compte de la vieille objection scolastique contre l'identification de l'intelligence et de l'instinct' ['There is no call then for taking seriously the old scholastic objection against equating intelligence and instinct'] (de Gourmont, 1903: 251). De Gourmont and Epstein both seek to go around the entrenched dualism between thought and body that runs from Scholasticism to Cartesian thought and nineteenth-century Positivism. Epstein's queer sensibility would also have found in his elder's work a crucial confirmation that so-called aberrant sexuality, from masturbation to fetishism and homosexuality, was indeed strictly natural, that is, present in the animal world. The fact that Epstein reintegrated the closet likely for reasons of social acceptability, again, does not mean that he was not harnessing all the philosophical resources available to revolutionize the place of embodiment and desire in modernity.

Another thinker has been cited as an important influence on Epstein: Henri Bergson (see chapter 2). Malcolm Turvey, notably, underlines Epstein's reliance on a metaphysics of flux and mobility that agrees with Bergson's overall theory of duration and becoming (2008: 20–1, 24–5, 49–51). The problem, as Turvey is careful to note (*ibid.*: 24), is that Bergson's thought was famously anti-cinematographic since he mistakenly believed that cinema transforms unbroken duration into a series of still images. Certainly, the filmstrip does so, but *projection* restores the phi-effect through which natural human vision cognitively perceives movement as such – whether it is artificial or real matters little. The phi-effect is the crucial difference between chronophotographs shown at a few frames per second (fps) that are perceived stroboscopically and thus distinct, and cinema which, at around 15 fps, suppresses any awareness of the interval. But the problem is not just that Bergson was wrong about film. In a very direct way, Epstein's *photogénie*, which rests on the unique properties of the film apparatus – slow motion and even more so reverse motion – runs against Bergson's eminently naturalist and anti-mechanistic view of duration. The spiritualist side of Bergson's model of natural duration, memory, and becoming is absent in Epstein. Almost polar opposite notions obtain: suspension and syncope, and bodily experiencing in the present. Indeed, Epstein cites Bergson only in passing and with very little specificity. In *La Lyrosophie*, indicating that science has supplanted theology he mentions the work 'd'un Bergson ou d'un [Édouard] Branly' (*ibid.*: 133) as examples, and in *Alcool et cinéma* Bergson figures in a list of followers of the temporal flux of Heraclitus rather than the intervals of Zeno: 'Bruno, Hegel, Schopenhauer, Bergson, Engels, etc.' (Epstein 1976: 210). Éric Thouvenel's in-depth analysis of Epstein's writings and positions reveals that he was in fact rather anti-Bergsonian – in fact virulently so – siding instead with Gaston Bachelard's defence of rhythm and discontinuous time against unruptured becoming (Thouvenel, 2010).[2] In his notes on a book by Bachelard, Epstein writes for instance: 'Mais il y a une *intelligence cinématique* (et une expérience des états visqueux, liquides) à côté de l'intelligence géométrique à laquelle Bergson accorde la suprématie' ['But there is a *cinematic intelligence* (and an experience of viscous, liquid states) besides the geometrical intelligence Bergson sees as having supremacy'] (*ibid.*: 64). Clearly he remains on the side of absolute fluidity/malleability against the relative mobility of duration of Bergson.

Rather than Bergson, we should look to thinkers such as Albert Einstein (whom Epstein mentions much more often), and especially Baruch Spinoza. Abel Gance called Epstein 'a young Spinoza', likely because both embraced Spinoza's monism, the belief in a single substance uniting immanence and transcendence. Such a thought informs Epstein's last work, *Le Cinéma du diable*, as Jacques Aumont keenly pointed out, but it is already clearly recognizable in *La Poésie d'aujourd'hui*, with its notion of the 'unique plane' where thoughts, sensations, images, and language ostensibly meet (1998: 91, n. 13). Chiara Tognolotti has also shown that, perhaps later in life, the thought of Nietzsche was crucial to Epstein, especially his denunciation of false morals and the emphasis on the conflict between the

---

2 Thouvenel's essay invalidates Turvey (2009).

Apollonian removal from, and the Dionysian engulfment into the real, in *The Birth of Tragedy* (Tognolotti, 2005).

Other important sources of inspiration for Epstein's early thought were esoteric movements, in particular pre-Socratic schools such as the Pythagoreans, and medieval Jewish mysticism.[3] In both cases, it seems that Epstein was interested in ways of getting around the entrenched dualism of body–mind that came in the wake of Descartes and Kant. This is clear in the chapter 'Kabbale' from *La Lyrosophie*, as well as in two slightly different versions of another chapter, 'Nous Kabbalistes', appearing in *La Lyrosophie* and the journal *L'Esprit nouveau* (Epstein, 1922b: 83–95). His interest in the pre-Socratics also likely involves the queer phil-hellenism that informs *Ganymède*, and had attracted other queer thinkers such as André Gide or Claude Cahun recognizing in ancient Greece a golden age of tolerance for same-sex love.

What is a philosophy of the cinema?

Before going any further, we might do well to ask ourselves what a philosophy of the cinema is, or even what it might be attempting to achieve. Certain commentators of Epstein, based on selected sections of his writings, assume that he is propounding a theory. Turvey writes repeatedly of 'Jean Epstein's film theory', in an anachronistic way since it presumes a contemporary understanding of cinema and all the various theoretical positions that have developed since the 1920s (2008: 21, 23, 26). A theory of cinema, we might suppose, would tell us what cinema is or should be, how it works or should work, what place it occupies or should occupy in the social and cultural horizon, and which movies best exemplify it as a medium of representation and perhaps as an art form. However, such a theory, as most theories in the modern sense do, takes its object (cinema) to be relatively bounded, that is, definable and separate from the physical world and the social and cultural sphere. This creates a historiographic problem in the case of Epstein and others in the 1920s, because cinema was precisely *not* the bounded object it ultimately became after World War Two. At that time (*c.*1945) L'Institut de filmologie, for instance, decided to

---

3 See 'L'Écho de Pythagore', Fonds Epstein, Collection Cinémathèque Française, BiFi, 228B60.

conduct a pluri-disciplinary investigation into the various phenomena of cinema, and Kracauer was drafting the book that became *Theory of Film: The Redemption of Physical Reality* (1960). Richard Abel confirms our need to be careful with the term when he writes that, 'Such a notion of theory, however, seems premature for the period [1907–29], as well as highly dubious as an aesthetic absolute' (1998: xviii). Epstein himself warned against theory in 1926 when he writes: 'Les théories qui précèdent les œuvres sont aléatoires et légères ...' ['Theories that precede the works are arbitrary and fickle...'] (1974: 126).

Yet in asserting that, 'certain texts by Epstein, Dulac, Canudo, and Moussinac may come close' to 'a rigorously systematic, coherent theory of film' (Abel, 1998: xviii), Abel leaves unaddressed the expression that Epstein uses for his writings: '*la philosophie du cinéma*' (Epstein, 1921b: 35). The difference is sizeable between theory and philosophy. While theory applies rigorously systematic methods to a bounded object, philosophy questions all at once the methods, the boundaries, the object itself, the observer, and all the links between them. Philosophy's general assumption is holistic, we might say, where theory's usefulness is instrumental. In any case, it is crucial to consider Epstein's writings as part and parcel of a holistic philosophy of cinema – that is, a thought about life just as much as a specialized thought about the film apparatus. We may then state that *photogénie* as enacted through specific technical means (CUs, speed alterations, montage stylistics, etc.) amounts to a theory of the apparatus of cinema, but only as one component within a broader philosophy requiring other independent components such as the fatigue of the modern masses, the reinterpretation of melodrama, the filmic exemplarity of Brittany, or indeed, the direct, oral, lyrical, and maxim-like stylistics of Epstein's written descriptions of the experience of movie-viewing. In the introduction to *L'Intelligence d'une machine*, he writes: 'L'image animée apporte les éléments d'une représentation générale de l'univers qui tend à modifier plus ou moins toute la pensée ... Une philosophie peut donc naître de ces jeux de lumière et d'ombre ...' ['The moving image brings the elements of a general representation of the universe which tends more or less to modify the whole of thought ... A philosophy may thus be born from these plays of light and darkness ...'] (Epstein, 1974: 255). The emphasis here is on 'all of thought'.

With Epstein, born two years after the implementation of the Lumière *cinématographe*, arises the idea of a philosophical purview that acknowledges the prior mediation of cinema in our perception of all things before, and proposes that the cinematic amounts to a new state or stage in human capacities. Cinema is not just any tool, machine, or apparatus: it is a transformative lens through which just about anything can be shown in various ways, and to large numbers of various people, in a portable (ambulant) way. Cinema is a new beginning for humanity in the sense that we cannot really imagine what the world truly felt like before moving images entered it. Cinema marks our own limits, our horizon, perhaps better than any other single threshold, object, or condition. That is why for Epstein, cinema does not necessarily precipitate specific technical or social or economic or artistic questions. Rather, it opens up anew the broadest and first questions of philosophy: what are we, what do we know, what do we want?

Epstein's central set of ideas

Although one is hard pressed to summarize a philosophy that was never shaped into a system and always eschewed any kind of method to remain fragmentary and 'lyrical', there are nonetheless a few key invariants in Epstein's philosophy of the cinema. I will set them out here as a series of theses listed in order of importance and often referring back to chapters in this book where certain aspects have been developed in more depth.

1 Cinema is about bodies

It is about my body and affects as a viewer – and not just my eyes and my mind – and a viewer who is part of an embodied collective, an audience and a social class. In this, Epstein prolongs the Unanimism of Jules Romains and is close to the 'intercorporeality' of Merleau-Ponty.[4] It is also about filmic bodies, foremost via close-ups that

4 Epstein planned a chapter on Unanimism in the first draft of Le 'Phénomène littéraire' (Fonds Epstein, Collection Cinémathèque Française, BiFi, 235B91). For Unanimism and cinema, see Wall-Romana (2012). Merleau-Ponty's uses of 'intercorporéité' is found in Merleau-Ponty (1964: 10, 222, 228) (the neologism was not rendered in the English translation). Note that Epstein cites Merleau-Ponty (Fonds Epstein, Collection Cinémathèque Française, BiFi, 98B24) and that Merleau-Ponty wrote to Epstein (Fonds Epstein, Collection Cinémathèque Française, BiFi, 242B61).

bring focus onto small areas (face, hands) to heighten the visibility of affects. Cinema is not about stories, but about affect situations. If movie-making devolves into the representation, rather than presentation, of bodies, or accentuates the scopic pleasure straight males take in viewing female bodies (*pace* Laura Mulvey's famous proposal), this has little to do with the essential corporeality of cinema. For Epstein, our body is dominated by affective intensities, that is, a corporeal subconscious, much more so than the Freudian unconscious, which is too narrative. The subconscious is the cognitive reverse side of coenaesthesis, that is, the flow of sensations (including affects) that arise from the inside out within our body and about our body.

2 Cinema is non-human

It is 'un œil en dehors de l'œil' ['an eye outside of the eye'] providing a unique quality, 'celle d'échapper à l'égocentrisme de notre vision personnelle' ['to escape the tyrannical hold of our personal vision'] (Epstein, 1974: 129). While it is a man-made invention, which requires manning and human craft, cinema is properly non-human, like much mechanical technology, since it captures, records, and manipulates reality in four dimensions in a way humans cannot do, for instance by showing in acceleration the growth of a plant (*ibid.*: 250). Cinema's supra-human objectivity (with a wilful play of Epstein on the word *objectif*, lens, in French) is such that it is better than mirrors, which lie, since they reverse left and right. Cinema is *non-human*, but that does not mean that it is *inhuman* in itself, anymore than the automobile, which can become either a tank or an ambulance. The non-humanity of cinema provides us with a unique potential for 'knowing more', which is why Epstein calls 'le cinéma, instrument non seulement d'un art, mais aussi d'une philosophie' ['cinema, instrument not only for an art but for a philosophy'] (*ibid.*: 258).

3 Cinema creates physical and affective realities (not just illusion)

As an apparatus, in its actual images, and via its spectatorial effects, cinema must be considered real. The early suspicion that cinema belongs to the magic tricks of Houdin and Méliès was revived by Jean-Louis Baudry and other contemporary critics of the 1970s, who tended to view cinema as mainly an illusion-making machine. Epstein would dismissively call this aspect of cinema 'theatre'. In part because he was trained as a scientist, Epstein considers cinema as an actual physical apparatus, which produces images that confound and augment our knowledge of physics, matter, spatial and temporal continuity–discontinuity, cause and effect, and finally whose impact on viewers is real since it has a restorative effect on their fatigued bodies. But how can cinema be deemed 'real' if, for example, reverse motion violates the entropy laws of physics? Epstein's answer is that 'The cinematograph too is an experimental apparatus which constructs, that is, thinks an image of the universe; hence there is some reality pre-determined by the structure of its plasmatic mechanism' (ibid.: 333). What cinema 'thinks' into existence is a new matter or plasma – a four-dimensional stream of images. As a parenthesis, this idea is both para-Bergsonian, in that Bergson defines perception or images as a way of projecting oneself virtually into the world, and anti-Bergsonian since for Bergson only the human mind is capable of doing so. We should add that quantum physics today has found ways to make particles go back in time, slow them down, and bend light beams around objects. Its definition of 'reality' might well end up being closer to Epstein's than to our commonsensical view of what is an illusion.

4 Cinema alters knowledge

For Epstein cinema is both hardware – physical and sensorial reality – and software, that is, mental and epistemological. He writes in 1947: 'Le développement du cinéma marque, à mon sens, la fin du cartésianisme par l'assouplissement de l'armature logique de notre esprit. Ce sont les bases mêmes de la philosophie qui sont ébranlées' ['The development of cinema marks, in my opinion, the end of Cartesianism, by easing the logical framework of our mind. The very bases of philosophy are undermined'] (ibid.: 335). The important words here are *assouplissement* (easing) and *armature* (framework), because they metaphorically suggest the replacement of static structures by movement and plasticity. Indeed, this makes Epstein quite literally an early post-structuralist. If Epstein insists everywhere that cinema's presentation of movement is such a novelty, it is because philosophical knowledge, based on a model of geometrical axioms as in Descartes and Leibnitz, had until then been thought of as an immobile edifice, 'hence the *ne varietur* character of [its] geometrical analysis of the mind' (ibid.: 361). Against this solid or geometrical model, Epstein argues that cinema shows the fluidity, mobility, and plasticity of time, space, and human experiences, and therefore raises a radical challenge to philosophical models inflexibly beholden to frozen reason. Jacques Derrida's critique of structuralism and architecture rests on a similar dismissal of the metaphorical sway of solids and buildings.

5 Cinema responds to a modern ethical and social need

From his very first book to his last – that is, from World War One to World War Two (about war he has, however, remained strikingly silent) – Epstein has never veered off his utopian belief that cinema was an ethical and social salve, in fact of a homeopathic kind. It is ethical ('moral' in his vocabulary) through *photogénie*, which amplifies our engagement with inanimate objects or scenes by disclosing in them a kind of imaginary or residual affect tied to their mobile plasticity. But it is also socially useful in a more conventional way, as mass catharsis, granted that some aesthetic qualities be present in what he calls, with great provocation, 'poésie en quantité industrielle' ['poetry in industrial quantities'] (Epstein, 1976: 247). While early on, he aligned cinema's poetry with the specific innovations of avant-garde modernism in Proust, Cendrars, Aragon, and others, he later expanded both his sense of 'poetry' and of catharsis. Although he remains vague about what the aesthetic qualities of 'poetry' should be when they apply to cinema, *Le Tempestaire* might serve as a precious exemplum. As for catharsis, after being dubious of Freud's psychoanalysis as a whole (see 'Freud ou le nick-cartérianisme en psychologie' (1922c)), Epstein invokes in 1946 a very Freudian parade of repression, sublimation, day-dreaming, and fantasy in order to argue for lyrosophy, against the imposition of moral codes on movies (Epstein, 1974: 397–403). His little-known documentary œuvre, finally, brings a crucially political and ethical supplement to what might otherwise be mistaken as aestheticism (see chapter 5).

6 Cinema is democratic

Oppositions between documentary and dramatic movies, or mainstream narrative and alternative/experimental fiction, or studio production vs. structural avant-garde film are pre-empted by Epstein's holistic notion of cinema. For him, the pro-filmic is neither an artificial set nor merely some part of the built world or nature used as background: it has a robust reality. But it doesn't mean it is favoured over the filmic. Epstein's cinema occupies the whole spectrum of realism from a transparent and immediate haptic contact with things themselves, to vivid counterpoints in which the actively transformative role of cinema is showcased. Similarly, his films cover the whole range of storytelling: from the strong suggestion of a possible world outside of our own which we apprehend through protagonist identification (classic fiction), all the way to moments of free affective resonance when our investment in the narrative is near zero because the movie releases us from the story with poetic images that generate affects and associations at a far remove from the plot. This is obvious in the quick edit of tree branches and lake surfaces during Roderick's song in *La Chute de la maison Usher*. The reason Epstein is so central to a thinker such as Gilles Deleuze has to do, I believe, with Epstein's refusal to pare down cinema's holism into a more digestible realm on either side of the divide between transparent mainstream narration, and medium-centred experiments with sensorial intensity. Friedrich Schlegel wrote that 'poetry is republican speech: a speech which is its own law and end unto itself, and in which all the parts are free citizens and have the right to vote' (1991: 8 fr. 65). Epstein too compares cinema to the French Revolution because it is democratic and 'speaks' a universal language (1974: 359–60). From this we can construe that he subscribes to Schlegel's Romantic utopianism in seeing in art's rejection of established languages and hierarchic forms a possible liberation of the masses. This emancipating dimension may not be immediately plain outside of his documentary work. Yet it is rigorously implied in every one of the key ideas above. *Photogénie* itself may be considered ultimately empowering to viewing subjects because it discloses to them their own embodied situation, without binding it to dramatic states and ideological stakes. Epstein revered Chaplin all his life for that very reason: film drama has never entirely recovered from the way Chaplin's subaltern somatic body punctures narrative to stay on the side of the dispossessed.

7 Time is multiple

Dans un même temps, dans un temps unique, dans le temps enfin, toutes choses deviennent. [Within the same time, within a single time, within time simply, all things become]. (Alain, 1916: 74)

Epstein is clearly anti-Bergsonian. He inverts Bergson's main thesis by asserting that for time in cinema, 'quantité et qualité deviennent des notions corrélatives, interchangeables' ['quantity and quality become correlative and interchangeable notions ...' (Epstein, 1974: 312). Bergson strenuously insisted that quality and quantity are absolutely exclusive of each other. Nor does Epstein subscribe to intuition and inner duration directed by time's arrow. For him, fatigue triggers among other things blanks, distraction, and intermittence – the very opposite of intuition's clean and crisp attentiveness (Epstein, 1921a: 192–3). It is because of fatigued viewing that Epstein especially believes in using CUs and altered or reverse motion, since they fit damaged attention better. About slow motion, a quantitative reduction of cinema's duration, he writes: 'Un tel pouvoir de séparation du sur-œil mécanique et optique fait apparaître clairement la relativité du temps ... Le drame est situé en dehors du temps commun' ['Such a power of separation from the optical and mechanical super-eye lets transpire clearly the relativity of time ... Drama is located outside of common time'] (Epstein, 1974: 191). Hence, Epstein calls cinema 'la machine à penser le temps' ['the time-thinking machine'] (*ibid*.: 282), for its unique capacity of making us live various temporalities, 'temps locaux et incommensurables' ['local and incommensurable times'] (*ibid*.: 285). This is, again, a profoundly post-humanistic view of time since it decentres Man as 'unique repère ... souverain arbitre' ['unique reference, [and] sovereign arbiter'] (*ibid*.: 314) of the cosmos, and brackets human history as central to cosmic events.

We will end the list here. There are of course many more important critical and philosophical ideas at play in Epstein's writing and films, and many more that await study. For instance, the notion that high art and mass culture share the same psychophysiological root; that language is anchored to the body as much as to the mind; that cinema will keep evolving, etc. We limited ourselves here to those that palpably inform the entirety of his œuvre. Let us conclude this section on an important citation:

> le cinématographe marque, au contraire, sa représentation de l'univers de caractères propres, d'une originalité qui fait de cette interprétation non pas un reflet, une simple copie des conceptions de la mentalité-mère organique, mais bien un système différemment individualisé, en partie indépendant, qui contient en germe le développement d'une philosophie s'éloignant assez des opinions courantes, pour qu'il convienne peut-être de l'appeler anti-philosophie.[5]

[5] 'the cinematograph inscribes its own characters upon its representation of the

This might be the farthest point in Epstein's thought. With cinema, he claims, a new kind of being is born, with a mechanical intelligence that challenges our anthropo-centrism, and opens a new realm beyond the reaches of classical philosophy.

Epstein's critical and philosophical legacy

One way to gauge the productivity of Epstein's ideas is to trace their role and evolution within the thoughts of others. In spite – or perhaps because – of the breadth of his influence, this is easier said than done. The publication in 1921 of his work 'Le Phénomème littéraire' over six issues of *L'Esprit nouveau*, one of the leading international avant-garde journals of the time, placed it front and centre among the new intellectual currents of post-war modernism. By 1922, his work was translated into English, appeared in Russian journals, was reviewed in the German press, and read by Brazilian intellectuals.[6] His core thesis on modernity's new reliance on the subconscious in literature and mass culture quickly disseminated to the far margins of international networks. This thesis, developed especially in *La Poésie d'aujourd'hui*, played a decisive role in the genesis of one of the most important terms and movements of the twentieth century: Surrealism. This episode is worth examining closely because it goes a long way towards explaining the relative oblivion from which Epstein and his work have subsequently suffered.

Guillaume Apollinaire coined the word *surréalisme* in a March 1917 letter to poet Paul Dermée, and soon used it in print in a note about Cocteau's ballet *Parade* in May 1917, before including it in the preface to his own play *Les Mamelles de Tirésias* in June 1917. While in March, he uses 'surrealism' as synonym with supernaturalism, something outside of reality, by June it acquires the meaning of prosthetic technology: 'Lorsque l'homme a voulu imiter la marche, il a créé la roue qui ne ressemble pas à une jambe. Il a fait ainsi du surréalisme

---

universe, with an originality that makes of this interpretation not a mere reflection or copy of the conceptions of the organic mother-mind, but really a differently individualized system, in part independent, that contains the germinal development of a philosophy so distant from common opinions that we might well call it an anti-philosophy' (*ibid.*: 310).

6 Mário de Andrade, for instance, closely engaged with and appropriated Epstein's theses in 'Le Phénomène littéraire'; see Suárez and Tomlins (2000: 48–50).

sans le savoir' ['When man tried to imitate walking, he created the wheel which does not resemble a leg. Hence he applied surrealism without knowing it'] (Apollinaire, 1972: 94). Apollinaire points here to a mode of non-mimetic analogy, like the metaphor, aiming to 'revenir à la nature elle-même, mais sans l'imiter comme font les photographes' ['go back to nature itself, but without imitating it like photographers do'] (*ibid.*). This characterization already wavers around the cinematic, by embracing the kinetics of mechanical movement but rejecting the mimetic fixity of photographic reproduction. In May, correcting Cocteau's ironically calling *Parade* 'un ballet réaliste', Apollinaire wrote: 'De cette alliance nouvelle, car jusqu'ici les décors et les costumes d'une part, la chorégraphie d'autre part, n'avaient entre eux qu'un lien factice, il est résulté, dans Parade, une sorte de sur-réalisme' ['From this new alliance, since until now sets and costumes on the one hand, choreography on the other, had only a fictitious link, there results, in *Parade*, a kind of sur-realism'] (1991: 865–6; Albright, 2004: 320–1). Here surrealism is equated with a *Gesamtkunstwerke*, a collaborative total work of art. Yet what binds Picasso's sets and costumes, Satie's music and Diaghilev's choreography was the libretto of Cocteau, which he expressly wrote with cinema in mind. For instance, one main character is the 'Young American Girl', likely named after movie credits, who is said to have directed 'a 50,000 metre-long movie', and parodies on stage the filmic adventures of Pearl White and Elaine. Cocteau even had the dancer, Maria Chabelska, imitate Chaplin's walk and mimic the flickering of movie projections. Now, Apollinaire would have good reasons to equate surrealism with film, since he was at that time co-writing and selling a movie scenario, *La Bréhatine*. In November 1917 he gave a famous talk, 'L'Esprit nouveau et les poètes' calling on poets to embrace cinema as modernity's new 'book of images'.[7] Breton, tasked with organizing poetry readings around that talk, was horrified by its nationalism and Germanophobia, as well as its recourse to 'science' that is, film- and phonograph-aided poetry (1999: 452–3). Apollinaire died a few months later, leaving the exact meaning of the word *surréalisme* tantalizingly unsettled.

For a few years the word *surréalisme* remained peripheral to Breton, since dada had come on the scene and he allied himself with

---

7 Apollinaire (1991: 941–54 (942); 1972: 227–37). In a letter to Maurice Raynal, Apollinaire mentions the scenario first, then tells of his coining the term 'surrealism' (Frutkin, 1998: 201).

Tzara. Only in late 1922, after that collaboration fizzled, did he reclaim the word surrealism, defining it as 'automatisme psychique' ['psychic automatism'] (Breton, 1988: 274). However, by then, Paul Dermée and Jean Epstein had both recuperated Apollinaire's term and intentions, using it to denote both technological and psychic automatism. In 1920, Dermée writes the following:

> Cette activité de second plan devenue autonome et fonctionnant à l'aveugle en l'absence de toute volonté consciente, voilà ce qu'on appelle de l'automatisme'. (1920: 32)
>
> Nous rêvons, le kaléidoscope d'images, de sensations, et de sentiments fonctionne, le film se déroule, varié et captivant et toute la richesse profonde de la vie intérieure traverse la conscience en un vaste courant: notre âme s'emplit d'une mélodie spontanée, c'est le 'flux lyrique' qui chante! (*ibid.*: 34)
>
> Quant aux images, il faut les prendre avec grand soin, en évitant qu'elles donnent aux objets une existence dans le monde extérieur. Rien, en effet, ne doit faire sortir le lecteur de son moi profond. Donc, pas d'images réalisables par la plastique: mais leur *surréalisme*. (*ibid.*: 37)[8]

Dermée not only outlines four years before Breton the twofold definition of surrealism the latter will promulgate – psychic automatism giving rise to a new register of images – but he does so by expressly invoking the cinema apparatus throughout, extending Apollinaire's kinetic anti-mimetism towards the virtuality of film as another way of avoiding static representation.

A year after Dermée, Epstein called on 'cinema and poetry to superimpose their esthetics', in *La Poésie d'aujourd'hui* (1921a: 170). In this book's key chapter on what he terms 'Metaphor-Thought' we read the following:

---

8 'This background activity that became autonomous and functions blindly without the use of conscious will, this is what we call "automatism"'. / 'We dream, kaleidoscope of images; sensations and emotions function. The film unfolds, varied and captivating and the whole richness of inner life traverses consciousness as a broad current: our soul fills up with a spontaneous melody, it is the lyrical flux that sings!' / 'As for images, they must be handled with great care, by preventing them from giving to objects an existence in the exterior world. For nothing must make the reader come out of his deep self. Thus no images realizable through plastic means: only their *surrealism*'.

Une idée qu'on croyait usée, vide et vieillie, projetée contre une autre aussi finie, et du choc de ces décrépitudes naît une jeune étincelle. L'image doit être brusque sous peine de ne pas être ... Ces rapprochements ne sont pas un simple jeu. (*ibid.*: 132)

on faisait poser la réalité comme chez un photographe de village; aujourd'hui la métaphore est instantanée. (*ibid.*: 134)

Le ralentisseur P. F. au cinéma découvre ce que le cinéma ordinaire ne savait pas voir ... C'est un peu voisin de ce que Guillaume Apollinaire appelait surréalisme, et la compréhension cinématographique est de lui ... L'analogie enjambe les distances et les espèces. (*ibid.*: 135)⁹

Here Epstein propounds as surrealism: (1) a kind of explosive montage or juxtaposition of ideas, compared to a spark and crossing long distances; (2) the overcoming of photographic realism; (3) slow motion as making strange ordinary reality. His book was published in April 1921 by La Sirène, a well-established publisher. In May 1921, Breton wrote the following about the first Max Ernst exhibition in France:

l'écriture automatique apparue à la fin du XIXe siècle est une véritable photographie de la pensée. (1988: 245)

Mais la faculté merveilleuse, sans sortir du champ de notre expérience, d'atteindre deux réalités distantes et de leur rapprochement de tirer une étincelle... (*ibid.*: 245–6)

On sait aujourd'hui, grâce au cinéma, le moyen de faire *arriver* une locomotive sur un tableau. A mesure que se généralise l'emploi des appareils ralentisseur et accélérateur, qu'on s'habitue à voir jaillir des chênes et planer des antilopes, on pressent avec une émotion extrême ce que peuvent être ces temps locaux dont on entend parler. (*ibid.*: 246)

[Ernst] projette sous nos yeux le film le plus captivant du monde... tout en éclairant au plus profond ... notre vie intérieure ... (*ibid.*)¹⁰

---

9 'An idea thought to be used up, empty and old, is projected against another just as finished; and from the shock of their decrepitude a young spark is born ... Such juxtapositions are not a simple game.' / 'reality was made to pose as for a village photographer; today metaphor is instantaneous'. / 'The slow motion device of cinema uncovers what ordinary cinema could not see ... This is close to what Guillaume Apollinaire called surrealism, and the cinematographic comparison is his ... Analogy crosses distances and species'.

10 'automatic writing which emerged at the end of the nineteenth century is a true photography of thought'. / 'But the marvellous faculty, without leaving the field

The similarities of Breton's text with Epstein's passage through the same five pivotal and highly specific terms – photograph[i]e, étincelle, distan[ce], rapprochement, ralentissement – suggests to me a direct borrowing. What's more, as Breton is talking about collages and paintings, he puts Epstein's robust cinematic terms under the erasure of tropes: the more Breton refers to cinema, the more insubstantial and metaphorical it becomes. By the time he writes *Le Manifeste du surréalisme* in 1924, poetry has been purged of the model of cinema, on the one hand, and the cinema of the first narrative avant-garde of Gance, L'Herbier, Epstein, and Dulac has been frozen out of surrealism, on the other. Either way, Breton never acknowledged Epstein or his work, erasing his contribution to surrealism the same way he erased that of Apollinaire and Dermée. (Breton's 1921 piece on Ernst may have also borrowed from Dermée's 1920 text, since the expressions 'film ... captivant' and 'vie intérieure' appear in both within the same paragraph.)

From the mid-1920s until World War Two, Epstein's influence appeared to have progressively dwindled.[11] The arrival of sound marked the end of his more daring silent fiction, and the few commercial fiction films he directed gave no more signs of the experimentalism for which he was renowned – until *Le Tempestaire* (1947). After the Liberation, when he began collaborating with IDHEC and the Institut de Filmologie, both set up during the years 1946–47, and thanks to the intercession of Marie now collaborating closely with Langlois at the Cinémathèque, his film work enjoyed a modicum of renewed interest. The article he published in *Les Temps Modernes* attests to it: one of its editors, Maurice Merleau-Ponty gave a very Epsteinian conference at IDHEC in 1945 on cinema, philosophy, and poetry, and he was likely behind the decision to publish this article (rather than Sartre!). After this swansong, however, Epstein progressively slipped

---

of our experience, of reaching two distant realities and from their juxtaposition, generating a spark ...' / 'We know today, thanks to cinema, how to make a locomotive *arrive* upon a painting. The more we generalize the use of slow motion [*ralentisseur*] and accelerating devices, the more we get used to seeing oaks unfold and antelopes fly, the more we foresee with extreme emotion what might be these local times we hear about ...' / [Ernst] projects for our eyes the most captivating film in the world ... while throwing light on the depths ... of our inner life ...'

11 Epstein is mentioned by poets on the margins of surrealism such as Henri Michaux, Antonin Artaud, and Jean Cocteau; see Bellour (2001).

out of the post-war intellectual landscape and his writings and philosophy fell into critical oblivion until his death in 1953.

Still, his film work and thought began almost immediately percolating throughout the transformations of French cinema in the 1950s and early 1960s. It began when the *Cahiers du cinéma* dedicated a commemorative issue to his work in June 1953. Later in the year, a number of filmmakers that included Alain Resnais, Chris Marker, Agnès Varda, and Alexandre Astruc formed *Le Groupe des trente* meant to rescue the short film. Their manifesto read:

> Next to the novel and other extensive works, there is the poem, the short story, or the essay, which often plays the role of a hothouse; it has the function of revitalizing a field with the contribution of fresh blood, since an art that ceases to change is a dead art. (Alter, 2006: 14)

Epstein 22-minute-long masterpiece *Le Tempestaire* was, as we've seen, likely on Marker's mind. A few years later, Truffaut would characterize the work of these filmmakers – later known as the Left Bank group – as the 'Delluc branch' by comparison to the New Wave's Lumière branch, and the first name he mentioned was Epstein's (*ibid.*: 13).

In the 1950s, Edgar Morin, a young anthropologist of Western culture who had worked at the Institut de Filmologie, published a far-reaching analysis of the cognitive embeddedness of cinema in contemporary culture (1957). In *Cinema, or the Imaginary Man* (2005a), Morin deepened the Epsteinian thesis that modes of being-in-the-world in the twentieth century co-evolved at the contact of the imaginary realms opened by film as medium, and the impact of half a century of transformative movie-viewing. Underneath the book's vast erudition about the history and evolution of cinema and film thought, it is clear that Epstein is the main tutelary figure. This prescient work merging cognitive, psychological, and cultural perspectives, was at cross-purpose with the existentialist phenomenology in vogue in the 1950s, and with the rise of Bazin as France's main thinker of cinema. Largely neglected then, *Cinema, or the Imaginary Man* is now receiving renewed critical attention, especially after it was translated into English (2005a). Morin followed suit with a second work, *The Stars* (2005b), which also takes up where Epstein had left off with his feverish and lyrical 'love' in *Bonjour Cinéma* for silent stars such as Sessue Hayakawa, Charlie Chaplin, and Alla Nazimova. Of course, the dark social affects and eroticism of these stars was now replaced by the pulp sex appeal of Brigitte Bardot's role in Roger Vadim's *Et Dieu créa la femme* (1956). And while Epstein loved silent film actors for the singular eloquence of their bodily affects, the new star-system produced mostly models for commercial emulation.

In spite of the marked interest by a few film theoreticians such as Siegfried Kracauer, who points out repeatedly in his *Theory of Film: The Redemption of Physical Reality* (1960), that Epstein's movies anticipate aspects of neo-realism, the 1960s were unfavourable to Epstein's philosophy of the cinema. Retrospectives in the US and Italy did maintain a historical attention to Epstein's film œuvre, but structuralism and post-structuralism made the recovery of Epstein's thought unlikely, even though his thinking about language prolongs that of Saussure, and his attack on Cartesianism announces those of Foucault and Derrida. Once apparatus theory developed in the 1970s, concepts such as *photogénie* would be looked upon as unredeemably mystical if not guilty of sheer mystification. Jean-Luc Godard acknowledged later in his *Histoire(s) de cinema* the importance of Epstein: the book version of that film, mixing lines in verse and movie frames, is in fact an unmistakable homage to *Bonjour cinéma*.[12] Yet in 1958 he wrote desultorily that Epstein's aesthetic was simply 'périmée' – obsolete.[13]

The recovery of Epstein's thought began around the time the Brighton Conference (1978) brought the focus of cinema studies back to the silent period. The publication of Epstein's collected *Écrits* in two volumes (1974, 1976) a few years before, was certainly part of the impetus to re-evaluate the silent era. In the US, Richard Abel gave a detailed analysis of key French narrative films between 1915–29, and he indicates that Marie Epstein showed him the films of her brother around 1976 (1984: xi). Stuart Liebman subsequently wrote the first analysis of Epstein's early film theory for a Ph.D. dissertation (1980), while in France Noureddine Ghali embarked in 1984 on an ambitious analysis of French avant-garde theory and criticism, revealing the broad critical currents from which, in part, sprung Epstein's work. Finally, Richard Abel published in 1988 a large selection of key articles and essays on cinema from 1907 to 1929 in two volumes (nine articles are by Epstein), with over 160 pages of introductory material that represents a monograph of its own.

---

12 Godard (1998); Epstein is mentioned in 1: 120–1, 275; 3: 133, 169; 4: 43, 184.
13 See Laurent Le Forestier, 'Jean Epstein: son influence sur les cinéastes', at: www.bifi.fr/public/ap/article.php?id=145 (consulted 20/08/2011).

Thus through the 1980s, rather paradoxically, Epstein's utopian philosophy was all at once gathering dust in the sub-basement of the history of French thought, and enjoying a critical reappraisal, though largely within the confine of silent-film studies. Coincidentally, this was at the very time Gilles Deleuze set out to give a multi-year seminar on cinema (autumn 1981 to the beginning of 1985), which resulted in his monumental two-volume *Cinéma*, with *L'Image-mouvement* (1983) and *L'Image-temps* (1985), arguably the defining work for the reinvented notion of a philosophy of the cinema. Epstein is very present in this work, first and foremost through the many references to the two-volume *Écrits*, whose breadth and importance Deleuze was manifestly among the first to understand fully. For instance, when he defines the movement-image that becomes for him the essential emblem of silent cinema as a whole, he writes that 'Epstein has the most deeply and poetically extracted this nature of the shot [*plan*] as pure movement' (1986: 23).

But I would argue that, in spite of numerous citations, Epstein is very much the absent figure in Deleuze's two *Cinema* books. The concluding discussion about what a philosophy of the cinema ought to be takes up Epstein's reflection in *L'Intelligence d'une machine* but fails to mention it. This is not the place for an in-depth analysis of Deleuze's oblique reliance on Epstein in the *Cinema* books and beyond. But let me give another example and suggest a reason for Deleuze's obliquity. In order to contrast the classical tradition of the movement-image based on action–actuality, with the new time-image based on virtuality, Deleuze develops his famous model of the crystal. He indicates that it is derived from Guattari while it constitutes an adaptation of Bergson's dyad actual–virtual (1989: 92, 110). The illustrative films he lists tend to include glass objects, in particular a snow-globe (*Citizen Kane* – Deleuze calls it 'petite boule de verre', in the French edition), mirrors (*The Lady of Shanghai*) and windows, as well as figures of circularity (the merry-go-round in *Lola Montès*) (*ibid.*: 68–75). The formula Deleuze proposes for the time-crystal is that of 'the germ and the mirror', that is, a process of growth juxtaposed to a bifurcated mimetic image. By now, we are familiar enough with Epstein's concepts, films, and writings to recognize in Deleuze's instantiations of the time-crystal the gamut of Epsteinian preoccupations. Mirrors are at the centre of *Le Miroir à trois faces* (a film Deleuze does not cite), and self-mirroring informs the beginning section of *Le Cinématographe vu de l'Etna*. The glass ball is the nexus of *Le Tempestaire* (a film Deleuze does not cite either), and the merry-go-round has become a kind of signature of Epsteinian quick editing in *Cœur fidèle* (to which he does refer). More crucially, the *philosophical importance* of the growth of crystals and wheat germs captured in accelerated motion on film lies at the very core of Epstein's (and Dulac's) consideration of cinema's mobility and alternative temporality. We thus begin to suspect that Deleuze's time-crystal encapsulates the essence of Epstein's philosophy and film work, and puts it paradoxically to use during the time when Epstein was in eclipse (1945–80). Or, to put it another way, Epstein's cinema and his philosophy of the cinema have, according to Deleuze's tacit proposal, become subsumed within post-war films as their latent principle of composition. Hence, when Deleuze defines the time–image of post-war cinema, his formulation appears to describe Madeline's animated portrait in *La Chute de la maison Usher* (to which he refers elsewhere in the *Cinema* books):

> A two-sided image, actual *and* virtual is formed. It is as if an image in a mirror, a photograph, a postcard, came to life, assumed independence and passed into the actual, even if it meant that the actual image returned into the mirror and resumed its place in the postcard or photo, following a double movement of liberation and capture. (*ibid.*: 68)

This summarizes exactly the dilemma of Roderick Usher and the way Epstein animates Madeline's portrait with superimposed footage before immobilizing it again. Deleuze uses a palimpsestic method consisting in transforming actual movies into virtual concepts that structure later movies. 'What we see in the crystal is always the teeming of life, of time, in their doubling or their differentiation' (*ibid.*: 121). Is this not again a description of the key moment in *Le Tempestaire*, when the storm appears in the crystal ball of the storm-tamer? The question might then be to what extent exactly Deleuze distilled Epstein's entire philosophy of cinema, substance, time, and language into some of the conceptual innovations of the *Cinéma* books.

Epstein's notion of the 'plan intellectuel' or 'plan unique' – an expression that rests on the double denotation of 'plan' meaning both 'a plane' *pace* Spinoza, and 'a shot' when applied to cinema – has certainly found its way into Deleuze's concept of 'the plane of immanence'. Epstein provides the following definition in *La Poésie d'aujourd'hui* on the heels of a poem by Aragon: 'Ainsi il apparaît nettement que la littérature moderne admet un seul plan intellectuel. Tout: pensée et acte, idée et sensation, aujourd'hui et demain et hier, prévisions et certitudes et souvenirs, tout est projeté ensemble, côte à côte, sur le même carré d'écran.'[14] To be sure this echoes Simultaneism, although Epstein stipulates that it was wishful thinking to want to flatten out time into a single moment (1921c: 61). More striking is the fact that the cinema apparatus provides here the *modus operandi* for the new philosophy that organizes modernist aesthetics. A movie, made of disparate cuts and shots, exists nonetheless seemingly on the same imaginary 'plane' in which all its footage miraculously coheres. Together with the imaginary world of the movie, Epstein's unique plane refracts Spinoza's monism which considers that everything is linked to everything else – is of the same ultimate substance – in particular, for Epstein, in the case of language, images, and reality. Hence in *La Lyrosophie*, Epstein connects the unique plane with the way the Kabbalah bestows on individual Hebrew letters an efficient power of association with ideas and objects in the real world (1922b: 76). Spinoza, cinema, and the Kabbalah converge. In Deleuze and Guattari, the 'plane of immanence' comprises a similar convergence. They define it as 'an unlimited One-All, an "Omnitudo" that includes all the concepts on one and the same plane. It is a table, a plateau, or a slice ...' (Guattari and Deleuze, 1996: 35). Broad as these last three terms are, they refer *in nuce* to cinema: the editing table (*une table*), the shooting set (*un plateau*), and the cut (*une coupe*). Deleuze and Guattari's formulations come very close to Epstein's: 'The plane of immanence is not a concept that is or can be thought but rather the image of thought, the image thought gives itself of what it means to think, to make use of thought, to find one's bearings in thought' (*ibid.*: 37). This image of thought, for them, requires 'infinite movement or the movement of the infinite' (*ibid.*), while 'the plane of immanence is always single' (*ibid.*: 39). The resemblance between Epstein's film-like 'unique intellectual plane' and Deleuze and Guattari's single 'plane of immanence' could of course be explained away through Spinoza: let's recall that Gance called Epstein 'a young Spinoza', and Deleuze and

---

14 'Hence it appears clearly that modern literature accepts a single intellectual plane. Everything: thought and action, idea and sensation, today and tomorrow and yesterday, forecasts and certainties and memories, everything is projected together, side by side, upon the same square of screen' (1921a: 144–5).

Guattari call Spinoza 'the infinite becoming-philosopher' (*ibid.*: 60). But it might be indeed Epstein's interest in both Spinoza and cinema that proved the determining factor for Deleuze.

The case is much more straightforward in the philosophy of politics and aesthetics of another philosopher who arrived on the scene in the 1980s: Jacques Rancière. He addresses Epstein head-on (together with Deleuze and Jean-Luc Godard) in his recent collection of essays *Film Fables* (2006). This book follows the general thesis he has cultivated for many years called 'the aesthetic regime of the arts', whereby, he argues, ruptures in aesthetics are not between classicism, modernism, and postmodernism (all terms he rejects), but between a regime where each art was seen as high craft in a given medium of representation, 'the representative regime', and a new regime, 'the aesthetic regime of the arts' in which art became unified in its search for specificity, and radically separated from other activities of production. For Rancière, this realignment closely corresponds to the rise of democratic states in the second half of the nineteenth century, and to a host of secondary changes about classes, language, and science. Rancière is adamant that the turn towards the aesthetic regime of the arts and democracy occurred for epistemic reasons, not at all as a result of modernization and technology. Cinema thus represents for him a major challenge because he must neutralize its possible role in suggesting, hastening, or generalizing the aesthetic regime of the arts. Accordingly, the main thesis of *Film Fables* is that:

> Cinema literalizes a secular idea of art in the same stroke that it actualizes the refutation of that idea: it is both the art of the afterwards that emerges from the Romantic de-figuration of stories, and the art that returns the work of de-figuration to classical imitation. (*ibid.*: 11)

So cinema is a 'thwarted fable' because 'at the end of the day, the whole logic of representative art finds itself restored, piece by piece, by this machine' (*ibid.*: 10). Rather than being on the side of art's new autonomy in searching for its medium specificity, cinema ends up bringing back representation and imitation, the key notions in the obsolete regime of art. Although we have seen the originality of Epstein's avant-garde melodramas, for Rancière the development of medium specificity is simply pre-empted by the very recourse to the melodramatic frame, and he would, for instance, deny any truly innovative status to *Coeur fidèle*.

Rancière opens the book with an epigraph of Epstein – who is his first and clearly most important target. Epstein's philosophy is crucial to the overall argument of Rancière since for the latter, 'Deleuze and Godard both repeat Jean Epstein's dramaturgy, they both extract, after the fact, the original essence of the cinematographic art from the plots the art of cinema shares with the old art of telling stories' (ibid.: 6). Rancière asserts that while Epstein celebrated the camera-eye for disclosing a unity with things that is at once the old unity restored and a new gaze on reality mediated by technics, in point of fact he could do so only because of the facilitation of narratives, in the interstices of which pure moments of 'photogénie' can take place. In other words, narrative is necessary as the backdrop against which appears, 'the solid base of the means specific to [the technical apparatus]' (ibid.: 4). Or to put it more plainly:

> Epstein extracts the theoretical and poetical fable that describes the original power of the cinema from the body of another fable, from which he erased the traditional narrative aspect in order to create another dramaturgy, another system of expectations, actions, and states of being. (ibid.: 5)

For instance, Rancière would consider that Epstein translates Poe's grotesque fetishistic bonds – themselves a compromise formation resulting from the failure of Romanticism's dream of a perfect fusion (in love and knowledge, see Hegel) – into the very essence of cinema: *photogénie*. The problem, for Rancière, is that cinema as an art then remains parasitical of narrative, and its break with the previous regimes must be considered incomplete. Moreover, he asserts, the new dramaturgy of Epstein's *photogénie* tacitly relies on the idea of the transformation of energy that inspired the likes of Marinetti (whom Epstein despised), Khlebnikov, Cendrars, Delaunay, Loïe Fuller, *et al.* (ibid.: 4). He adds that all of them indeed recycled ideas already present in the theatre of Maeterlinck (ibid.: 7), showing again that literature precedes and informs any novelty claimed by cinema as an apparatus.

It is both a brilliant reading and a masterful misreading. Yes, Epstein relies on narrative and nineteenth-century literature to generate *situations*, and yes, it is undeniable that situations rely on the fictive efficacy of the narrative background that is temporarily suspended. But for all that, photogenic situations cannot simply be reduced to an old faith in narrative and representation. And, no, *photogénie* does not celebrate vitalism as part of modernity's 'great ode to energy' (ibid.: 3), since it rests on messy affects from the subconscious and the dysfunctions of coenaesthesis, best revealed in states of *fatigue*. Like Turvey, Rancière errs by thinking Epstein is a Bergsonian. His analyses remain too macroscopic, selective, and overdetermined by a prior thesis. His view of Epstein's philosophy is much too narrow since his argument relies mostly on the epiphanies of *Bonjour cinéma*. He is unaware of Epstein's documentary work during the Front Populaire era, which would complicate his argument by forcing him to rethink the interconnection of residual narrative with the focus on the under-represented demos whom Rancière champions. Finally, Rancière is unfamiliar enough with the breadth of Epstein's written œuvre, that he fails to mention that Epstein considers, in *La Poésie d'aujourd'hui*, '*Le Phénomène littéraire*', and *La Lyrosophie*, that literature was much more profoundly altered by cinema than cinema was informed by the stories it drew from literature. Ultimately, Rancière dismisses the notion of 'the intelligence of a machine' because he is unwilling to recognize a part of agency to 'the glass eye' of cinema in the mutations of aesthetics at the end of the nineteenth century. His readings thus belie an old-fashioned humanism that seeks – as did Bergson's – to leave the human immune from the sensorial, cognitive, and prosthetic transformations brought about by technology.

There are, to conclude this chapter, two broad kinds of contemporary reading of Epstein's incipient anti-philosophy. Thinkers such as Jacques Rancière and Malcolm Turvey condemn Epstein on account of his deluded technophilia, medium fetishism, and epistemological naïveté, for the former, and because of his supposed perceptual errors and utopian flaunting of rational categories for the latter. Although Epstein's thought is indeed technophilic, fetishistic, utopian, and paralogical, Rancière and Turvey prosecute their case in an exceedingly narrow way in terms of the corpus of both his writings and films, and they are profoundly mistaken about the place of Bergson in his thought. Epstein's work also partakes of the social ethics of the 'demos', by giving the under-represented classes some means of self-representation – in the Breton films most clearly. It is also committed to the sensorial realism that, as Rancière himself affirms, is the basis of the political (via the 'sensible'). Ultimately, it is clear that Turvey and Rancière have admired Epstein's work at some point, but now find a common need for burning their youthful idol: this appears to taint their analyses.

Fortunately, on the other side, we find many more thinkers and critics who are able to recognize that some of Epstein's writings and films may well display utopian excesses, technophilic biases, even at times shoddy argumentation, without feeling compelled to use this as an alibi for dismantling his imaginative, generous, emancipating, and highly inspiring œuvre. Jean-Luc Godard, Jacques Aumont, and Tom Gunning, as we have seen, have been vocal advocates of Epstein since at least the mid-1990s. It is fair to say that the last two generations of film critics and theoreticians in France – Raymond Bellour, Jean-Marie Schefer, Érik Bullot, Alain Fleischer, and Nicole Brenez, to cite a few – and somewhat less generally elsewhere in Europe – Francesco Casetti, for instance – have been decisively influenced by Epstein, and are much better informed about his work than are Rancière and Turvey.[15] What these thinkers have in common is that they consider Epstein prescient in understanding cinema as a powerful affect-making apparatus that inflects the social sphere as well as all of the arts, and is ideally suited to reveal the broad range of epistemic mutations that is synonymous with modernity. In this regard, it is perhaps not so surprising that Epstein's name should pop up in the work of an improbable thinker whose project is a vast symptomatology of modernity: Slavoj Žižek.[16]

References

Abel, Richard (1984), *French Cinema: The First Wave, 1915–1929*, Princeton: Princeton University Press.
— (ed.) (1988a), *French Film Theory and Criticism*, vol. 1, 1909–29, Princeton: Princeton University Press.
— (ed.) (1988b), *French Film Theory and Criticism*, vol. 2, 1929–39, Princeton: Princeton University Press.

15 For some of these thinkers and critics, Epstein's influence runs deeper than the few direct references to his work. This is true for example of Bellour (1999), Scheffer (1997), and Fleischer (2009), in which Epstein is omnipresent but very much in filigree. This may be compared to Aumont (2002), Brenez (1998), Casetti (2005), Albera (2005), and Bullot (2009), which are all explicitly in dialogue with Epstein's theories and films.
16 See Žižek (2002: xxxii): 'Scopic drive ... is making oneself visible to the Other's gaze, which functions here as *objet petit a*, best exemplified by the dead man's empty eye-sockets: "The faces of the dead have but a gaze and no eyes".' This is a quote from a rather obscure passage of Epstein's writings (1974: 199).

— (ed.) (2005), 'Newsreels', *Encyclopedia of Early Cinema*, London and New York: Routledge, 477–8.
Alain (Émile Chartier) (1916), *Éléments de philosophie*, Paris: Gallimard.
Albera, François (2005), *L'Avant-garde au cinéma*, Paris: Nathan.
Albright, D. (ed.) (2004), Guillaume Apollinaire, 'Program Notes for Parade' (1917), in Daniel Albright (ed.), *Modernism and Music: An Anthology of Sources*, Chicago: University of Chicago Press, 320–1.
Alter, Nora M. (2006), *Chris Marker*, Urbana-Champaign: University of Illinois Press.
Apollinaire, Guillaume (1971) 'The New Spirit and the Poets', *Selected Writings of Guillaume Apollinaire*, Roger Shattuck (trans.), New York: New Directions, 227–37.
— (1972), *L'Enchanteur pourrissant*, suivi de *Les Mamelles de Tirésias* et de *Couleur de Temps*, Paris: Gallimard, 1972.
— (1991) 'Parade', *Œuvres en prose complètes*, vol. 2, Paris: Gallimard, 865–6.
Aumont, Jacques (ed.) (1998), 'Cinégénie, ou la machine à re-monter le temps', in Jacques Aumont (ed.), *Jean Epstein: cinéaste, poète, philosophe*, Paris: La Cinémathèque française, 87–108.
— (2002), *Les Théories des cinéastes*, Paris: Nathan.
Bellour, Raymond (1999), *L'Entre-Images 2: Mots, Images*, Paris: POL.
— (2001), 'Jean Epstein chez Henri Michaux', in Nicole Brenez and Christian Lebrat (eds), *Jeune, pure et dure! Une histoire du cinéma d'avant-garde et expérimental en France*, Paris: La Cinémathèque française, 430.
Brenez, Nicole (1998), *De la figure en général et du corps en particulier*, Paris: De Boeck Université.
Breton, André (1988), *Œuvres*, vol. 1, Paris: Gallimard.
— (1999), *Œuvres*, vol. 3, Paris: Gallimard.
Bullot, Érik (2009) *Renversements 1: notes sur le cinéma*, Paris: Paris expérimental.
Casetti, Francesco (2005), *Eye of the Century: Film, Experience, Modernity*, New York: Columbia University Press.
Deleuze, Gilles (1986), *Cinema 1: The Movement-Image*, Hugh Tomlinson and Barbara Habberjam (trans.), Minneapolis: University of Minnesota Press.
— (1989), *Cinema 2: The Time-Image*, Hugh Tomlinson and Robert Galeta (trans.), Minneapolis: University of Minnesota Press.
Delluc, Louis (1919), *Cinéma & cie: les confidences d'un spectateur*, Paris: Bernard Grasset.
— (1920a), *Charlot*, Paris: Éditions Maurice de Brunoff.
— (1920b), *Photogénie*, Paris: Éditions Maurice de Brunoff.
Dermée, Paul (1920) 'Découverte du lyrisme', *L'Esprit Nouveau* 1 (October), 29–37.
Diamant-Berger, Henri (1919), *Cinéma*, Paris: La Renaissance du livre.
Epstein, Jean (1921a), *La Poésie d'aujourd'hui, un nouvel état d'intelligence*, Paris: Éditions de la Sirène.
— (1921b), *Bonjour cinéma*, Paris: Éditions de la Sirène.
— (1921c), 'Le Phénomène littéraire', in Aumont (ed.), *Jean Epstein*, 39–85.
— (1922a), *La Lyrosophie*, Paris: Éditions de la Sirène.
— (1922b), 'Nous Kabbalistes', in Aumont (ed.), *Jean Epstein*, 119–24.
— (1922c), 'Freud ou le nick-cartérianisme en psychologie', in Aumont (ed.), *Jean Epstein*, 139–46.

— (1974), *Écrits sur le cinéma*, vol. 1, Paris: Éditions Seghers.
— (1976), *Écrits sur le cinéma*, vol. 2, Paris: Éditions Seghers.
Fleischer, Alain (2009), *L'Empreinte et le tremblement*, Paris: Galaade.
Frutkin, Mark (1998), *Atmospheres Apollinaire*, Vancouver: Beach Holme.
Gauthier, Christophe (1999), *La Passion du cinéma: cinéphiles, ciné-clubs et salles spécialisées à Paris de 1920 à 1929*, Paris: AFRHC.
Ghali, Noureddine (1995), *L'Avant-garde cinématographique en France dans les années vingt: idées, conceptions, théories*, Paris: Paris expérimental.
Godard, Jean-Luc (1998), *Histoire(s) du cinéma*, Paris: Gallimard/Gaumont.
Gourmont, Remy de (1903), *Physique de l'amour: essai sur l'instinct sexuel*, Paris: Le Mercure de France.
Guattari, Felix and Gilles Deleuze (1996), *What Is Philosophy?* New York: Columbia University Press.
Kracauer, Siegfried (1960), *Theory of Film: The Redemption of Physical Reality*, New York: Oxford University Press.
Liebman, Stuart (1980), 'Jean Epstein's early film theory, 1920–1922', Ph.D. dissertation, New York University.
Merleau-Ponty, Maurice (1964), *Le Visible et l'invisible*, Paris: Gallimard.
Morin, Edgar (1956), *Le Cinéma, ou l'homme imaginaire*, Paris: Minuit, 1956.
— (1957), *Les Stars*, Paris: Minuit, 1957.
— (2005a), *The Cinema, or the Imaginary Man*, Lorraine Mortimer (trans.), Minneapolis: University of Minnesota Press.
— (2005b), *The Stars*, Richard Howard and Lorraine Mortimer (trans.), Minneapolis: University of Minnesota Press.
Rancière, Jacques (2006), *Film Fables*, Emiliano Battista (trans.), Oxford: Berg.
Scheffer, Jean-Louis (1997), *L'Homme ordinaire du cinéma*, Paris: Cahiers du cinéma/Gallimard.
Schlegel, Friedrich (1991), *Philosophical Fragments*, Peter Firchow (trans.), Minneapolis: University of Minnesota Press.
Suárez, José I. and Jack E. Tomlins (2000), *Mário de Andrade: The Creative Works*, Cranbury: Associate University Presses.
Thouvenel, Éric (2010), 'A toute intelligence je préfère la mienne': quand Jean Epstein lisait Gaston Bachelard', *1895* 62 (December), 53–75.
Tognolotti, Chiara (2005), 'L'alcool, le cinéma et le philosophe: l'influence de Friedrich Nietzsche sur la théorie cinématographique de Jean Epstein', *1895* 46 (June) 37–53.
Turvey, Malcolm (2008), *Doubting Vision: Film and the Revelationist Tradition*, Oxford: Oxford University Press.
— (2009) 'Epstein, Bergson, and Vision', in Temenuga Trifonova (ed.), *European Film Philosophy*, New York: Routledge, 93–107.
Wall-Romana, Christophe (2012), *Cinepoetry: Imaginary Cinemas in French Poetry*, Fordham, Fordham University Press.
Žižek, Slavoj (2002), *For They Know Not What They Do: Enjoyment as a Political Factor*, 2nd edn, London: Verso.

Conclusion: Epstein as pioneer of corporeal cinema

Epstein's influence on specific filmmakers and films is harder to trace, and certainly more diffuse, than the impact of his philosophy and *photogénie* on the development of film theory and philosophies of cinema. In Luis Buñuel and Salvador Dalí's *Un Chien Andalou* (1929), for instance, there is a short sequence in which the body of the main protagonist is carried through a clearing by six men wearing hats (Talens, 1993: photogram no. 308). It includes an MS of the procession as it walks towards the hand-held camera. This shot undoubtedly mimics the same set-up in the coffin-carrying sequence of *La Chute de la maison Usher*, for which Buñuel served as Epstein's assistant. Similarly, in Jean Cocteau's *Le Sang d'un poète* (1930), 30 seconds after the beginning of the fourth episode, Cocteau inserts a very short (less than one second long) but critical MCU of Dargelos's face out of focus, while the background is in focus. This device again recalls the key shots of Roderick's out-of-focus face in CU with the background in focus. While neither Buñuel nor Cocteau has claimed Epstein as a major influence, it is clear that his aesthetic choices pervade some of theirs, as a pre-eminent Cocteau critic confirms (Williams, 2006: 48). When Hitchcock, 'the master of suspense', explains the genealogy of his interest in suspense, he points both to Poe and to Epstein's film *La Chute de la maison Usher* (Gottlieb, 1995: 144). Yet both Poe and Epstein, as we have seen, favour a suspension or delay in the entire dramatic action, a 'drame en suspens' as Epstein puts it in *Bonjour cinéma*, rather than a tension or charge regarding the narrative resolution of a scene or episode. It then appears that Hitchcock redirected Epstein's notion of 'suspens' to craft a new sub-genre which entered common parlance via expressions such as 'suspense story' and 'suspense novels' in the 1950s, according to the *OED*. But then again, Tom Gunning reminds us that the 'original "master of suspense"' was D.W. Griffith – and certainly Epstein himself was beholden to Griffith for this overall sense of rhythm of his filmic œuvre (1993: 27).

There are, however, documented cases allowing us to affirm a direct genealogy. This is the case with Jean Vigo. Not only did he point to Epstein's *Le Cinématographe vu de l'Etna* as a major textual influence, it is plain that his *L'Atalante* (1934) owes much to Epstein's *La Belle Nivernaise* whose river barge microcosm proves paradoxically at once freeing and constraining. Michael Temple indicates that the discovery of Epstein came into Vigo's life at a particularly crucial moment of illness (2005: 9). As for filmmaker and theoretician Maya Deren, whose philosophy of cinema comes perhaps the closest to Epstein's among later experimental filmmakers, she has left a direct account of her discovery of Epstein's writings. In her treatise entitled *An Anagram of Ideas on Art, Form and Film* (1946), she writes:

> The complexity of the camera creates, at times, the illusion of being itself a living intelligence which can inspire its manipulation on the explorative and creative level simultaneously. (I have just received from France a book entitled 'L'Intelligence d'une Machine' by Jean Epstein. I have not yet read it, but the approach implied in the title and the poetic, inspired tone of the style in which Mr. Epstein writes of a subject usually treated in pedestrian, historical terms leads me to believe that it is at least interesting reading for those who share, with me, a profound respect for the magical complexities of the film instrument).[1] (47–8)

Since Deren proceeds to describe the specificities of slow motion and reverse motion, we gather that she has read more of Epstein's book than she lets on. Intriguingly – almost telepathically? – she ends her oblique gloss of Epstein on musings about filming ocean waves in reverse motion, which was precisely what Epstein was thinking about at that very moment in late 1946 as he prepared shooting *Le Tempestaire*! Although the *Cahiers du cinéma*'s special 1953 issue on Epstein brought his work to the attention of the budding New Wave critics and soon-to-be filmmakers, he does not appear to figure very high in their pantheon – as Godard's dismissive quip (see chapter 5) attests. Only around the 1990s do we find conspicuous testimonies of filmmakers from both within and without the mainstream about

---

1 See Michelson (2001: 21–45).

the importance of Epstein to them. For instance, Leos Carax recognizes Epstein's movies as a major influence on his film aesthetics, and Philippe Grandrieux, like Deren, refers to his writings as a source of inspiration.[2] In a recent interview about his film *Hors Satan* (2011), Bruno Dumont is asked whether he is influenced by Dreyer's *Ordet*. He responds:

> Of course, I know the movie, but foremost I've had in mind the films of Jean Epstein with Breton peasants: *L'Or des mers* and *Le Tempestaire*. They display a kind of magical realism, shot with real people, but with a completely hallucinated *mise en scène* from the 20s. He shoots the ocean in an incredible way, which made me want to film the sea, even if that scares me a little ... Since *Hadewijch*, a supernatural theme was present [in my work]; but the idea was to go beyond to find the spiritual in plasticity rather than in the subject-matter. (Royer and Tobin, 2011: 32–3)

Dumont narrows down very pragmatically, as a filmmaker, the assistance that Epstein can provide in getting rid of the shackles of narration and professional acting in order to embrace the physical world, embodiment as such, and the plastic dimensions of their encounter.

For some critics, it is the loose school with which Epstein has been associated that represents the nexus of influence in the history of cinema. Robert Ray has advanced the thesis that *photogénie*, emphasizing the alluring and suspensive qualities of the filmic image rather than its narrative load, provided Hollywood with a complement to continuity through a kind of fetishistic resonance. Ray traces this in particular in a movie produced and closely supervised by Irwin Thalberg, *Grand Hotel* (US, 1932), in which there is an 'unmotivated overhead shot of Garbo in her ballerina costume, alone for the first time, opening like a flower as she settles wearily on the floor. The narrative idles, enabling this instance of *photogénie* to unfold because, as Thalberg knew, the movie would be the better for it' (2001: 6–7). Ray might have mentioned also the movie's cinematographer, William H. Daniels, since he was responsible for the photography of Eric von Stroheim's *Greed* (US, 1924), Ernst Lubitsch's *Ninotchka* (US, 1939), Jules Dassin's *The Naked City* (US, 1948), Anthony Mann's *Winchester '73* (US, 1950), Lewis Milestone's *Ocean's 11* (US, 1960),

2 For Carax, see Rosenbaum (1997: 187). For Grandrieux, see Nicole Brenez, 'The Body's Night: An Interview with Philippe Grandrieux', at: www.rouge.com.au/1/grandrieux.html (consulted on 03/09/2011).

and Mark Robson's *Valley of the Dolls* (US, 1967) – thus spanning the whole period of Hollywood's signature productions. Ray asserts that *photogénie* was the secret ingredient that Thalberg extracted from the French 'Impressionist–Surrealist model' (*ibid.*: 13) to captivate viewers' sensations through the alluring detail. This is certainly a seductive thesis, especially since it revalues the contribution to Hollywood's hegemony from so-called Impressionist filmmakers and thinkers of the like of Epstein – whom Ray sees as the best theoretician for the model (*ibid.*: 3, 12). As for the question how a French avant-garde aesthetics migrated to a US mainstream studio system, studies from the 1990s onwards show that quick transnational transmission is more often the rule than the exception in film history. The substantial emigration of movie industry personnel from Europe to the US during the 1930s, due to global depression and the rise of Nazism, represents an obvious conduit.[3] It should be added that Ray is careful to assimilate Surrealism and Impressionism (and Bazinian aesthetics to some extent) only around a single trait: their appreciation for the wayward or odd detail pioneered by the proponents of *photogénie* in their veneration of the CU, and reprised by Surrealism and Bazin. Certainly the notion that the studio system found ways to balance its streamlining process and stock stories with hints of contingency feels in equal part intuitively logical and deeply troubling. One aspect that Epstein never guarded against (as Pudovkin and others may have sensed) is *photogénie*'s potential for pre-emption, and worse yet, for devolving into sheer glamour or advertising slickness.

Epstein's fascination with CUs, details, and unforeseen aspects of filmic images has undoubtedly influenced the very idea of cinephilia. In an essay rethinking film theory in the wake of Bazin, Mary Ann Doane writes,

> Whether the moment chosen by the cinephiliac was really unprogrammed, unscripted, or outside codification is fundamentally undecidable. It is also inconsequential since cinephilia hinges not on indexicality but on the knowledge of indexicality's potential, a knowledge that paradoxically erases itself. The cinephile maintains a certain belief, an investment in the graspability of the asystematic, the contingent, for which the cinema is the privileged vehicle. (2003: 84)

---

3 See Phillips (2004). Billy Wilder's *Mauvaise Graine* (1933) exemplifies the Berlin–Paris–Hollywood axis in the 1930s; see Wimmer (2011).

In this dense excerpt, Doane asserts that cinephilia is closely linked to a kind of virtuality the viewer perceives in film images. It is another way to arrive at *photogénie*'s charge in the unexpected detail. Significantly, Doane's apology of cinephilia as virtuality comes on the heels of her glossing a long passage of Paul Willemen that concerns Epstein's love for Hayakawa from *Bonjour cinéma*.

I would like to propose in this conclusion that the most lasting effect Epstein has had on the cinema as a whole was through his efforts to displace the centre of gravity of a movie away from questions of illusion, narrative, action, continuity, and even image composition, to focus on physical encounters both within the shot – between the lens, bodies, matters, and objects – and to a lesser extent between shots. In other words, Epstein has opened the way for a corporeal cinema predicated on cinematography and montage rather than narration and *mise en scène*.

Coeur fidèle (1923), as we have seen, revolves around the melodramatic impossibility of Marie and Jean to meet up without interferences. Yet all these obstacles – Jean's fights with Petit-Paul, Petit-Paul forcing himself on Marie, the wound to the police officer, Marie's baby, the baby's sickness, and the killing of Petit-Paul by Marie's neighbour – are, before anything else, sensorial and corporeal events. Moreover, this list of bodily collisions explains why psychic fatigue is all that is left on Jean and Marie's faces by the time they are reunited – a far cry from a happy ending. This second, concluding merry-go-round sequence with the two lovers should be understood to generate not only a *visible* circular movement, which most critics have celebrated, but also an almost *invisible* bodily and facial pull. It seems likely to me that Epstein's instruction to his actors was to show no emotion at all so as to let the centrifugal force leech their faces of any affect, almost physically pulling each of the lover's face into itself. In the first merry-go-round sequence, by contrast, Petit-Paul is grabbing at Marie, and their faces are redolent with tension and emotions; lust and fear respectively. Of course, Epstein does not end the movie on the empty-faces sequence, but the epilogue must be read as a direct and didactic answer to that corporeal display.

Every one of Epstein's more important films may be approached as enacting a series of corporeal events, within bodies, between bodies, between bodies and the camera, and between shots, that is in some key way tangential to or even distinct from the narrative.

The subjective spiral shot in the garage in *La Glace à trois faces* (1927) mobilizes centrifugal force too, in order to evince in viewers the bodily memory of feeling lodged and pressed in the seat of an automobile. It is as if we 'viewed' the image with our backs and sides. This spiral shot, foreshadowing the fatal collision of the driver with the bird, connects also with the sequence of shots from the beginning of the movie showing us the protagonist's body *visually embedded* among several cars before getting into his own. Such scenes tend to leave the narrative economy behind either through ellipses – shortening of duration and causality – or, more radically, through tangents difficult to situate either within the story (the order in which events are shown to us) or the tale (the temporal order of events). When the protagonist walks among the cars, it is unclear whether Epstein is establishing his routine, describing a specific day, making a psychological sketch, or presenting a riddle. This uncertainty, we had indicated in chapter 3, invites us to attend to the bodiliness, and by extension psychosexuality, of the protagonist all the more.

This sense of a layered or faceted or parallel corporeal plot seems much more prominent in the case of Epstein than among other filmmakers of the French narrative avant-garde such as Germaine Dulac, Marcel L'Herbier, or René Clair, who also pay a great deal of attention to embodied events and experimental storytelling structures. To this extent, we might be able to say that Epstein has been the main pioneer in the 1920s in pushing fiction films in the direction of corporeal cinema, which Buñuel and Dalí's *Un Chien Andalou* and Cocteau's *Le sang d'un poète* took even further albeit in a more sensational and oneiric vein. Corporeal cinema does not mean only or simply that filmic bodies are prominent or foregrounded: there are too many genres, from porn to gore and sport films of which this could be said. Keeping in mind the importance of affects for Epstein, as distinct from emotions, we should consider corporeal cinema as comprising a broad range of fiction movies (and documentaries to a lesser extent) in which underneath or on the margins of a main plot, there is a palpable sense that something is at play through bodily affects that cannot be captured in a subplot.[4] This cardinal sense of embodiment

---

4 For a slightly different use of 'corporeal cinema' in a book that invokes Epstein nonetheless, see Beugnet (2007). She writes: 'This book's focus, then, is on an aesthetic of sensation, where the material dimension of a cinematic work is initially given precedence over its expository and mimetic/realist functions' (*ibid.*: 14).

for Epstein's *photogénie* and philosophy at large partakes of a form of what may be called *corporeal realism*. Introducing a collection of essays on realism and corporeal cinema, Ivone Margulies has argued in a text entitled 'Bodies Too Much', that 1970s theory 'has framed realist cinema as needing demystification rather than explanation' (2003: 7). For much 1970s film theory, realism was inherently suspect, manipulative, bourgeois, that is, ideologically conservative. But that was an ideological position that could not account for the brute fact of filmic reality, of bodies in front of the camera, and of viewers not only viewing but also sensing and being affected by bodies on film. Margulies and others consider that corporeal realism can be strongly oppositional, as in Buñuel's *Las Hurdes* (1932), Hara Kazuo's *Sayonara CP* (1972), or Abbas Kiarostami's *And Life Goes on* (1992) — all films that call upon viewers not to doubt the real or the power of film, but to be challenged by the corporeal resonance of filmic encounters. Epstein's cinema belongs to this *oppositional corporeal realism* placing conditions of embodiment before all other imperatives, whether of truth effect, documentary mimesis, or narrative structure.

As we have seen in chapter 3, corporeal cinema and queer aesthetics have more than passing affinities, if we think of the cinema of Cocteau, Pasolini, Kenneth Anger, or Derek Jarman. The two contemporary filmmakers who have decided to call the entirety of their collaborative œuvre, 'le cinéma corporel', Maria Klonaris and Katherina Thomadaki, are lesbians (Klonaris and Thomadaki, 2006). Epstein belongs to discussions of the role of embodied experiencing in queer cinema that should extend to both silent movies and films that are not obviously queer. In view of the fact that Epstein's closet was a result of censorship — that is, of the legal and cultural opprobrium against homosexuality which Epstein himself outs as entirely unfounded — the corporeal dimension of his work might be thought of as queer, indeed, as a paradigmatic example of queer play with the visibility and concealment of gay aesthetics. The themes, figures, and submerged plots of his films echo many of the concerns of queer cinema, namely the primacy of embodiment for identity; self-mirroring and the figure of Narcissus as complicating issues of narcissism; the contingency and uncontrollability of affects; the reliance on principles of fluidity rather than solidity; the role of double meanings, doubling, and figures of doubles; the mythical if not sacred haunting of death and suicide; hyperesthesia, or acute sensibility/sensitivity, etc. On this basis Epstein's corporeal cinema has a clear place in the queer canon.

The corporeal aesthetics of liminal/closeted queerness in some of Epstein's films likely influenced subsequent filmmakers. An obvious example would be Robert Bresson's *Pickpocket* (1956). Anglo-American critics at least from 1962 onwards have commented on the 'repressed homosexuality' or 'repressed homoeroticism' that is at the core of the submerged plot of Bresson's film (Reader, 2000: 55–7; Pipolo, 2010: 125–6). This is particularly clear in the sequence in which Michel, the protagonist, aided by an all-male gang of pickpockets cruises through Paris stealthily manhandling the bodies of their targets. When Michel returns to his room he looks as if he has just been to an orgy. The point is less whether director Bresson is concealing or recoding (his) homosexuality – it is plain that he is – but *how* he does so: by entrancing and even entrapping viewers into sharing in the bodily control and grace of the pickpocket qua queer, via *photogénie*, rhythm, de-emphasized dialogues and narrative, and the sheer corporeal comportment of his 'models', as he calls his non-professional lead actors.

In all this, including the use of non-professionals, Bresson proves to be clearly Epsteinian, as can be gathered explicitly from his famous *Notes sur le cinématographe*. For example, Bresson takes the camera to be a 'sublime ... machine' for 'divination', and approaches filming as a way to create self-disclosing situations: 'Tourner c'est aller à une rencontre. Rien dans l'inattendu qui ne soit attendu secrètement par toi' ['shooting means going towards an encounter. There is nothing in that unexpected [encounter] that you did not expect secretly'] (1988: 104).[5] Even the inversion of cause and effect, one of Epstein's central ideas, which seemed destined to wane with the silent era's fascination with reverse motion, reappears: 'Que la cause suive l'effet et non l'accompagne ou le précède' ['May the cause follow the effect rather than accompanying or preceding it'] (*ibid.*: 102). The very definition Bresson gives of the *cinématographe* as art in opposition to *le cinéma* as industrial production – 'Le cinématographe est une écriture avec des images en mouvement et des sons' ['The *cinématographe* is writing with moving images and sounds'] (*ibid.*: 18) – harks back to the sources of Epstein's thought about film, namely that it offers a new sensorial appreciation of movement and new possibilities for language. It is then all the more strange that none of the major books on Bresson

---

5 Since the only English edition botches the title as *Notes on the cinematographer*, translations are mine.

CONCLUSION 195

in either English or French analyses what the two filmmakers have in common nor traces the influence of the former on the latter's emphasis on corporeality, including liminal queerness.[6]

Epsteinian aesthetics in recent cinema

I would like to close this conclusion with a limited look at several films that display singularly Epsteinian aspects, in particular the intersection of technical choices and corporeal realism. My point here is to show that the set of preoccupations that shaped Epstein's films has clearly re-emerged within the work of recent filmmakers similarly favouring corporeal aesthetics over narration. I can only speculate here about the complex reasons for such a resurgence: they likely involve, together with a mix of direct and indirect influence from Epstein, a renewed interest in corporeality connected with digital images and digital art, and a return to concepts close to *photogénie* caused by the perceived end of analogue cinema.[7]

We might begin with Steven Soderbergh's *Solaris* (2002), a readaptation of Polish writer Stanislaw Lem's sci-fi novel of the same title, rather than a remake of Tarkovsky's *Solaris* (1972). The premise of Lem's novel is quite Epsteinian since it has to do with an oceanic planet interacting directly with the affects of protagonists, and disrupting their sense of time, causality, and self. Moreover, Soderbergh's film moves the centre of gravity of the book from scientifico-philosophical questions to corporeal elements found in many of Epstein's films, such as a crisis of heterosexuality leading to suicide. Soderbergh's film constitutes in fact a remarkably parallel reflection to that of Epstein's *La Chute de la maison Usher*, and both films may be used to illuminate each other. As the film opens, a voice-over of Rheya (Natasha McElhone) asks the question that Madeline never got to ask Roderick: 'Don't you love me anymore?' Kris Kelvin (George Clooney), her husband, is shown prostrate with grief, which suggests that she is dead. We later learned she committed suicide. The gist of

6 Pipolo (2010): mentions Bresson's commitment to the medium specificity of cinema as akin to that of Epstein, but does not question a more direct filiation.
7 See Hansen (2004) and Jones (2006) for an overview of intersections between digital imaging and the corporeal. Statements by artist Bill Viola on the use of close-ups and altered speed in his own work seem eminently Epsteinian without there being any direct trace of Epstein; see Wall-Romana (2012).

Solaris is to confront Kris's mourning, like Roderick's, to the ambiguous possibility of resuscitating a dead lover, or perhaps a dead love. Rainy scenes and a flowing tap in ECU announce early on a thematic fluidity that progressively converge into the liquid/gaseous and synaptic-looking ocean of Solaris. The first image of Rheya we see, in a dream sequence of Kris, is an MCU on the slit of a lock she holds with both hands between her legs, sitting in a bus (21:50). The obvious sexual symbolism represents heterosexuality as a lock for which the key is absent – at least from Kris's purview. His dream soon merges into memories, while interspersed ECUs of Kris's sleeping head have us wonder when exactly the film's referential present is and through whose POV we are witnessing the action. We see the first meeting of Kris and Rheya's re-enacted at their friend Gibarian's home. Rheya gets up, aware Kris is looking at her, and walks away in an MS just as Gibarian tells him about Solaris: 'it's reacting, almost like it knows it's being observed' (24:12). This merging of Rheya with the mysterious Solaris in manipulating the gazer Kris, recalls a similar merging of Madeline with the mysteriously animated painting in Roderick's mesmerized gaze. When the Rheya ghost appears to Kris as a dream in his cabin, Soderbergh shoots her from Kris's POV: she goes from a fuzzy half-lit shape in the background to a hyper-crisp ECU of her eyes and mouth. With this shot, the close-up becomes the technique of choice to rethink affect, death, doubling, and causality in *Solaris*. When Kris wakes again to behold Rheya's fleshy ghost, consciously this time, his expression in MCU staring at the camera (29:43) displays the same mixture of pain and fascination as Roderick's CU looking at the camera that stands for Madeline's painting. Oddly, Rheya's ghost immediately tells Kris that in their apartment on Earth, 'it's dark, very dark, and there are no paintings on the wall' (30:42), as if painting somehow held the key to their relationship. As the film goes on, CUs and ECUs of Rheya's full face and profiles multiply, the close-up revealing affects on the human face to be the correlates of the colourful oceanic swirls in the atmosphere of Solaris. At the conclusion of the film (1:30:35), we return to a CU of Kris, back at home, again gazing straight at the camera while beholding Rheya anew. Both actors look straight at the camera, and thus at us, while narratively we're not sure whether Kris is looking at a real woman, her fleshy ghost, or a fantasy representation of women. The limits and magic of cinema are laid bare in this riddle of the invisible field behind the lens: is it the camera, a protagonist, us, or an idea? Soderbergh's final sequence starts on this pivotal shot of Kris's face in CU, then uses the classic shot–counter-shots and two-shots for depicting heterosexual relationships, even though here the status of the two protagonists is as unclear as in *La Chute de la maison Usher*:

1   (1:30:35) Kris in full face CU at centre of screen
2   (1:30:42) Rheya in full face CU at centre of screen
3   (1:30:48) same as 1
4   (1:30:54) same as 2
5   (1:31:06) same as 1
6   (1:31:10) same as 2
7   (1:31:17) Slight HA ¼ face CU of Kris screen left looking screen right
8   (1:31:22) Slight HA ¼ face CU of Rheya screen right looking screen left; Kris and Rheya kiss; we see her face on his shoulder
9   (1:31:37) Slight HA ¼ face CU of Kris screen centre on Rheya's shoulder
10 (1:31:41) same as 8
11 (1:31:52) same as 9
12 (1:32:00) 11 slowly dissolves into an ELS of Solaris
13 (1:32:42) title: SOLARIS

The sequence's excruciatingly normative shooting and editing of the heterosexual rite of kissing on-screen should be considered emblematic if not parodic. After all, it takes place after the spacecraft with Kris on board has plunged into Solaris, thus when both spouses are dead. (But perhaps not: we can never be sure when anything takes place, nor how strictly to believe in chronology or cause and effect.) In this respect, it could also be compared to the epilogue that closes *Cœur fidèle* and re-sutures heterosexuality in a different key but similarly *after* the narrative has ended. Because of a common interest in corporeal cinema and in questioning depictions of heterosexual love, Epstein and Soderbergh crafted remarkably similar filmic meditations using some of the same techniques to address some of the same ambiguities.

Let us turn now to Ang Lee's corporeal opera, *Crouching Tiger, Hidden Dragon* (2000). This is also a film that questions heterosexuality or pushes it to extremes, and displays a corporeal *photogénie* with shots in altered speed that closely parallel Epsteinian sensibility. The two lead heterosexual couples either refuse to touch at all, as with the two fighters Li Mu Bai (Yun-Fat-Chow) and Shu Lien (Michele Yeoh), at least until he is literally on his last breath, or else touch too much – punching, kicking, tumbling, knifing each other, and ultimately making love, in the case of Jen (Ziyi Zhang) and Lo (Chen Chang). But that does not suffice either and Jen must, in the end, commit a sublime suicide. While *emotions* appear narratively displaced from the sexual–affective to the agonistic–martial register, in cinematographic terms, *affects* keep storming spectacularly over the CU faces if not eyes (when Jen goes 'ninja') of the protagonists, waxing eloquent to compensate for their formulaic words. Rarely has the 'theatre of the skin' been so fascinating to decipher. One exception is the relationship between the two women, Shu Lien and Jen, which progressively takes over the heterosexual romances by conspicuously mobilizing through direct bodily contacts a wide range of affects from seduction to aggression, and filial/maternal love to same-sex desire.

The originality of Lee's film is that the corporeal bleeds back, as it were, all at once within the choreography of fighting, facial affects, the imaginary capacities of fighters' bodies – their hyperesthesia – even the fluid agency of nature (water plays a crucial role in the fates of Li Mu Bai and Jen). Lee's film proceeds clearly from sensory awareness and the embodied subconscious oozing from and animating everything: objects, landscapes, water, garments, and moving bodies themselves. The slightly *accelerated* motion of the Wudan fighters forms an exact counterpart to Epstein's slightly *slowed-down* motion, with the same aim of revalorizing bodily affect. The placement of the camera at the very heart of the action, and the rapid montage that results from the many cuts on movement and change-of-shot scale, perfectly illustrate the philosophy of Epstein's 'dance of the landscape' meant to capture and render the kinaesthetic enmeshing of bodies and space. *Crouching Tiger* pioneered the subgenre of international digital Wuxia films, which also include Zhang Yimou's *Hero* (2003) and *The House of Flying Daggers* (2004). All three films may be considered Epsteinian in their de-emphasizing of melodrama to favour corporeal situations (fighting, albeit in set pieces), fluidity (water and wind constantly refract the flow of moving images), and sensorial acuity (materials and textures, layered aural and visual spaces, hyperesthesia and temporary impairment, etc.). Wuxia increasingly relies on kinaesthesia via flying or levitating scenes from the wavering bamboo tops in *Crouching Tiger*, to the fight around a row of tall curtains in *Hero* (perhaps a recollection of the sentient curtains of *The Fall of the House* of Usher), as well as through projectiles, objects becoming projectiles, and projectile POV shots. At the same time, and perhaps as a reaction to this *projectility* (to coin a word), the use of Epsteinian slow motion, which had largely vanished from mainstream cinema since the 1920s, massively reappears in digital films, accompanying technical leaps such as the 'bullet time' of *The Matrix* (US, 1999).[8]

The Epsteinian legacy is not limited to digital FX movies, and a host of full live-action films could be mentioned as well, such as Terrence Malik's *The Thin Red Line* (US, 1998) for its Epsteinian animism; Bruno Dumont's *Humanité* (Fr., 1999) for the corporeal realism of the working-class protagonists and environments; Tony Gilroy's *Michael Clayton* (US, 2007) for its rhythm of 'suspens' (rather than suspense) and the *photogénie* cinematography of Robert Elswit.

Epstein's work in cinema, film 'theory', and philosophy, offers today a surprisingly contemporary set of movies, cinematographic idioms, and reflections on all the phenomena of cinema. Emblematic of this artistic freshness is the percolation of *photogénie* in Bill Viola's work, or of *phonogénie* for instance in the work of experimental musician and performance artist Adrian Shephard, whose beautiful 1998 sound piece was written to accompany *La Chute de la maison Usher*.[9] Even now that we have seemingly gone over the brink of the digital, Epstein remains vital for anyone wishing to make movies or understand the past and present mutations of cinema and moving images.

References

Beugnet, Martine (2007), *Cinema and Sensation: French Film and the Art of Transgression*, Edinburgh: Edinburgh University Press.

Bresson, Robert (1988 [1975]), *Notes sur le cinématographe*, Paris: Gallimard/Folio.

Deren, Maya (1946), *An Anagram of Ideas on Art, Form and Film*, Yonkers: Alicat Book Shop Press.

Doane, Mary Ann (2003), 'The Object of Theory', in Ivone Margulies (ed.), *Rites of Realism: Essays in Corporeal Cinema*, Durham and London: Duke University Press, 80–9.

Everett, Anna (2003), 'Digitextuality and Click Theory', in Anna Everett and John Thornton Caldwell (eds), *New Media: Theories and Practices of Digitextuality*, New York: Routledge, xi–xxx.

8 Everett (2003: xxiii) keenly points out the connection of Epstein with 'bullet time'.
9 See Adrian Shephard's work, at: www.testcard.com

Gottlieb, Sidney (ed.) (1995), *Hitchcock on Hitchcock: Selected Writings and Interviews*, Berkeley: University of California Press.
Gunning, Tom (1993), *D.W. Griffith and the Origins of American Narrative Films*, Urbana-Champaign: University of Illinois Press.
Hansen, Mark B.N. (2004), *New Philosophy for New Media*, Cambridge: MIT Press.
Jones, Caroline A. (ed.) (2006), *Sensorium: Embodied Experience, Technology, and Contemporary Art*, Cambridge: MIT Press.
Klonaris, Maria and Katheria Thomadaki (2006), *Le cinéma corporel: corps sublimes, intersexe et intermédia*, Paris: L'Harmattan.
Margulies, Ivone (2003), 'Bodies Too Much', in Ivone Margulies (ed.), *Rites of Realism: Essays in Corporeal Cinema*, Durham and London: Duke University Press, 1–25.
Michelson, Annette (2001), 'Poetics and Savage Thought: About *Anagram*', in Bill Nichols (ed.), *Maya Deren and the American Avant-Garde*, Berkeley: University of California Press.
Phillips, Alastair (2004), *City of Light, City of Darkness: Émigré Filmmakers in Paris, 1929–1939*, Amsterdam: Amsterdam University Press.
Pipolo, Tony (2010), *Robert Bresson: A Passion for Film*, Oxford: Oxford University Press.
Ray, Robert (2001), *How a Theory Got Lost and Other Mysteries in Cultural Studies*, Bloomington and Indianapolis: Indiana University Press.
Reader, Keith (2000), *Robert Bresson*, Manchester, Manchester University Press.
Rosenbaum, Jonathan (1997), *Movies as Politics*, Berkeley: University of California Press, 1997.
Royer, Philippe and Yann Tobin (2011), 'Entretien avec Bruno Dumont: mon métier c'est de fabriquer des apparitions' *Positif* 608 (October), 29–33.
Talens, Jenaro (1993), *The Branded Eye: Buñuel's Un Chien Andalou*, Giulia Colaizzi (trans.), Minneapolis: University of Minnesota Press.
Temple, Michael (2005), *Jean Vigo*, Manchester: Manchester University Press.
Wall-Romana, Christophe (2012), 'Epstein's *Photogénie* as Corporeal Vision: Inner Sensation, Queer Embodiment, and Ethics', in Sarah Keller and Jason Paul (eds), *Jean Epstein: Critical Essays and New Translations*, Amsterdam: Amsterdam University Press, 51–72.
Williams, James S. (2006), *Jean Cocteau*, Manchester: Manchester University Press.
Wimmer, Leila (2011), '"I Don't Have a Home!": Paris interregnum in *Mauvaise Graine*', in Karen McNally (ed.), *Billy Wilder, Movie-Maker: Critical Essays on the Films*, Jefferson: McFarland, 161–75.

Filmography

Pasteur (1922), France, 1,200 m, 35 mm, b/w, silent
Production: L'édition française cinématographique
Supervision: Jean Benoit-Lévy
Artistic direction: Adrien Bruneau
Direction: Jean Epstein
Scenario: Edmond Épardaud
Camera: Edmond Floury
Cast: Henri Monnier (Pasteur), Maurice Touzé (Pasteur as child), Jean Rauzéna (Meister as child), Robert Tourneur (Pasteur's father)
Filmed in 1922 at the Studio Nadal, Joinville-le-Pont, with exteriors in Arbois, Dôle, Strasburg, Alais, Pouilly-le-Fort, and the Institut Pasteur of Paris and Lille
Premiere: 27 December 1922 (pre-premiere at La Sorbonne), 31 August 1923 (release)
Distribution: Le Film du centenaire and Pathé Consortium-Cinéma
Notes: DVD available through l'Institut National de l'Audiovisuel

Les Vendanges (1922), France, b/w, silent
Production: L'édition française cinématographique
Direction: Jean Epstein
Camera: Edmond Floury
Filmed on location around Narbonne
Notes: No copy of this film has been located

L'Auberge rouge (1923), France, 1,642/1,800 m, tinted b/w, silent
Production and distribution: Pathé Consortium-Cinéma
Artistic Direction: Louis Nalpas

Adaptation: Jean Epstein (short story *L'Auberge rouge*, Honoré de Balzac)
Direction: Jean Epstein
Camera: Raoul Aubourdier
Assistant cameras: Roger Hubert, Robert Lefebvre
Cast: Léon Mathot (Prosper Magnan), Gina Manès (daughter of the innkeeper), David Evremont (FrédéricTaillefer), Pierre Hot (Innkeeper), Jacques Christiany (André Taillefer), Marcelle Schmidt (Victorine), Robert Tourneur, Bourdelle, Dartagnan, René Ferté, Henri Barat, André Volbert
Filmed at the Studio des Vignerons in Vincennes, with exteriors at the Château de Vincennes
Premiere: 28 September 1923

Cœur fidèle (1923), France, 2,000 m, 35 mm, b/w, silent

Production and distribution: Pathé Consortium-Cinéma
Scenario and direction: Jean Epstein
Camera: Paul Guichard
Assistant cameras: Stuckert and Léon Donnot
Cast: Léon Mathot (Jean), Gina Manès (Marie), Edmond Van Daële (Petit-Paul), Benedict (Le père Hochon), Mme Maufroy (La mère Hochon), Melle Marice [Marie Epstein] ('the cripple'), Madeline Erickson (Woman in the port)
Filmed at the Studios des Vignerons et des Auteurs in Vincennes, with exteriors in the old port of Marseilles and in Manosque
Premiere: 23 November 1923
Notes: available in DVD (France) and Blu-Ray (UK)

La Montagne infidèle (1923), France, 600 m, 35 mm, b/w, silent

Production and distribution: Pathé Consortium-Cinéma
Direction: Jean Epstein
Camera: Paul Guichard
Notes: Documentary on the eruption of Mount Etna, June 1923; no copy of this film has been located

La Belle Nivernaise (1923), France, 1,569/1,800 m, 35 mm, b/w, silent

Production and distribution: Pathé Consortium-Cinéma
Adaptation: Jean Epstein (short story *La Belle Nivernaise*, Alphonse Daudet)

Direction: Jean Epstein
Assistant direction: René Allinat
Camera: Paul Guichard
Assistant camera: Léon Donnot
Cast: Blanche Montel (Clara), Maurice Touzé (Victor), David Evremont (Maugendre), Max Bonnet (L'Équipage), Pierre Hot (Le Père Louveau), Mme Lacroix (La Mère Louveau)
Filmed at Studio des Vignerons in Vincennes, with exteriors on the Seine between Paris and Rouen, and in Vincennes
Premiere: 5 January 1924

[*Photogénies* (1924), France]

Notes: This was a montage of rushes, various footage and newsreels. According to Leprohon (1964) it was commissioned by Jean Tédesco for the Vieux-Colombier; according to Vichi (2003: 171), it illustrated Epstein's conference 'L'élément photogénique' given to CASA on 11 April 1924 (at the Théâtre Raymond Duncan); see Epstein (1974: 144, n. 1)

La Goutte de sang (1924), France, 1,800 m, 35 mm, b/w, silent

Production: Société des Cinéromans
Adaptation: Jean Epstein (novel *La Goutte de sang*, Jules Mary)
Direction: Jean Epstein and Maurice Mariaud
Camera: Paul Guichard
Assistant camera: Léon Donnot
Cast: Andrée Lionel (Mme Chenavat), Symiane (Marie), Roger Karl (Justin Chenavat), Paulette Ray (Gisèle), Georges Chaliat (Richard), Michael Floresco (Renaud), Daniel Mendaille (Judge), Jean-François Martial (Bernier)
Distribution: Pathé Consortium-Cinéma
Premiere: 26 September 1924
Notes: Epstein abandoned the direction and his name is not mentioned in the credits

Le Lion des Mogols (1924), France, 2,000/2,272 m, 35 mm, b/w, silent

Production: Films Albatros
Treatment: Ivan Mosjoukine
Direction: Jean Epstein
Cameras: Joseph-Louis Mundviller and Fedor Bourgassof

Sets: Alexandre Lochakoff
Costumes: Boris Bilinsky
Cast: Ivan Mosjoukine (Prince Roundghito-Sing), Nathalie Lissenko (Anna), Camille Bardou (the Banker Morel), Melle Alexiane (Zemgali), François Zelas (Kalavas), François Viguier (the Great Khan)
Premiere: 12 December 1924
Filmed at Studios Albatros in Montreuil and Menchen d'Épinay, with exteriors in the port of Marseilles
Distribution: Film Armor

L'Affiche (1924), France, 2,000 m, 35 mm, b/w, silent

Production: Films Albatros
Scenario: Marie Epstein
Direction: Jean Epstein
Camera: Maurice Defassiaux
Assistant camera: Chelles
Sets: Boris Bilinsky
Cast: Nathalie Lissenko (Marie), Camille Bardou (the CEO), Genica Missirio (Richard), Sylvane de Castillo (Richard's mother), Roger Huguenet (child), Pierre Hot, Georges Saillard, François Viguier
Filmed at Studios Albatros in Montreuil, with exteriors in Bougival
Premiere: 26 February 1925
Distribution: Film Armor

Le Double amour (1925), France, 2,000/2,127 m, 35 mm, b/w, silent

Production: Films Albatros
Scenario: Marie-Antonine Epstein
Direction: Jean Epstein
Camera: Maurice Desfassiaux
Assistant camera: Roudakoff
Sets: Pierre Kéfer
Costumes: Drécoli and Paul Poiret
Cast: Nathalie Lissenko (Laure Maresco), Jean Angelo (Jacques Prémont-Solène), Camille Bardou (Decurgis), Pierre Batcheff (Jacques Maresco)
Filmed at Studios Albatros in Montreuil, with exteriors in Nice
Premiere: 27 November 1925
Distribution: Film Armor

Les Aventures de Robert Macaire (1925), France, 4,079/4,500 m, 35 mm, b/w, silent

(Five Episodes)
Production: Films Albatros
Scenario: Charles Vayre
Adaptation: Raoul Ploquin (novel, *L'Auberge des Adrets*, Benjamin Antier, Saint-Amand, and Polyanthe)
Direction: Jean Epstein
Cameras: Paul Guichard, Jehan Fouquet, and Nicolas Roudakoff
Assistant camera: Roudakoff
Sets: Jean Mercier, Georges Geffroy, and Lazare Meerson
Cast: Jean Angélo (Robert Macaire), Alex Allin (Bertrand), Suzanne Bianchetti (Melle de Sermèze), Nino Constantini (René de Sermèze), Sacha Dulong (Marquis de Sermèze), Camille Bardou (Le Gendarme Verduron), Lou Davy [Lou Dovoyna] (Victoire), Jean-Pierre Stock (Henri), François Viguier (Le Baron de Cassignol), Marquisette Bosky (Jeanne, Robert's daughter), Maximilienne Max (farmer's wife), Melle Niblia (Eugénie Mouffetard), Jules de Spoky
Filmed at Studios Albatros in Montreuil, with exteriors in the Dauphiné
Premiere: 11 December 1925
Distribution: Film Armor
Notes: Five episodes were released separately; a shorter version of 3,000m was subsequently made

Mauprat (1926), France, 2,000 m, 35 mm, b/w, silent

Production: Les Films Jean Epstein
Adaptation: Jean Epstein (novel *Mauprat*, George Sand)
Direction: Jean Epstein
Assistant direction: Luis Buñuel
Camera: Duverger
Sets: Pierre Kéfer
Cast: Sandra Milowanoff (Edmée de Mauprat), Maurice Schutz (Hubert de Mauprat/Tristan de Mauprat), Nino Constantini (Bernard de Mauprat), René Ferté (Adhémar de la Marche), Alex Allin (Marcasse), Halma (Jean de Mauprat), Bondireff (L'Abbé Aubert), Line Doré (Melle Leblanc), Marice [Marie Epstein], Jane Thiery
Filmed at Studio Menchen d'Épinay with Exteriors in the Indre
Premiere: 6 March 1927
Distribution: Sélection Maurice Rouhier

Au pays de George Sand (1926), France

Production: Les Films Jean Epstein
Direction: Jean Epstein
Camera: Georges Périnal
Notes: documentary of the Castle of Nohant; no copy of this film has been located

Six et demi onze (1927), France, 1,800/2,000 m, 35 mm, tinted b/w, silent

Production: Films Jean Epstein
Scenario: Marie Epstein
Direction: Jean Epstein
Camera: Georges Périnal
Sets: Pierre Kéfer
Edmond van Daële (Jérôme de Ners), Nino Constantini (Jean de Ners), Suzy Pierson (Marie), René Ferté (Harry Gold)
Filmed at Studio Roudès, Neuilly, with exteriors in Paris and Fontainebleau
Distribution: Compagnie universelle cinématographique

La Glace à trois faces (1927), France, 900/1,200 m, 35 mm, b/w, silent

Production: Films Jean Epstein
Adaptation: Jean Epstein (short story, La Glace à trois faces, Paul Morand)
Direction: Jean Epstein
Camera: Marcel Eywinger
Sets: Pierre Kéfer
Set manager: Maurice Morlot
Cast: René Ferté (the Man), Olga Day (Pearl), Suzy Pierson (Athalia), Jeanne Helbling (Lucie), Raymond Guérin (a bore [un fâcheux]), Paul Garat
Filmed at Studio Roudès, Neuilly, with exteriors in Paris
Premiere: 22 November 1927
Distribution: Studio des Ursulines

La Chute de la maison Usher (1928), France, 1,271/1,500 m, 35 mm, tinted b/w, silent

Production: Films Jean Epstein

Adaptation: Jean Epstein (tales of Edgar A. Poe)
Direction: Jean Epstein
Assistant direction: Luis Buñuel
Camera: Georges Lucas
Assistant camera: Jean Lucas
Slow-motion operator: Hébert
Sets: Pierre Kéfer
Set manager: Maurice Morlot
Costumes: Fernand Ochsé
Cast: Jean Debucourt (Roderick Usher), Marguerite Abel-Gance (Madeline Usher), Charles Lamy (Visitor), Fournez-Goffard (the Doctor), Luc Dartagnan (Butler) Pierre Hot, Halma
Filmed at Studios Éclair and Menchen d'Épinay, with exteriors in Sologne and Vexin
Premiere: 5 October 1928
Distribution: Exclusivité Seyta

Finis Terræ (1929), France, 1,820/2,400 m, 35 mm, b/w, silent

Production: Société Générale de Films
Direction: Jean Epstein
Assistant direction: Pierre Hot
Camera: Joseph Barth and Joseph Kottula
Assistant camera: Louis Née and Raymond Tulle
Cast: Kelp harvesters and fishermen of the Archipelago of Ouessant
Filmed in exteriors in the islands of Bannec, Balanec, Ouessant, and the sea of Iroise
Distribution: Mappemonde-Films

Sa Tête (1929), France, 823/900 m, 35 mm, b/w, silent

Production: Gaston Roudès
Direction: Jean Epstein
Assistant direction: Marcel Cohen
Camera: Albert Brès
Assistant camera: Fred Alric
Cast: France Dhélia (Blanche), René Ferté (Jean), Nino Constantini (Paul), Irma Perrot (Mme Bonnard), Camille Brant (Lawyer), Pierre Hot (Judge)
Filmed at Studios Roudès, Neuilly, with exteriors in Seine-et-Oise
Premiere: December 1929
Distribution: Exclusivité Seyta

L'Arbre ou le pas de la mule (1930), France, 35 mm, b/w, [sound?]

Production: Le Théâtre du Vieux Colombier
Adaptation: Jean Epstein (non-fiction, *La Forêt de Tronçais en Bourbonnais*, Jacques Chevalier)
Direction: Jean Epstein
Camera: Albert Brès
Filmed in the Tronçais
Notes: no copy of this film has been located

Mor'Vran (La Mer des corbeaux) (1930), France, 900 m, 35 mm, b/w, sound

Production and distribution: Compagnie Universelle Cinématographique
Direction: Jean Epstein
Camera: Alfred Guichard, Albert Brès, Marcel Rubière
Assistant camera: Henri Chauffier
Music: Alexis Archangelsky
Sound system: Synchronista
Cast: Fishermen of the island of Sein
Filmed in exteriors in the island of Sein and off the coast of Finistère

Notre-Dame de Paris (1931), France, 300 m, 35 mm, b/w, sound

Production and distribution: Synchro-Ciné
Direction: Jean Epstein
Camera: Émile Monniot
Assistant camera: Raymond
Notes: no copy of this film has been located

La Chanson des peupliers (1931), France, 300 m, 35 mm, b/w, sound

Production and distribution: Synchro-Ciné
Adaptation: Jean Epstein (poem, 'La Chanson des peupliers', Camille Soubise [Alphonse Vanden Camp])
Direction: Jean Epstein
Music: Doria
Camera: Émile Monniot

Le Cor (1931), France, 300 m, 35 mm, b/w, sound

Production and distribution: Synchro-Ciné, C.-F. Tavano
Adaptation: Jean Epstein (poem, 'Le Cor', Alfred de Vigny)
Direction: Jean Epstein

Camera: Christian Matras
Vocals: Jean Claverie (Paris Opera)
Music: A. Flégier
Sound: Cinevox-Haïk
Orchestra: Edouard Flament

L'Or des mers (1932), France, 2,000 m, 35 mm, b/w, sound

Production and distribution: Synchro-Ciné
Artistic direction: C.-F. Tavano
Direction: Jean Epstein
Camera: Christian Matras
Assistant camera: Albert Brès and Joseph Braun
Texts: Étienne Arnaud
Music: Th. Kross, Hartmann and Marcel Devaux
Synchronization: Charles Delacommune
Filmed in exteriors on the island of Hoedick

Les Berceaux (1932), France, 300 m, 35 mm, b/w, sound

Production and distribution: Synchro-Ciné
Direction: Jean Epstein
Camera: Joseph Barth
Music: Gabriel Fauré
Vocals: André Gaudin
Filmed in exteriors in Cancale and Saint-Malo

La Villanelle des rubans (1932), France, 200/300 m, 35 mm, b/w, sound

Production and distribution: Synchro-Ciné
Adaptation: Jean Epstein (song, 'Les rubans de la vie', Junka)
Direction: Jean Epstein
Camera: Joseph Barth
Music: Zimmermann
Vocals: L. Gaudin
Lyrics: René Paul Groffe (excerpts from 'Le Beau jardin de France')

Le Vieux Chaland (1932), France, 300 m, 35 mm, b/w, sound

Production and distribution: Synchro-Ciné
Direction: Jean Epstein
Camera: Joseph Barth
Music: Zimmermann

Vocals: André Gaudin
Lyrics: René Paul Groffe

Le Petit Chemin de fer (1932), France, 300 m, 35 mm, b/w, sound
Production and distribution: Synchro-Ciné
Direction: Jean Epstein
Lyrics: Fredy

L'Homme à l'Hispano (1932), France, 2,400 m, 35 mm, b/w, sound
Production: Vandal et Delac
Adaptation: Jean Epstein (novel L'Homme à l'Hispano, Pierre Frondaie)
Scenario and direction: Jean Epstein
Assistant direction: Louis Delaprée and Robert de Knyff
Editing: Marthe Bassi
Cameras: Armand Thirard and Joseph Barth
Assistant cameras: Philippe Agostini and Arthur
Music: Jean Wiener
Orchestra: Roger Désormière
Sound: Marcel Courmes and Norbert Gernolle
Sets: Georges Wakhévitch and Marc Lauer
Recording system: Tobis-Klangfilm
Cast: Marie Bell (Lady Oswill), Jean Murat (Georges Dewalter), Georges Grossmith (Lord Oswill), Jean Helda (Mme Deléone), Louis Gauthier (Lawyer Montnormand), Gaston Manger (Deléone), Mme Beaume (Governess)
Filmed in the Studio of Billancourt, with exteriors in Cannes, Provence, Biarritz, and the Pays basque
Premiere: April–May 1933
Distribution: Films J.-P. de Venloo

La Châtelaine du Liban (1933), France, 2,400 m, 35 mm, b/w, sound
Production: Vandal et Delac
Adaptation: Jean Epstein (novel, La Châtelaine du Liban, Pierre Benoît)
Scenario and direction: Jean Epstein
Assistant direction: Ary Sadoul and Pierre Duval
Cameras: Armand Thirard, Joseph Barth and Christian Matras
Sets: d'Aguettand
Music: Alexandre Tansman
Sound: Baugé

Cast: Melle Spinelly (Athelstane), Jean Murat (Captain Domèvre), Georges Grossmith (Colonel Hobson), Ernest Ferny (Captain Walter), Marguerite Templey (General's wife), Michèle Verly (Michèle), Gaby Basset (Maroussia), Chakatouny (Djoun), Georgé (Gardafuy), Marnay (Colonel Hennequin), Prieur (Colonel Marret), Decœur (General)
Filmed at Studio Pathé-Francœur in Paris, with exteriors in Lebanon, Syria, and Avignon.
Premiere: February 1934
Distribution: Films J.-P. de Venloo

La Presse Moderne, comment se fait un grand régional (Une visite à Ouest-Éclair) (1934), France, 200 m, 35 mm, b/w, sound

Alternative title: *La Vie d'un grand journal (Une visite à Ouest-Éclair)*
Production: Ouest-Éclair
Direction: Jean Epstein
Camera: Georges Lucas

Chanson d'Armor (1934), France, 1,200 m, 35 mm, b/w, sound

Production: Ouest-Éclair (Rennes)
Scenario: Jean des Cognets
Adaptation and direction: Jean Epstein
Assistant direction: Pierre Duval
Camera: Jean Lucas
Assistant cameras: Georges Lucas and Raymond Raynal
Music: Jacques Larmanjat
Orchestra: Roger Désormière
Choirs and dances: Émile Cueff, dancers of Pont-Aven, and the 'Queens' of Cornwall.
Assistant choir and dances: Suscinio
Sound: Behrens
Editing: Marthe Poncin
Breton language coach: Fanch Gourvil
Cast: Yvon Le Mar'hadour (Jean-Marie Maudez), Solange Montchâtre (Rozen), Fanch Gourvil (Tutor), François Viguier (Innocent), Georges Prieur (Fiancé),
Marinette Fournis (Melle Maudez)
Exteriors in Brittany
Premiere: 2 February 1935
Distribution: Pathé

Cœur de gueux / Cuor di vagabondo (1936), France, 2,400 m, 35 mm, b/w, sound

Production: G.-B. Seyta and Films Renaissance–Pisorno-Forzano
Scenario: G.-B. Seyta and Camille François
Adaptation: Jean Epstein (film *Le Cœur des gueux* [Fr., 1925], Alfred Machin and Henry Wulschleger)
Direction: Jean Epstein
Assistant direction: Pierre Duval
Assistant direction for Italy: Giacomo Forzano
Editing: Giacinto Solito
Camera: Mario Albertelli
Assistant camera: Angarelli
Sets: Lacca
Music: Jean Lenoir and Jacques Dallin
Orchestra: F. Audier
Vocals: Jean Lenoir
Lyrics: Camille-François
Cast: Madeleine Renaud (Claude), Ermete Zacconi (Father Larue), André Burgère (Jean Berthier), Violette Napierska (Marthe), Charles Deschamps (Charles), Pitouto (Prosper), Jacky Vilmont (Cloclo), Suzy Wall (Claude's friend), Teddy Michaux (fairground talent), Philippe Janvier (Paul)
Filmed at the Studio Tirrenia, Marina di Pisa, with exteriors in Pisa and Livorno
Premiere: September 1936
Distribution: Compagnie Universelle Cinématographique
Notes: This was a parallel French–Italian production; no copy of the Italian version has been located

La Bretagne (1936), France, 900 m, 35 mm, b/w, sound

Production: Films Jean Benoit-Lévy, SNCF
Direction: Jean Epstein
Camera: Georges Lucas
Assistant camera: Robert Ruth
Voice-over: Léandre Vaillat
Voice talent: Jacques Bernier
Music: Henri Casadesus
Vocals: Yvon Le Mar'hadour
Choreography: Émile Cueff

Sound: Fred Berhens
Distribution: Atlantic-Film
Filmed in Brittany
Notes: The film was shown at the Exposition des Arts et Techniques in Paris in 1937

La Bourgogne (1936), France, 900 m, 23 min., 35 mm, b/w, sound

Direction: Jean Epstein
Assistant direction: Pierre Duval
Camera: Georges Lucas
Assistant camera: Robert Ruth
Voice-over: Léandre Vaillat
Music: Henri Casadesus
Sound: Fred Berhens
Production and distribution: Atlantic-Film
Filmed in Burgundy
Notes: The film was shown at the Exposition des Arts et Techniques in Paris in 1937

Vive la vie (1937), France, 1,200 m, 35 mm, b/w, sound

Production: Films Jean Benoit-Lévy
Scenario: Marie Epstein and Jean Benoit-Lévy
Direction: Jean Epstein
Assistant direction: Pierre Duval
Camera: Jean Lucas and Georges Lucas
Assistant camera: Robert Ruth
Music: Jean Wiener
Sound: Fred Berhens
Distribution: Ministère des loisirs
Cast: The 'Ajistes' Pierre-Olivier de Marichard, Boris Kossloff, Jean Bessière, Georges Leroy, Jacques Brochard, Henri Signoret
Filmed in the Studio of Billancourt, with exteriors in, among others, the Auberges de jeunesse of Aix-en-Provence, Apt, Vallée des Loups

L'Île perdue (1937), France, 2,400 m, 35 mm, b/w, sound

Alternative title: *La femme du bout du monde*
Production: Jean Rossi and Films FRD
Adaptation: Jean Epstein (novel, *La femme du bout du monde*, Alain Serdac)

Scenario and direction: Jean Epstein
Assistant direction: Pierre Duval
Camera: Riccioni and Cotteret
Assistant camera: Franqui and Joseph Baun
Editing: Henriette Caire
Music: Jean Wiener
Sound: Fred Berhens
Sets: Roger Berteaux
Cast: Charles Vanel (Mechanic Durc), Germaine Rouer (Anna), Jean-Pierre Aumont (Lieutenant Jacquet), Alexandre Rignault (Bourrhis), Philippe Richard (Captain Sueur), Douking (Planque), Jacky Vilmont (Jimmy), Robert Le Vigan (Shipowner), Paul Azais (Radio Operator Molinier)
Filmed in the Studio of Courbevoie, with exteriors on the island of Ouessant
Premiere: January 1938
Distribution: Films Osso
Notes: Laura Vichi (2003: 177) indicates that *L'Île perdue* is half of *La Femme du bout du monde*; the Cinémathèque copy entitled *L'Île perdue* is about 70 min. long, which is 2,400m.

La Relève (1938), France, 340 m, 35 mm, b/w, sound

Production: Fédération nationale du bâtiment (CGT)
Direction: Jean Epstein
Camera: Georges Lucas
Music: The International
Cast: Peyrard, Jeanne Murrey, Péricat, Toussel, Bollman, Drouin, Rose, and workers of the national building trade union
Exteriors: Paris, Père-Lachaise demonstration
Notes: available online with the Ciné-Archives of the French Communist party (www.cinearchives.org)

Les Bâtisseurs (1938), France, 1,500 m, 35 mm, b/w, sound

Production: Fédération nationale du bâtiment (CGT)
Scenario: Jeander
Direction: Jean Epstein
Assistant direction: Pierre Duval
Camera: Georges Lucas
Assistant camera: Robert Ruth
Music: Hoéré and Honegger

Lyrics: Robert Desnos
Choir: Chorale enfantine de Villejuif-Gentilly
Sound: Fred Berhens
Assistant sound: Maxime Bachellerie
Cast: MM Drouin and Rose (unemployed construction workers)
Sets: Roger Berteaux
Credit sequence: Marcel Griffoul
Documentation and research: Fouquet and Lenoir
Filmed in the Studio of Garenne, with exteriors in, among others, Paris, Chartres, Saint-Cloud
Distribution: Ciné-Liberté and Maison des techniques
Notes: available online with the Ciné-Archives of the French Communist party (www.cinearchives.org)

Eau-vive (1938), France, 1,200 m, 35 mm, b/w, sound

Production: Films Jean Benoit-Lévy
Scenario and direction: Jean Epstein
Assistant directions: Pierre Duval and Jacques Brochard
Cameras: Georges Lucas and Pierre Bachelet
Sets: Le Barbanction
Music and orchestral direction: Maurice Jaubert
Cast: Florence Page (Denise Lafont), Jacques Mancier (Philippe), Philippe Richard (Tulle), Paul Barge (unionist Barbabé), Georges Bowden (Martin), Georges Zehr (Eugène), André Marmay (Lafont), François Viguier (Charles), Paul Marthes (president waterworks union)
Filmed in the Studio of La Garenne, with exteriors in Rochefort-en-Yvelines
Exteriors: Rochefort-en-Yvelines

Artères de France (1939), France, 600 m, 35 mm, b/w, sound

Production: Coopérative des Artisans d'Art du Cinéma
Scenario: Henry Champly
Direction: Jean Epstein with René Lucot
Assistant direction: Pierre Duval
Cameras: Jean Lucas and Georges Lucas
Music: Henri Casadesus
Sound: Fred Behrens
Distribution: Robert de Nesles
Notes: Documentary for the French section of the New York International Fair

Le Tempestaire (1947), France, 600 m, 35 mm, b/w, sound

Production: Filmagazine
Head of production: Nino Constantini
Direction: Jean Epstein
Cameras: A. S. Militon and Schneider
Sound: Léon Vareille and Frankiel
Sound assistant: Dumont
Score: Yves Baudrier
Cast: fishermen and lighthouse keepers of Belle-Île-en-Mer
Filmed in Belle-Île-en-Mer
Premiere: 13 March 1947
Distribution: Le Trident

Les Feux de la mer (1948), France, 600 m, 35 mm, b/w, sound

Production: Films Étienne Lallier for the United Nations
Direction: Jean Epstein
Assistant direction: Pierre Duval and Jacques Duchateau
Cameras: Pierre Bachelet and André Bernard
Animation: Henry Ferrand
Musical score: Yves Baudrier
Sound: Léon Vareille
Cast: Lighthouse keepers of the island of Ouessant and the Finistère coast
Distribution: UN

Efforts de productivité dans la fonderie (1953), France, 600 m, 35 mm, b/w, sound

Production: Association Française pour l'Accroissement de la Productivité
Direction: Jean Epstein
Camera: Ed. Floury and A. Militon
Editing: Y. Martin
Voice-over: M. Dorléac
Notes: Edmond Floury took over the direction when Epstein died

Select bibliography

Abel, Richard (1984), *French Cinema: The First Wave, 1915–1929*, Princeton: Princeton University Press.
— (ed.) (1988), *French Film Theory and Criticism*, vol. 1 (1909–29), vol. 2 (1929–39), Princeton: Princeton University Press.
Aumont, Jacques (ed.) (1998), *Jean Epstein: cinéaste, poète, philosophe*, Paris: La Cinémathèque française.
Bellour, Raymond (2001), 'Jean Epstein chez Henri Michaux', in Nicole Brenez and Christian Lebrat (eds), *Jeune, pure et dure! Une histoire du cinéma d'avant-garde et expérimental en France*, Paris: La Cinémathèque française, 430.
Brenez, Nicole and Ralph Eue (eds) (2008), *Jean Epstein: Bonjour cinéma und andere Schriften zum Kino*. Wien: Österreichisches Filmmuseum/Synema Publikationen.
Bullot, Érik (2009) *Renversements 1: notes sur le cinéma*, Paris: Paris expérimental.
Casetti, Francesco (2005), *Eye of the Century: Film, Experience, Modernity*, New York: Columbia University Press.
Deleuze, Gilles (1986), *Cinema 1: The Movement Image*, Hugh Tomlinson and Barbara Habberjam (trans.), Minneapolis: University of Minnesota Press.
Delluc, Louis (1919), *Photogénie*, Paris: Éditions Maurice de Brunoff.
Dillon, Steven (2004), *Derek Jarman and Lyric Film: The Mirror and the Sea*, Austin: University of Texas Press.
Epstein, Jean (1921), *La Poésie d'aujourd'hui, un nouvel état d'intelligence*, Paris: Éditions de la Sirène.
— (1921), *Bonjour cinéma*, Paris: Éditions de la Sirène.

— (1921), 'Le Phénomène littéraire', in Aumont (ed.), *Jean Epstein*, 39–85.
— (1922), 'Freud ou le nick-cartérianisme en psychologie', in Aumont (ed.), *Jean Epstein*, 139–46.
— (1922), *La Lyrosophie*, Paris: Éditions de la Sirène.
— (1922) 'The New Conditions of Literary Phenomena', *Broom*, April, 3–10.
— (1922), 'Nous Kabbalistes', in Aumont (ed.), *Jean Epstein*, 119–24.
— (1926) *Le Cinématographe vu de l'Etna*, Paris: Les Écrivains réunis.
— (1930–40) (Alfred Kléber), *Ganymède, essai sur l'éthique homosexuelle masculine*, Fonds Epstein, Collection Cinémathèque Française, BiFi, 227 B 60.
— (1974), *Écrits sur le cinéma*, vol. 1, Paris: Éditions Seghers.
— (1976), *Écrits sur le cinéma*, vol. 2, Paris: Éditions Seghers.
— (1995) *L'Or des mers*, Quimperlé: La Digitale.
— (1996) *Les recteurs et la sirène*, Quimperlé: La Digitale.
Fitterman-Lewis, Sandy (1996), *To Desire Differently: Feminism and the French Cinema*, New York: Columbia University Press.
Gauthier, Christophe (1999), *La Passion du cinéma: cinéphiles, ciné-clubs et salles spécialisées à Paris de 1920 à 1929*, Paris: AFRHC.
Ghali, Nourredine (1995), *L'Avant-garde cinématographique en France dans les années vingt, idées, conceptions, théories*, Paris: Paris expérimental.
Guigéno, Vincent (2003), *Jean Epstein, cinéaste des îles*, Paris: Jean-Michel Place.
Heller-Roazen, Daniel (2007), *The Inner Touch: Archaeology of a Sensation*, New York: Zone Books.
Hillairet, Prosper (2008), *Cœur fidèle de Jean Epstein: le ciel et l'eau brûlent*, Crisnée: Yellow now.
Keller, Sarah (2012), 'Introduction', in Keller and Paul (eds), *Jean Epstein*, 23–47.
Keller, Sarah and Jason Paul (eds) (2012), *Jean Epstein: Critical Essays and New Translations*, Amsterdam: Amsterdam University Press.
Le Forestier, Laurent (2009), 'Entre cinéisme et filmologie: Jean Epstein, la plaque tournante', in François Albera and Martin Lefebvre (eds), *La Filmologie, de nouveau Cinémas* 19(2–3) (spring), 113–40.
Leprohon, Pierre (1964), *Jean Epstein*, Paris: Éditions Seghers.
Liebman, Stuart (1980), 'Jean Epstein's early film theory, 1920–1922', Ph.D. dissertation, New York University.

— (1999), 'Sublime et désublimation dans la théorie cinématographique de Jean Epstein: *Le Cinématographe vu de l'Etna*', in Aumont (ed.), *Jean Epstein*, 125–37.
Moore, Rachel (2000), *Savage Theory: Cinema as Modern Magic*, Durham: Duke University Press.
Morin, Edgar (1956), *Le Cinéma, ou l'homme imaginaire*, Paris: Minuit, 1956
— (2005), *The Cinema or the Imaginary Man*, Lorraine Mortimer (trans.), Minneapolis: University of Minnesota Press.
Noé, Alva (2006), *Vision in Perception*, Cambridge: MIT Press.
Rancière, Jacques (2006), *Film Fables*, Emiliano Battista (trans.), Oxford: Berg.
Ray, Robert (2001), *How a Theory Got Lost and Other Mysteries in Cultural Studies*, Bloomington and Indianapolis: Indiana University Press.
Singer, Ben (2001), *Melodrama and Modernity: Early Sensational Cinema and Its Contexts*, Berkeley: University of California Press.
Thouvenel, Éric (2010), 'A toute intelligence je préfère la mienne': quand Jean Epstein lisait Gaston Bachelard', *1895* 62 (December), 53–75.
Tognolotti, Chiara (2005), *Al cuore dell'immagine: L'idea di fotogenia nel cinema europeo degli anni Venti*, Bologna: La luna nel pozzo.
— (2005), 'L'alcool, le cinéma et le philosophe: l'influence de Friedrich Nietzsche sur la théorie cinématographique de Jean Epstein', *1895* 46 (June) 37–53.
Turvey, Malcolm (2009), 'Epstein, Bergson, and Vision', in *European Film Philosophy* (ed.) Temenuga Trifonova, New York, Routledge, 93–107.
Vichi, Laura (2003), *Jean Epstein*, Milano: Editrice Il Castoro.
Vignaux, Valérie (2007), *Jean Benoit-Lévy ou le corps comme utopie: une histoire du cinéma éducateur dans l'entre-deux-guerres en France*, Paris: AFRHC.
Wall-Romana, Christophe (2012), *Cinepoetry: Imaginary Cinemas in French Poetry*, Fordham, Fordham University Press.
— (2012), 'Epstein's Photogénie as Corporeal Vision: Inner Sensation, Queer Embodiment, and Ethics', in Keller and Paul (eds), *Jean Epstein*, 51–72.

Index

3D (three-dimensionality) 41, 44, 71–2, 138
see also fourth dimension

Abel, Richard 7, 11, 26, 38, 40, 43, 50–1, 58, 115–16, 130, 164, 177
accelerated motion 73, 179
see also reverse motion; slow motion
J'Accuse 5, 18
Adorno, Theodor 22, 53
L'Affaire Dreyfus 129
affects 14, 19–20, 27, 29, 33n.18, 41–4, 74–6, 91, 52–3, 58, 111, 123, 137, 155, 160, 165–9, 177, 183–4, 191–2, 195–8
see also body; corporeality; corporeal cinema; illness and sickness; queer
L'Affiche 8, 14, 50, 64–5
Albatros (film production company) 34–5
Alcool et cinéma 10, 25, 42, 73, 141
Apollinaire, Guillaume 17, 135, 171–5
apparatus 14, 20–4, 43, 49, 61, 71–7, 84, 153, 159, 162, 164–7, 180–4
apparatus theory 12, 29, 177
Aragon, Louis 21, 168, 180
L'Arbre ou le pas de la mule 139
Artaud, Antonin 34, 43, 109, 112, 137
Artères de France 8
L'Auberge rouge 8
Aumont, Jacques 13, 162, 184
aura 29–34, 101
automobile 14, 63, 67, 69, 76–7, 82–7, 91, 101, 142, 166, 192
see also glass closet; heterosexuality
avant-garde 3, 5, 17–18, 22, 42, 69, 71n.3, 158, 168, 171
cinema 2, 11–12, 136–7, 190
melodrama 5, 10, 14, 22–3, 25, 49–66, 75, 79, 81, 85, 87, 91–4, 111, 113, 142, 164, 181, 191, 198
see also narrative avant-garde
see also Futurism; Surrealism
Les Aventures de Robert Macaire 50

Les Bâtisseurs 8, 143, 145–8
Baudelaire, Charles 31n.16, 36, 40–2, 76
Bazin, André 12, 42, 176
'Le Bel Agonisant' 35
La Belle Nivernaise 14, 34, 49, 62–3, 66, 110, 188
Benjamin, Walter 14, 22, 29–34, 49, 67
Benoit-Lévy, Edmond 131
Benoit-Lévy, Jean 7, 131–2, 142
Les Berceaux 140
Bergson, Henri 68, 71–3, 161–2, 167, 169, 170, 178, 183
body 14–15, 19, 23, 30, 35, 75, 86, 118, 121, 131, 161, 163, 165–6, 169–70
and illness and sickness 57, 66, 76–7, 115, 117–19, 188, 191
and photogénie 27–8
see also coenaesthesis; corporeality; corporeal cinema;

INDEX 221

photogénie; queer sexuality
Bonjour cinéma 6, 19, 23, 39, 50, 53, 87, 91, 158–9, 176–7, 183, 187, 191
La Bourgogne 1, 3, 138, 142–3
Bresson, Robert 6, 15, 122, 194–5
La Bretagne 138, 143–4
Breton, André 12, 17–18, 22, 34, 160, 172–5
Brittany 6, 8, 109–27
Buñuel, Luis 12, 34, 43, 51, 109, 187, 192–3

Cendrars, Blaise 17, 18, 21, 25, 86, 161, 168, 182
  and Abel Gance 6
censorship 35, 53, 57, 59, 78–9, 193
CGT 145–7
Chanson d'Armor 113, 120, 124, 144
La Chanson des peupliers 138–9
chansons filmées 128, 138–41
Chaplin, Charlie 5, 18, 50, 53, 136, 169
La Châtelaine du Liban 129
La Chute de la maison Usher 4, 8, 14, 26, 34–46, 49–50, 76–77, 89, 109, 111, 126, 128, 139, 141, 154, 169, 179, 187, 195, 197, 199
cine-clubs 5
Le Cinéma du diable 162
Le Cinématographe vu de l'Etna 26, 30, 33, 94, 135–6, 179, 188, 194
cinepoetry 23
Clair, René 7, 17, 76, 142, 192
class 18, 22, 65–6, 86, 93, 111, 142, 146–8, 165, 181, 183
  working-class 11, 14, 49–66, 123n.5, 142, 147, 199
close-ups 30, 58, 72–3, 111, 122, 123n.5, 165, 195n.7, 196
Cocteau, Jean 4, 6, 10, 17, 51, 89, 94, 112, 138, 155, 157, 172, 187, 192
coenaesthesis 21, 28, 41, 74–6, 83, 95, 118, 123, 166
Cœur fidèle 8, 14, 30, 35, 49, 53, 66–2, 65, 76, 83, 134, 136, 141–2, 151, 179, 181, 191, 197
Congress of Brighton 12–13, 177
contingence 10, 11, 64, 137, 139–40, 190, 193
Le Cor 139

Le Corbusier (Charles-Édouard Jeanneret) 6, 32, 108, 146, 148
corporeal cinema 20, 30, 38, 44, 95, 129, 145, 175, 191–9
  see also body; corporeality; *photogénie*; queer sexuality
corporeality 4, 14, 22, 28, 46, 75
  see also body; corporeal cinema; *photogénie*; queer sexuality
Crouching Tiger, Hidden Dragon 197–9
'culture industry' 53

Deleuze, Gilles 4, 13, 15, 68, 73, 110–11, 123, 140, 169, 177, 179–82
Delluc, Louis 7, 25, 35, 132, 157–8, 176
Démolition d'un mur 135
Dermée, Paul 171–3, 175
Derrida, Jacques 68n.1, 168, 177
Descartes, René 74, 136, 163, 167
Desnos, Robert 8, 145, 147
documentary film 1–3, 7–14, 75, 109–15, 120, 124, 127–55, 168–9, 183
Le Double amour 8, 14, 50, 88, 91–4, 126
Dulac, Germaine 6, 11, 32, 51, 61, 76, 89, 128, 137, 141, 164, 175, 192

The Edge of the World 112
Eisenstein, Sergei 3, 4, 24, 34
Epstein, Marie 5, 8–10, 57, 64–5, 109, 131, 175, 177

'The Fall of the House of Usher'
  Edgar Allan Poe 36–9
  James Sibley Watson 36–7
  see also La Chute de la maison Usher
La Femme du bout du monde 120, 128
Les Feux de la mer 120, 124, 149, 152
Feyder, Jacques 11, 51, 53, 86
Film d'Art 5, 7, 158
filmologie 10, 12, 163, 175–6
Finis Terræ 8, 14, 43, 76, 105–6, 113–22, 125, 127, 142n.13
First World War 5, 11, 17–18, 67, 70, 91, 130–1, 157–8, 168
Flammarion, Camille 70
flow 68, 110, 135–7, 140, 166, 196
Foucault, Michel 73n.1, 177
fourth dimension 71–2, 167

Freud, Sigmund 18, 20, 22, 119, 137, 160, 168
Front Populaire 7, 8, 12, 138, 141, 147–8, 183
Futurism 18n.1, 69, 159
see also avant-garde; Marinetti

Gance, Abel 5, 6, 9, 17–18, 25, 30, 32–3, 51, 70, 76, 132, 138, 162, 175, 180
Ganymède, Essai sur l'éthique homosexuelle masculine 89–90
Gardiens de phare 112
Gaudreault, André 23, 129
genres 2, 3, 11, 37, 51–4, 61, 109, 127, 129–30, 136, 138, 141, 187, 192, 198
Germany Year Zero 127
La Glace à trois faces 3, 8, 14, 77–83, 85, 92–3, 117, 121, 128, 178, 192
glass closet 14, 80–3, 86, 88, 93, 117
Godard, Jean-Luc 4, 51, 154, 177, 181–2, 184, 188
de Gourmont, Remy 40, 42, 161
La Goutte de sang 35
Greek (thought) 3, 69, 81, 90, 163
see also Homer; philosophy
guitar 39, 93, 139, 141
lute 104
viola 126
Gunning, Tom 13, 23, 129, 184, 187
Guy, Alice (Blaché) 139

health see body: illness and sickness
Heidegger, Martin 68–9
L'Herbier, Marcel 7, 10, 51, 76, 79, 89, 151, 175, 192
heterosexuality 10, 14, 24, 76, 79–87, 90–2, 117, 195–8
critique 40, 50, 62, 82–7, 111, 125–6
see also glass closet; homosexuality; melodramas; queer sexuality
Hillel-Erlanger, Irène 61, 89
Hitchcock, Alfred 54–5, 61, 118, 187
Homer 125, 150
L'Homme à l'Hispano 14, 85–8
homosexuality 10, 25, 42, 75–6, 78–80, 85–90, 93, 116, 161, 193
repressed 14, 78, 83, 89, 116, 194
see also glass closet; heterosexuality; homosocial; queer

homosocial 40, 116

IDHEC 10, 151, 175
L'île perdue 124, 127
Impressionist cinema see narrative avant-garde
innervation 32–3
L'Intelligence d'une machine 71–4, 153, 164, 167

Jewishness 4, 5, 43, 131–2, 163
and Nazi Occupation 9–10
see also Kabbalah

Kabbalah 34, 160, 163, 180
kaleidoscope 60–1, 173n.8
Kracauer, Sigfried 4, 34, 164, 177

Lang, Fritz 34, 70
Langlois, Henri 10, 175
lens 7n.1, 64, 84, 91, 106, 119, 121, 139, 141, 165–6, 191, 197
Leprohon, Pierre 12–13, 43, 57, 88, 109, 114, 122–3, 125
Lermina, Jules 43–4, 50
Levinas, Emmanuel 31
Le Lion des Mogols 8, 33, 50
literature 2, 6, 13, 18, 20, 23–4, 36, 40–2, 45, 50, 70, 75, 76, 79, 80, 112, 140, 159, 171, 180n.14, 182–3
adaptation 7, 9n.6, 14, 36–7, 49–52, 56, 62, 70, 77–83, 86, 109–10, 140, 158, 124, 127, 195
sub-literature 22, 52, 56, 59
see also 'Le Phénomène littéraire'; *La Poésie d'aujourd'hui*; poetry
Lumière, Auguste 1, 2, 5, 42, 83, 129, 131, 135, 155, 164, 176
La Lyrosophie 6, 159–62, 180, 183

Mallarmé, Stéphane 36, 40–2
Marinetti, Filippo Tomaso 68–70, 182
Marius et Olive 129
Marker, Chris 153, 176
Marnie 55
La Maternelle 7, 131
Mauprat 8, 50, 110, 139
melodrama 5, 10, 14, 22–3, 25, 49–66, 79, 81, 85, 87, 91, 93, 109, 111, 113, 142, 164, 181, 198

INDEX

Merleau-Ponty, Maurice 10, 28, 165, 175, 178–9
merry-go-round 30, 56–60, 83, 99, 151, 191
mirror 77, 80–7, 94, 102, 135, 151, 155, 166, 178–9, 193
modernism 6, 14, 18, 20–2, 36–7, 40, 42–3, 46, 159, 168, 171, 181
modernity 8, 13, 18–19, 22–3, 34, 40, 52, 83, 143–4, 149, 161, 171–2, 182, 184, 192
La Montagne infidèle 110, 135–6
Morin, Edgar 4, 176–7
Morv'ran (La Mer des corbeaux) 120–1, 127
Mosjoukine, Ivan 8, 35
mothers 5, 14, 63–5, 92, 93, 95, 103, 110, 115, 117–19, 140, 170n.5
Mumford, Lewis 67, 74

narrative avant-garde 7, 11–12, 24, 51, 89, 94, 109, 128, 175
neo-realism 14, 114, 127, 177
Nietzsche, Friedrich 59, 137, 162
The Night of the Hunter 46

L'Or des mers 113–14, 120–3, 127, 189

panoramic shot 1, 60, 63, 83, 139, 144, 151
pantomime dialoguée 51
Pasteur 75–6, 132–4
de Pawlowski, Gaston 68, 70–2
The Perils of Pauline 53
phantasmagoria 44
'Le Phénomène littéraire' 6, 19, 32, 183
phenomenology 27, 35, 68, 73, 176
philosophy 29, 31, 53, 68–9, 136
  Epstein's philosophy of cinema 2, 4–5, 15, 43, 71, 73–4, 94, 110, 117, 155, 157–84
  see also photogénie; theory
  see also Bergson; Deleuze; Derrida; Descartes; Foucault; Freud; Levinas; Merleau-Ponty; Nietzsche; Rancière; Sartre; Spinoza
phonogénie 129, 138–9, 149–55
photogénie 3, 4, 24–35, 42–3, 45, 49, 55, 59, 79, 83, 87, 89, 91, 95, 111, 124, 129, 134, 136, 158, 161, 168–9, 177, 182, 187, 190–1, 193–5, 197
photography 14, 25, 41, 65, 76–7, 84–5, 151, 172–5, 179
  chronophotography 39, 161
Pierre-Quint, Léon 31–3
plot 2–3, 5, 44, 51, 55–9, 61–4, 81, 111, 113–18, 122, 169, 182, 192–4
  see also literature; narrative avant-garde
Poe, Edgar Allan 36–9, 41–2, 152
poems 2, 6, 87–8, 113, 139, 140
  verse 23, 81, 86, 140, 158, 177
  intertitle verse 106, 120
La Poésie d'aujourd'hui 6–7, 19, 22–3, 28, 50, 56, 59, 74–5, 162, 164, 171, 173, 179–80, 183
poetic 3, 5, 23–4, 36, 51, 61, 86, 95, 158, 169, 178, 182, 188
poetics 52
poetic quality (vs. narrative value) 2
  see also literature; poems; poetry; poets; realism: poetic realism
poetry 3, 6, 14, 20–23, 27, 36, 39–42, 50, 69, 159, 168–75
poets 5, 8, 13, 19, 21, 23, 24, 25, 36, 40, 41, 42, 69, 71, 73n.7, 140, 145, 155, 159, 171–2, 175n.11
politics 4, 8, 12–15, 22, 35, 49, 53–4, 74, 77, 112, 129, 138, 142–7, 168, 181–3
  see also CGT; Front Populaire
La Presse Moderne, Comment se fait un grand régional 144–5
Le Promenoir 7, 88
Proust, Marcel 2, 30, 32, 34, 79, 89, 168
'pure cinema' 51

queer
  aesthetics 94, 193–5
  sexuality 13, 35, 62, 76–7, 85–95, 116–17, 161–2, 194–5
  vision 79, 81, 83, 94–5, 126

Rancière, Jacques 4, 13, 15, 53, 181–4
realism 11, 29, 63, 110, 130, 169, 183, 193
  corporeal realism 193, 195, 199
  magical realism 189

poetic realism 86, 113, 128
  see also neo-realism; Surrealism
La Règle du jeu 39, 63
  see also Renoir
La Relève, 147
Renoir, Jean 1, 39, 63–4, 76, 142, 147, 157
reverse motion 72, 150, 155, 162, 167, 170, 188, 194
  see also accelerated motion; slow motion
Riefenstahl, Leni 70n.2, 143
Rimbaud, Arthur 40–2
Romanticism 29
La Rose du rail 5
La Roue 5, 30

Le Sang d'un poète 51, 155, 187, 192
Sartre, Jean-Paul 10, 175
Sa tête 62–5
screen 28–30, 40, 44–5, 52, 61, 71, 72, 85, 87, 95, 118, 180n.14
Sedgwick, Eve 80–1
senses 20, 25, 33, 39
  sensations 15, 27–9, 41–3, 52, 56–9, 71–6, 87, 110, 118, 127, 130, 160, 162, 166, 173, 180, 190, 192
  sensibility 14, 28, 33, 37–8, 49–52, 71–7, 86–90, 113, 133–4, 161, 183, 193, 197
  sensorial experiences 6, 14, 19, 20, 25–7, 32, 40, 45, 49, 52, 59, 75–6, 94–5, 115, 118–19, 134, 149, 154, 167, 183, 191, 194, 198
simultaneism 22, 159, 180
simultaneity 72
situation 2, 55–6, 140, 149, 166, 169, 182, 194, 198
Six et demi onze 8, 14, 76–7, 83–6
slow motion 7, 37–9, 44–5, 73, 139, 151–5, 162, 170, 174–5, 188
  slight 119, 198
  variable 115
  see also accelerated motion; reverse motion
Solaris 195–7
Spinoza, Baruch 15, 162, 179–81
subconscious 20–2, 28, 52, 135, 166, 171

sub-literature see literature
supplement 68n.1
  see also Derrida
Surrealism 7–8, 12, 33–4, 42–3, 109, 135, 145, 171–5, 190
suspension 133, 162, 189, 199
  vs. suspense 54–7, 187–8
Symbolism 14, 26, 36, 40–2, 45–6, 49
synaesthesia 41, 45, 95, 126

talkies 11, 85, 128–9, 138, 154–5
technology 14, 17, 24–5, 31, 34, 41, 42, 62, 67–77, 82, 84–5, 95, 112, 142–5, 166, 171, 173, 181
  film 22, 138
  technophilia 67–71, 74, 183–4
  technophobia 67–70
  see also apparatus; automobile
Le Tempestaire 8, 14, 76, 112–13, 120, 123–4, 127, 138–9, 149–55, 168, 175, 179, 189
temporality 27–9, 34, 68–9, 71–2, 152, 169–70, 178–81
Thalberg, Irwin 189–90
theory
  of cinema 2–3, 12–15, 23–4, 27–9, 32–3, 36, 43, 91, 157–64, 190, 193, 199
    see also apparatus theory; photogénie
  of modernist poetry 20–2, 23, 56
  of social embodiment and aesthetic transformation 19–20
Tognolotti, Chiara 13, 162
Turvey, Malcolm 161, 183–4
Tzara, Tristan 17–18, 22, 32, 173

unconscious 20, 32–4, 75

Verlaine, Paul 40–2
Vertov, Dziga 3
Vichi, Laura 13
La Vie d'un grand journal 138
La Villanelle des rubans 139
vision
  and photogénie 28–9
  see also queer vision

Les Yeux sans visage 46